Immunities and the Right of Access to Court under Article 6 of the European Convention on Human Rights

International Studies in Human Rights

Volume 103

Immunities and the Right of Access to Court under Article 6 of the European Convention on Human Rights

By

Matthias Kloth

MARTINUS
NIJHOFF
PUBLISHERS

LEIDEN • BOSTON
2010

This book is printed on acid-free paper.

Library of Congress Cataloging-in-Publication Data

Kloth, Matthias.
Immunities and the right of access to court under Article 6 of the European Convention on Human Rights / by Matthias Kloth.
p. cm. — (International studies in human rights ; v. 103)
Includes bibliographical references and index.
ISBN 978-90-04-18184-7 (hardback : alk. paper)
1. Convention for the Protection of Human Rights and Fundamental Freedoms (1950). Article 6. 2. Due process of law—European Union countries. I. Title.

KJE3832.D83K56 2010
347.24'052—dc22

2009053700

ISSN 0924-4751
ISBN 978 90 04 18184 7

PRINTED IN THE NETHERLANDS

To my parents

Contents

Preface xiii
Abbreviations xv

Part I: Introduction 1

I. The scope and objective of this work 1

II. The right of access to court under Article 6 (1) of the Convention: the case of *Golder v. the United Kingdom* 2

III. The meaning of "civil rights and obligations" 6
1. The "civil" character of a right under Article 6 (1) 6
2. "Civil rights" regarding employment disputes in foreign embassies or international organisations 7
a) The case-law of the Court 7
b) Conclusion 10
3. The meaning of the term "right" 11

IV. The "Ashingdane Test" 13
1. Legitimate Aim 13
2. Proportionality 15
a) The margin of appreciation 16
b) A margin of appreciation regarding the application of public international law? 16
3. The very essence of the right 17
4. Conclusion 19

Part II: International Immunities 21

I. State immunity 21

1. State immunity in public international law 21
a) Absolute and restrictive immunity 22
b) State immunity in international and national law 23

(1) International Legislation 23
(a) The European Convention on State Immunity 23
(b) The United Nations Convention on Jurisdictional Immunities of States and Their Property 24
(2) National Legislation 25
c) Waiver of State immunity 25
d) Immunity from attachment and execution 26
2. State immunity and the jurisdiction of the forum State (Article 1 of the Convention) 26
3. State immunity in the recent Convention case-law 31
4. Alternative approaches to the conflict between State immunity and Article 6 (1) of the Convention 34
a) The equality of arms-argument and the role of alternative remedies 35
b) The comments of Judge Ress in his concurring opinion in the case of *"Bosphorus Airways" v. Ireland* 36
c) Judge Loucaides' approach: every blanket immunity is a disproportionate restriction on Article 6 (1) of the Convention 38
(1) Discussion of the approach 38
(2) Conclusion 41
5. State immunity in employment-related proceedings and Article 6 (1) of the Convention 41
a) The case of *Fogarty v. the United Kingdom* 41
(1) International practice regarding State immunity in employment disputes 42
(2) The decision of the Court 43
(3) Discussion of the judgment 44
(4) Conclusion 46
(5) The dissenting opinion by Judge Loucaides 47
b) Discriminatory immunity rules in employment-related disputes 48
c) The case of *Cudak v. Lithuania* 50
6. The "personal injury exception" and Article 6 (1) of the Convention: the case of *McElhinney v. Ireland* 53
a) Domestic legislation and State practice regarding the personal injury exception 54
b) International instruments and the personal injury exception 57
c) The restrictive interpretation of the personal injury exception ("insurable" personal injury) 59
d) Acts of the armed forces of the foreign State and the personal injury exception 59

e) Discussion of the judgment 60
f) Conclusion 63
7. State immunity for serious human rights violations and its compatability with Article 6 (1) of the Convention 64
a) Practice outside of Europe 65
b) Conclusion 68
c) The case of *Al-Adsani v. the United Kingdom* 68
(1) The decision of the majority 70
(2) The reasoning of the minority 72
(3) *Jus cogens* v. State immunity 72
d) Does the UN Torture Convention restrict State immunity in civil proceedings? 77
(1) A historic and systematic interpretation of Article 14 of the United Nations Torture Convention 78
(2) Conclusion 80
e) Developments since the *Al-Adsani* judgment 81
(1) Developments at the international level 81
(2) Developments at the domestic level 82
(3) The case of *Germany v. Italy* before the International Court of Justice 84
f) Conclusion 85
8. The responsibility under the Convention of the foreign State which successfully invokes immunity in the proceedings before the courts of the forum State 86

II. Immunity from execution and the right to enforce a judgment under Article 6 (1) of the Convention 88

1. The right to execute a judgment 88
2. Immunity from execution 89
3. Case-law of the Court 92
a) The case of Kalageropoulou and Others v. Greece and Germany 92
(1) Background to the case 92
(2) The enforcement proceedings in Greece 95
(3) The decision of the Court 96
(a) The complaint against Germany 96
(b) The complaint against Greece 96
(4) Further developments on the matter 99
b) The case of *Treska v. Albania and Italy* 100
c) The case of *Manoilescu and Dobrescu v. Romania and Russia* 102

d) The case-law of the Commission: the case of *N, C, F and AG v. Italy* 103
e) Immunity from execution and State agencies: the case of *Hirschhorn v. Romania* 103
f) Conclusion 105
4. *Jus cogens* and the right to enforcement of a judgment 105

III. Immunities of Heads of State, foreign ministers, diplomats and other State officials 107

1. Immunity of incumbent Heads of States 107
a) The legal position under public international law 107
(1) International instruments 109
(2) Exemptions in the statutes of international criminal tribunals 109
b) The case of *Association SOS Attentats and Beatrix de Boery v. France* 110
(1) The decision of the Court 111
(2) The conflict between immunity of incumbent Heads of State and Article 6 (1) of the Convention in the present case 111
(3) Conclusion 114
2. Immunity of former Heads of States 114
a) The legal position under public international law 114
b) Conflict with Article 6 (1) of the Convention 114
c) Case-law of the Court 115
3. Immunity of diplomats and foreign ministers 119
a) Diplomatic and consular immunities 119
(1) Diplomatic immunities 119
(2) Consular immunities 120
b) Case-law of the Convention organs 120
c) Immunity of foreign ministers 123
4. Immunity of other State officials 124
a) The legal position under public international law 124
b) Case-law of the Court: the *Jones and Others* case 125
(1) The decision of the Court of Appeal 127
(2) Criticism of the judgment 129
(3) The decision of the House of Lords 130
(4) The case before the European Court of Human Rights, Conclusion 131

IV. Immunity of International Oganisations 132

1. Reasons for the immunity of international organisations 133
2. The scope of the immunity of international organisations 134
3. The conflict between immunity of international organisations and Article 6 (1) of the Convention 136
4. The case-law of the Convention organs 138
   a) Case-law of the Commission: the case of Spaans v. Netherlands 138
   b) The cases of *Waite and Kennedy v. Germany* and *Beer and Regan v. Germany* 140
      (1) The decisions of the Court 140
      (2) Discussion of the judgments 141
   c) The case of *Beer and Regan v. Germany (II)* 144
5. Liability for acts of international organisations 144
6. Requirements for alternative means in order to satisfy the "proportionality" criterion 148
7. The "proportionality" criterion in cases against international organisations which are not employment-related: the case of the *Association of Citizens "Mothers of Srebrenica" and Others v. the Netherlands and the United Nations* 149
8. Conclusion 153

V. Other restrictions on the right of access to court for reasons based in public international law 154

1. The case of *Prince Hans-Adam II of Liechtenstein v. Germany* 154
2. The case of *Markovic and Others v. Italy* 156

Part III: Domestic Immunities 159

I. The liability of public authorities under English Law 159

1. The former approach by the Commission 160
2. The initial approach taken by the Court 161
   a) The case of *Ashingdane v. the United Kingdom* 162
   b) The case of *Fayed v. the United Kingdom* 162
3. Immunity of the police: the case of *Osman v. the United Kingdom* 164
   a) The judgment of the Court 165
   b) Responses to the judgment 166
   c) How the Court was alleged to have misinterpreted English tort law 167

4. Immunity of the social services: the case of *Z and Others v. the United Kingdom* 168
5. The question of compensation 171
6. Crown immunity: the case of *Roche v. the United Kingdom* 173
a) The decision of the majority 174
b) The opinion of the eight dissenting judges 176
7. Various approaches to a resolution of the conflict between "immunity from suit" and "immunity from liability" 177
a) The "Gearty thesis" 177
b) A "common sense application" of Article 6 (1) 178
c) The "dual limb"-approach 179
d) Proposal for a solution: the establishment of a "but for" test as first proposed by Francoise Hampson 180
(1) The dissenting opinion of Judge Zupancic in *Roche v. the United Kingdom* 181
(2) The "but for" test 181
(3) Conclusion 182
8. Judicial immunity in English tort law and in other legal systems 184

II. Parliamentary immunity 186

1. The case-law of the Commission 187
2. The case-law of the Court 188
a) The content of the remarks by a Member of Parliament 189
(1) The case of *A v. the United Kingdom* 189
(2) Discussion of the judgment 190
(3) Conclusion 191
(4) The case of *Zollmann v. the United Kingdom* 192
b) The occasion on which the statements have been made: the "Italian cases" 192
c) The refusal of the request by a Member of Parliament to have his parliamentary immunity lifted: the case of *Kart v. Turkey* 195
3. Conclusion 198

Summary 199
Bibliography 207
Index 219

Preface

This book was presented as a doctoral thesis to the Faculty of Law at the University of Bonn in 2008. It has been revised and edited to incorporate the developments in the field of Article 6 of the European Convention on Human Rights and immunities as of August 2009. Obviously, this academic work was written in my personal capacity; any views expressed herein do not necessarily reflect the position of my current employer, the Council of Europe.

I would like to thank Professor Dr. Dr. Christoph Grabenwarter (under whose supervision this study was conducted) for his very important encouragement, advice and intellectual guidance. I am also grateful to Professor Dr. Matthias Herdegen for his coevaluation of the original thesis. My friends Ellen Asche, Elif Yarsuvat, Çağa Tanyar, and my partner, Ayşegül Elveriş, have greatly encouraged me to successfully complete this endeavour—thank you! Moreover, I would like to thank Jane Griffiths for the proof-reading of the manuscript and all the team at Martinus Nijhoff/BRILL for their great work. Any remaining errors in the text are mine.

This work is dedicated to my parents, Dr. Karen and Günter Kloth, who supported me extensively throughout my legal education and who gave me opportunities I would not have had otherwise. This book would not have been possible without their support.

August 2009 Matthias Kloth

Abbreviations

AC	Appeal Cases
AJIL	American Journal of International Law
All ER	All England Law Reports
BVerfGE	Report of decisions of the German Federal Constitutional Court (*Bundesverfassungsgericht*)
BalYbIL	Baltic Yearbook of International Law
BYIL	British Yearbook of International Law
CLJ	Cambridge Law Journal
D/R	Decisions and Reports (ECHR)
ECHR	European Court of Human Rights
EHRR	European Human Rights Reports
EHRLR	European Human Rights Law Reports
EJIL	European Journal of International Law
ELR	European Law Review
EPIL	Encyclopaedia of Public International Law
EU	European Union
EuGRZ	Europäische Grundrechte Zeitschrift
EWHC	EW High Court
FS	Festschrift
F.Supp.	Federal Supplement (USA)
GC	Grand Chamber of the European Court of Human Rights
GWJILE	George Washington Journal of International Law and Economics
HHRJ	Harvard Human Rights Journal
HL	House of Lords
HRLR	Human Rights Law Reports
HYIL	Hague Yearbook of International Law
ICJ	International Court of Justice
ICLQ	International and Comparative Law Quarterly
ILA	International Law Association
ILM	International Legal Materials
ILR	International Law Reports
IOLR	International Organizations Law Review

IPrax	Praxis des internationalen Privat- und Verfahrensrechts
I.R.	Irish Reports
JICJ	Journal of International Criminal Justice
JICL	Journal of International and Comparative Law
KCLJ	King's College Law Journal
LJIL	Leiden Journal of International Law
LQR	Law Quarterly Review
MJIL	Michigan Journal of International Law
MLR	Modern Law Review
NILR	Netherlands International Law Review
NJW	Neue Juristische Wochenschrift
NZLR	New Zealand Law Review
ÖJZ	Österreichische Juristenzeitung
RdC	Recueil des Cours
RJD	Reports of Judgments and Decisions
RTDH	Revue trimestrielle des droits de l'homme
SIA	United Kingdom State Immunity Act of 1978
TLR	Tulane Law Review
UKHL	United Kingdom House of Lords
UN	United Nations
WLR	Weekly Law Reports
YILC	Yearbook of the International Law Commission
ZaöRV	Zeitschrift für allgemeines ausländisches Recht und Völkerrecht

Part I

Introduction

I. *The scope and objective of this work*

Immunities are generally granted to certain legal bodies in order to protect them from outside interference and to ensure that they can function effectively. Immunities may be identified as falling into two basic groups. The first one would contain those immunities which are introduced to fulfil obligations under public international law. These include State immunity, but also the immunity of Heads of State, foreign ministers, diplomats, consuls and other State officials, as well as international organisations and its staff members. The second group consists of immunities which are granted to legal bodies or persons at the domestic level. These may be Members of Parliament, judges or public authorities such as the police or the social services.

The term "immunity" is used primarily to denote an exemption from legal process. The aspect of immunity which is relevant to this work is immunity from suit, *i.e.* an exemption from jurisdiction of domestic courts with regard to civil proceedings. Immunity from suit means an attempt by a claimant to bring a claim against the holder of that immunity will prove to be unsuccessful. The suing person will be denied access to court because his or her claim is barred by immunity. This raises the question whether immunities are compatible with the fundamental rights and freedoms laid down in the European Convention on Human Rights (hereafter "the Convention"), namely the right of access to court under Article 6 (1). This work aims to investigate the conflict that arises between the right of access to court and immunities. The jurisprudence of the European Court of Human Rights in Strasbourg (hereafter "the Court") on the above conflict has developed considerably in the past years, and the rising number of cases which have been brought before the Court suggests that there appears to be a current trend to challenge immunities under the Convention.

Although not expressly mentioned, Article 6 (1) includes the right of access to court which has been "read" by the Court into that provision ever since the case of *Golder v. the United Kingdom*. The Court has however established that the right of access to court is not absolute and may be subject to limitations if the restriction pursues a legitimate aim, is proportionate and does not have the effect of extinguishing the applicant's right of access to court altogether. That test is applied uniformly to all kinds of immunities.

The present work is divided into three parts. The first part gives a general introduction to the right of access to court under Article 6 (1) as relevant in the present context, and explains the applicability of Article 6 (1) and the different criteria which the Court applies in order to establish whether immunities violate the right of access to court.

The second part will then turn to international immunities. Starting with the law of State immunity, it will discuss the Court's jurisprudence as well as alternative approaches suggested by international lawyers and judges. It attempts to suggest general criteria for dealing with the conflict between international immunities and Article 6 (1), a conflict which involves complex legal questions not only under the Convention, but also in general public international law.

The third and last part will then discuss the case-law on the conflict between domestic immunities and the right of access to court. Unlike international immunities, domestic immunities may be categorised into "immunity from liability" (a substantive limitation) or "immunity from suit" (a procedural limitation). Whereas the categorisation as a substantive limitation means that there is no "civil right" (with the consequence that Article 6 (1) of the Convention is strictly speaking not applicable), procedural limitations interfere with Article 6 (1) and need to be justified. The Court has based its jurisprudence on that distinction with – as will be argued – the consequence of a series of controversial judgments and a case-law which becomes increasingly inconsistent. The present work suggests an alternative approach which attempts to facilitate dealing with domestic immunities.

II. *The right of access to court under Article 6 (1) of the Convention: the case of* Golder v. the United Kingdom

The right to a fair trial (Article 6) occupies a central place in the Convention system and is a basic element of the notion of the rule of law.[1] The first paragraph of this provision provides that:

[1] Jacobs and White, *European Convention*, p. 151. The right of access to court is also enshrined in other international human rights instruments such as Article 10 of the Universal Declaration of Human Rights of 1948, Article 14 of the International Covenant on Civil and Political Rights of 1966 and Article 8 of the Inter-American Convention on Human Rights of 1969.

> In the determination of his civil rights and obligations or of any criminal charge against him, everyone is entitled to a fair and public hearing within a reasonable time by an independent and impartial tribunal established by law. (...)

The language of this paragraph appears to be ambiguous, as it does not mention the right of access to court explicitly. Hence, the conclusion could be drawn from the wording that the right to a fair trial is only guaranteed for pending legal cases, but not for individuals wishing to bring an action before a court. The question of whether a right of access to court could be implied within the wording of Article 6 (1) arose in the case of *Golder v. the United Kingdom.*[2] The case dealt with a prisoner who had been refused permission by the Home Secretary to contact his solicitor in order to bring civil proceedings for defamation against a prison officer. In a judgment which was considered as one of the most significant and creative steps taken by the Convention organs,[3] the Court held by nine votes to three that the right of access to court could be inferred from the text of Article 6 (1) and that this provision had been violated by the refusal to allow the applicant to contact his lawyer. The decision illustrates that Article 6 (1) grants the right of access to court not only in law, but also in fact.[4] Although the extensive interpretation which was chosen by the majority of the judges in *Golder v. the United Kingdom* has been applied by the Court and has been unchallenged by the Contracting Parties ever since,[5] it is worthwhile to briefly summarise the arguments for and against the reading of a right of access to court into the fair-trial provision.[6]

In interpreting Article 6 (1), the Court had regard to Articles 31 to 33 of the Vienna Convention on the Law of Treaties 1969 which contain the guiding principles of interpretation of a treaty of international law.[7] Article 31 (1) lists the general means which have to be considered for interpretation: text, context as well as object and purpose. Considering the "text" of Article 6 (1), the Court pointed out that the French version ("*contestations sur ses droits*") had a wider meaning than the English version ("*in the determination of his civil rights and obligations*"). Thus, it also embraces claims which

---

[2] *Golder v. the United Kingdom* (no. 4451/70), Judgment of 21 February 1975, Series A 18.

[3] Reid, *Practitioner's Guide*, p. 75; Harris/O'Boyle/Warbrick, *European Convention*, p. 196.

[4] Jacobs, The Right to a Fair Trial in European Law, EHRLR 1999, p. 144.

[5] See Harris/O'Boyle/Warbrick, *European Convention*, p. 196.

[6] For a detailed summary of the judgment see also: Nedjati, *Human Rights under the European Convention*, p. 105 et seq.

[7] *Golder v. the United Kingdom*, para. 29; see generally Villiger, *Articles 31 and 32 of the Vienna Convention on the Law of Treaties in the Case-Law of the European Court of Human Rights*, Festschrift Georg Ress, p. 317.

have not yet reached the stage of trial.[8] From a contextual point of view, the UK government argued that if a right to access were to be recognised, one would expect such a right to be expressly provided in the Convention, especially if seen together with other provisions of the Convention such as Article 5 (4) and Article 13 of the Convention, which explicitly mention a right of access to court in their own context.[9] The Court dismissed these arguments by finding that the three provisions did not operate in the same field.[10] While referring to the Convention's Preamble, the Court also found that the principle of "rule of law" was hardly conceivable in the absence of a right to institute proceedings.[11] Having regard to Article 31 (3) (c) of the Vienna Convention, the Court further reasoned that Article 6 (1) had to be read in the light of two universally recognised fundamental principles of international law, namely the capability to submit a civil claim to a judge and the prohibition of the denial of justice.[12] The most convincing passage of the judgment reads as follows:

> Were Article 6 (1) to be understood as concerning exclusively the conduct of an action which had already been initiated before a court, a Contracting State could, without acting in breach of the text, do away with its courts, or take away their jurisdiction to determine certain classes of civil actions and entrust it to organs dependent on the Government. (…) It would be inconceivable, in the opinion of the Court, that Article 6 (1) should describe in detail the procedural guarantees afforded to parties in a pending lawsuit and should not first protect Government that which alone makes it in fact possible to benefit from such guarantees (…). The fair, public and expeditious characteristics of judicial proceedings are of no value at all if there are no judicial proceedings.[13]

The UK government and three judges in the *Golder* argued that an extensive interpretation would force new obligations on the Contracting parties and would therefore be illegitimate. The only explanation for an omission would be that the Contracting Parties took the existence of a right to access for granted.[14] Although a serious deficiency, the lacking of a right to access

[8] *Golder v. the United Kingdom*, para. 32; see also the separate opinion of Judge Zekia, Part A. But even the English version would not necessarily refer only to judicial proceedings since it could be taken as synonymous with "wherever his civil rights and obligations are being determined" (*Golder v. the United Kingdom*, para. 32). This would imply the right to have the determination of disputes relating to civil rights or obligations before a court or tribunal.

[9] Ibid., para. 33.

[10] Ibid.

[11] Ibid., para. 34.

[12] Ibid., para. 35.

[13] Ibid.

[14] Separate opinion of Judge Zekia in *Golder v. the United Kingdom*, part B.

ought to be put right by the Contracting States and not by the Court itself.[15] The Court rejected these objections. Its interpretation would not create new obligations, but was based on the wording and the context as well as the object and purpose of the Convention as described above.[16] This approach seems to be correct since it is difficult to understand why a right that is taken for granted by the Contracting Parties should not fall within the jurisdiction of the Convention organs.

The *Golder* judgment has been widely uncontested despite these weighty arguments brought forward by the UK government and the three dissenting judges.[17] The judgment has ever since been referred to as a landmark decision that considerably extended the scope of Article 6 (1).[18] It is however important to note that the right of access to court does not include the right for the victim of a criminal offence to pursue criminal proceedings or to claim prosecution.[19] Neither does Article 6 (1) apply to proceedings aimed at instituting criminal proceedings against third persons.[20] The "criminal aspect" of Article 6 (1) only concerns charges *against* an individual.[21] This could become relevant in the context of immunities which also protect certain persons from criminal prosecution. If the efforts of a person to institute criminal proceedings against a third person are frustrated because the latter is protected by immunity, any complaint of a violation of Article 6 (1) would be incompatible *ratione materiae* with the provisions of the Convention. However, this has to be distinguished from the situation where a legal system permits a victim of a crime to be joined as a civil party to criminal proceedings which are already permitted to proceed.[22] Providing the outcome of the criminal

[15] Separate opinion of Judge Fitzmaurice in *Golder v. the United Kingdom*, para. 48.

[16] *Golder v. the United Kingdom*, para. 36.

[17] See Harris/O'Boyle/Warbrick, *European Convention*, p. 196. The three dissenting judges mainly concluded from the wording of Article 1 that only such rights and freedoms which are "defined" explicitly in the Convention would be guaranteed therein. This would in practice amount to a prohibition on reading into the Convention any implied rights or freedoms (*Golder v. the United Kingdom*, separate opinions of Judges Verdross, Zekia and Fitzmaurice).

[18] Van Dijk, *The Maze of Paragraph 1 of Art. 6*, HYIL 1988, p. 141; Jacobs, *The Right to a Fair Trial in European Law*, EHRLR 1999, p. 142; Bröhmer, *State Immunity*, p. 184.

[19] Van Dijk, *Access to Court*, p. 370; Frowein/Peukert, *EMRK*, p. 209; *Kiss v. the United Kingdom*, (no. 6224/73), Commission decision of 16 December 1976, D/R 7, p. 55; *T v. Belgium*, D/R 34 (1983), pp. 171–172. Note however the positive obligation under Article 6 (1) in *X & Y v. the Netherlands* (Judgment of 26 March 1985, EHRR 1985, p. 235) to prosecute a rapist for the protection of the victim.

[20] *Rékási v. Hungary* (no. 31506/96), Commission decision of 25 November 1996, D/R 87 A, p. 171.

[21] Harris/O'Boyle/Warbrick, *European Convention*, p. 197.

[22] See Simor/Emmerson, *Human Rights Practice*, 6.026 and 6.038.

proceedings is decisive of the civil party's allegations as to damage suffered, the victim's civil rights are being determined and Article 6 (1) will apply.[23]

III. *The meaning of "civil rights and obligations"*

1. *The "civil" character of a right under Article 6 (1)*

Article 6 (1) does not guarantee the right to a fair trial in the determination of all rights and obligations which an individual might claim under domestic law. According to the wording in Article 6 (1), the provision only applies to the determination of "civil rights and obligations". One way of interpreting the phrase could be to limit the scope of the term to relationships between private parties only. That would have an important impact on the relationship between immunities and the right of access to court. Since almost all immunities which are dealt with in this conflict are privileges accorded to public bodies, Article 6 (1) would not apply at all in this kind of cases. Disputes between an individual and the State, its diplomats, its Members of Parliament, the police or international organisations are not disputes between private individuals. Such a view would however disregard the fact that States and international organisations may also act like private persons. Regarding the question whether the status of the defendant or the categorisation of an act as private or public by domestic law has any impact on the nature of the right, the Court made the following statement in *König v. Germany*:

> If the case concerns a dispute between an individual and a public authority, whether the latter had acted as a private person or in sovereign capacity is therefore not conclusive (...). In ascertaining whether a dispute ('contestation') concerns the determination of a civil right, only the character of the right at issue is relevant.[24]

The Court specified that approach:

> Whether or not a right is to be regarded as civil within the meaning of this expression in the Convention must be determined by reference to the substantive content and effects of the right – and not its legal classification – under the domestic law of the state concerned. In the exercise of its supervisory functions, the Court must also take account of the object and purpose of the Convention and of the national legal system of the other contracting states (...).[25]

---

[23] Simor/Emmerson, *Human Rights Practice*, 6.026; *Tomasi v. France* (no. 12850/87), Judgment of 27 August 1992, Series A 241–A, para. 121.

[24] *König v. Germany* (no. 6232/73), Judgment of 28 June 1978, Series A 27, paras. 89–90.

[25] Ibid., paras. 89–90.

Therefore, the fact that the defendant is a public authority and its act is categorised under domestic law as "public" does not bear any significance to the question whether or not a certain dispute involves the determination of a civil right. What is decisive is that the concept of "civil rights" must be interpreted independently of the rights existing in the domestic law, even though the Court takes into consideration general principles of national law of the Contracting States.

2. *"Civil rights" regarding employment disputes in foreign embassies or international organisations*

In practice, the determination of the "civil" character of a right (despite certain public law features) has often proved difficult.[26] With regard to immunities, that categorisation has rarely been problematic, with the exception of claims against foreign embassies and international organisations concerning employment disputes. This is because many claims against foreign States and international organisations are brought by civil servants or other employees and concern employment disputes regarding recruitment processes, termination of contracts or payment of salary.

a) *The case-law of the Court*

On several occasions, the Convention organs had to decide generally whether an employment dispute within the civil service concerned the determination of a "civil right" within the meaning of Article 6 (1). Whereas disputes relating to private law relations between employer and employee would fall within the scope of Article 6 (1), the original approach was that disputes relating to the recruitment, employment and retirement of civil servants generally would not. The right concerned, however, was found to be of a civil nature if the civil servant employment dispute related to "purely economic rights" such as the payment of salary[27] or where the issue raised was "essentially economic".[28] Since almost all disputes relating to recruitment or termination of service have economic implications too, the distinction became increas-

[26] See generally Jacobs and White, *European Convention*, pp. 144–150; Grabenwarter, *Europäische Menschenrechtskonvention*, § 24, 7–13; Peters, *Europäische Menschenrechtskonvention*, p. 103; for a detailed list (in German) regarding categories of disputes to which Article 6 (1) does and does not apply, see Mayer-Ladewig, *EMRK-Handkommentar*, pp. 103–105.

[27] *De Santa v. Italy* (no. 25574/94), Judgment of 2 September 1997, RJD 1997–V, para. 18; *Abenavoli v. Italy* (no. 25587/94), Judgment of 2 September 1997, RJD 1997–V, para. 16.

[28] *Nicodemo v. Italy* (no. 25839/94), Judgment of 2 September 1997, RJD 1997–V, para. 18; see also Simor/Emmerson, *Human Rights Practice*, 6.042.

ingly difficult, arbitrary and inconsistent.[29] In *Pellegrin v. France*[30], the Court adopted a new, functional test to determine whether an employment dispute involving civil servants fell within the scope of Article 6 (1). The test was based on the nature of the employee's duties and responsibilities:

> [T]he only disputes excluded from the scope of Article 6 (1) of the Convention are those which are raised by public servants whose duties specify activities of the public service, in so far as the latter is acting as the depositary of public authority responsible for protecting the general interests of the state or other public authorities. (...) Accordingly, no disputes between administrative authorities and employees who occupy posts involving participation in the exercise of powers conferred by public law attract the application of Article 6 (1) since the Court intends to establish a functional criterion.[31]

In *Van der Peet v. Germany*[32], a similar approach was taken by the European Commission of Human Rights (hereafter "the Commission") concerning employment disputes within an international organisation.[33] The Convention organs did however not apply the "Pellegrin principle" in the cases of *Beer and Regan v. Germany* and *Waite and Kennedy v. Germany*.[34] Both cases concerned employment disputes within the international organisation *European Space Agency* (ESA), but the facts of the case were special since the applicants had been hired out by a private firm which led the Convention organs to conclude that the relationship between ESA and the applicants resembled that between private persons. Hence Article 6 (1) was applicable.

In the case of *Fogarty v. the United Kingdom*,[35] which dealt with an employment dispute concerning the applicant's secretarial post at the United States embassy in the United Kingdom, the latter's government disputed that the right on which the applicant relied was of a civil nature, since questions of employment of members of diplomatic missions would consequently fall within the core of sovereign power and had a "public law" character.[36] Hence

---

[29] Simor/Emmerson, *Human Rights Practice*, 6.042. See for instance the Court in *Pellegrin v. France*: "The Court considers that, as it stands, the above case-law contains a margin of uncertainty for Contracting States as to the scope of their obligations under Article 6 (1) in disputes raised by employees in the public sector over their conditions of service." (*Pellegrin v. France* [GC] (no. 28541/95), Judgment of 8 December 1999, RJD 1999–VIII, para. 60).

[30] Ibid.

[31] Ibid., para. 63.

[32] *Van der Peet v. Germany* (no. 26991/95), Commission decision of 12 April 1996.

[33] See further Simor/Emmerson, *Human Rights Practice*, 6.045.

[34] *Waite and Kennedy v. Germany* [GC] (no. 26083/95), Judgment of 18 February 1999; RJD 1999–I; *Beer and Regan v. Germany* [GC] (no. 28934/95), Judgment of 18 February 1999.

[35] *Fogarty v. the United Kingdom* [GC] (no. 37112/97), Judgment of 21 November 2001, EHRR 2002.

[36] Ibid., para. 22.

the recruitment process for employment in an embassy did allegedly not concern a civil right. The Court avoided the issue by proceeding on the basis that Article 6 (1) applied, just to find that the right of access to court had not been violated by the granting of State immunity to the United States.[37]

As the only dissenting judge, Judge Loucaides had to decide on the existence of a "civil right" in the present case and answered the question in the affirmative.[38] His decision appears to be correct for several reasons. First, the secretarial post for which Mrs Fogarty had applied could arguably not be considered as involving the "exercise of powers conferred by public law" as required by the "Pellegrin principle". Moreover, as that principle only explicitly excludes a "civil right" from disputes in which a public servant already has been employed, recruitment processes do not necessarily fall within the scope of the definition.[39] This argument is not inconsistent, since the Court found that Article 6 (1) would remain applicable to pension disputes (regardless of the position of the employee) since the duty of loyalty which "typifies" the public service would cease to exist after termination of employment.[40] Hence one could draw the reverse conclusion that a bond of loyalty does not yet exist during the recruitment process and prior to employment.[41]

Recent changes in the Court's jurisprudence on civil rights and employment issues strongly suggest that future applications on international immunities will fall within the ambit of Article 6 (1). In *Vilho Eskelinen and Others v. Finland*, the Grand Chamber of the Court decided in April 2007 to significantly review its jurisprudence on the issue and to widen the applicability of Article 6 (1) with regard to civil servants.[42] The reason for that change was that the *Pellegrin* jurisprudence of the Court had always been controversial, in particular since the Court had abandoned the "economic criterion"

[37] Ibid., para. 28.

[38] *Fogarty v. the United Kingdom*, dissenting opinion of Judge Loucaides.

[39] Ibid.

[40] See Simor/Emmerson, *Human Rights Practice*, 6.043.

[41] Moreover, Judge Loucaides observed that the applicant's claim was not only an employment dispute, but also based on the United Kingdom Sex Discrimination Act 1975, involving a complaint about sex discrimination. It should be noted that the European Court of Justice in *Johnston v. Chief-Constable of the Royal Ulster Constabulary* (Case 222/84 [1986] ECR, p. 1651), a case concerning equal treatment for men and women concerning armament in a police reserve force, found that employment disputes involving sex discrimination – even where the dispute took place in the public sector – had to be measured by the principle of judicial control as embodied in Article 6 (1) (see *Fogarty v. the United Kingdom*, dissenting opinion of Judge Loucaides).

[42] *Vilho Eskelinen and Others v. Finland* [GC] (no. 63235/00), Judgment of 19 April 2007; see also the case analysis by Parmar, *Vilho Eskelinen v Finland: The Further Extension of ECHR Article 6 to Disputes concerning Civil Servants*, EHRLR 2007, p. 456.

and thereby removed several economic claims which formerly would have fallen under Article 6 (1).[43] The Court observed in *Vilho Eskelinen and Others v. Finland* that its *Pellegrin* approach had not simplified the analysis of the applicability of Article 6 (1) and that it could only be considered a first step away from its previous approach that that provision did not apply to the civil service. Given the fact that many Contracting States accorded access to court to their civil servants regarding claims for salary and allowances (even for dismissal and recruitment) similar to employees in the private sector without perceiving a conflict with the vital interests of the State, the Court decided to adopt a new approach in this area.[44] Article 6 (1) was presumed to apply unless the respondent government could demonstrate that two conditions had been fulfilled. First, access to court must be expressly excluded in national law for the post or category of staff in question. Second, the exclusion must be justified on objective grounds in the State's interest, *i.e.* the State would have to show that the subject matter of the respective dispute was related to the exercise of State power or that the dispute had called into question the "special bond of trust and loyalty" between the State and its employee. The Court stated that in principle there was no justification for the exclusion from Article 6 (1) of ordinary labour disputes between a State and its employees.[45]

b) *Conclusion*

Although the Court's new approach in *Vilho Eskelinen and Others v. Finland* is to be welcomed as it significantly widens the applicability of Article 6 (1), it is not preferable from a dogmatic point of view. The applicability of Article 6 (1) in cases concerning a civil servant's access to court now depends on the question whether the exclusion of that access was justified. This is, however, a question which the Court used to decide on the merits. The shifting of that issue to the admissibility stage might be practicable in cases concerning complaints about the length of the labour proceedings (as was the actual case in *Vilho Eskelinen and Others v. Finland*). Where a Contracting State however excludes a civil servant's access to court, the new test might create more confusion, as it appears that the same issues might arise both at the admissibility stage and the merits of the case.[46] For the purposes of international immunities such as employment disputes in international organisations or

[43] Simor/Emerson, *Human Rights Practice*, 6.043. This had been sharply criticised by the dissenting judges in *Pellegrin v. France* (see the dissenting opinion of Judges Tulkens, Fishback, Casadevall and Thomassen).

[44] *Vilho Eskelinen and Others v. Finland*, para. 57.

[45] Ibid., para. 62.

[46] See for example the case of *Sukût v. Turkey* (no. 59773/00), Decision of 11 September 2007.

embassies of foreign States, the recent case-law however clearly indicates that Article 6 (1) applies. In the case of *Cudak v. Lithuania*,[47] which concerns an application for compensation for allegedly wrongful dismissal of a call desk-secretary at the Polish embassy in Lithuania and which is currently pending before the Grand Chamber of the Court, the question of whether Article 6 (1) applies will presumably be decided by the Court in the light of its new approach in *Vilho Eskelinen and Others v. Finland*.[48]

3. *The meaning of the term "right"*

The right of access to court is a procedural right which seeks to ensure that the individual can pursue those substantive rights which are recognised as arguable under domestic law.[49] The Court has phrased this as follows:

> Article 6 (1) extends only to 'contestations' (disputes) over (civil) 'rights and obligations' which can be said, at least on arguable grounds, to be recognised under domestic law; it does not in itself guarantee any particular content for (civil) 'rights and obligations' in the substantive law of the Contracting States.[50]

Therefore, Article 6 (1) does not guarantee any particular content for civil rights and obligations in domestic law. Nor is it for the Convention organs to use Article 6 (1) as a control mechanism to supervise that a State provides for certain substantive rights under national law. The Court does not possess

[47] *Cudak v. Lithuania* (no. 15869/02), Decision of 2 March 2006.

[48] By reference to the *Pellegrin* case, the Lithuanian government stated that the facts of the case did not fall within the ambit of Article 6 because the employment dispute concerned the predominantly public-law links between Poland and the applicant (see *Cudak v. Lithuania*, p. 7).

[49] See Lidbetter/George, *Negligent Public Authorities and Convention Rights – The Legacy of* Osman, EHRLR 2001, pp. 604–605; see generally Grabenwarter, *Europäische Menschenrechtskonvention*, p. 286; Jacobs and White, *European Conventions*, p. 144.

[50] *H v. Belgium*, Judgment of 30 November 1987, Series A 127–B, para. 40; *James and Others v. the United Kingdom* (no. 8793/79), Judgment of 21 February 1986, Series A 98, para. 81; *Lithgow and Others v. the United Kingdom* (no. 9006/80), Judgment of 8 July 1986, Series A 102, para. 192; *Holy Monasteries v. Greece* (no. 13092/87), Judgment of 9 December 1994, Series A 301–A, para. 80. See also the Commission's statement in the case *Sporrong and Lönnroth v. Sweden*: "Whether a right is at all at issue in a particular case depends primarily on the legal system of the State concerned. It is true that the concept of a 'right' is itself autonomous to some degree. Thus it is not decisive for the purposes of Article 6 para. 1 that a given privilege or interest which exists in a domestic legal system is not classified or described as a 'right' by that system. However, it is clear that the Convention organs could not create by way of interpretation of Article 6 para. 1 a substantive right which has no legal basis whatsoever in the state concerned." (*Sporrong and Lönnroth v. Sweden* (nos. 7151/75 and 7152/75), Commission Report of 8 October 1980, para. 150).

the power to create any legal rights which have no basis in the legal system of a Contracting State. Although States must provide in their domestic legal systems for the substantive fundamental rights and freedoms laid down in the Convention, they cannot be obliged by the Court to institute other rights which do not have any connection with the Convention rights.[51]

Governments have occasionally submitted that Article 6 (1) does not apply to cases involving immunities. Their argument has been as follows: where a person or body is protected by immunity from suit, no civil right exists for anyone to bring an action against that person or body. Even though the right which is claimed by the plaintiff might generally exist under domestic law, the immunity in question leads to the extinction of the cause of action in the particular case. Therefore, Article 6 (1) is allegedly not even applicable, as the right which is invoked by the applicant does not exist under domestic law due to the operation of the immunity. As far as international immunities such as State immunity or the immunity of international organisations are concerned, that argument can be rejected easily. It is generally recognised under public international law that both immunities may be waived.[52] Therefore, international immunities serve as a procedural bar and not a limitation on a domestic cause of action. In its case-law on State immunity, the Court has frequently observed that in the case of a waiver of State immunity by the defendant foreign State, the applicants' actions would have proceeded to a hearing and a judgment.[53] The Court rightly concluded from this that Article 6 (1) was applicable because there existed a civil right within the meaning of that provision, despite the operation of State immunity. With regard to domestic immunities, the distinction between procedural limitations and substantive limitations (*i.e.* a limitation on a cause of action) is more complicated and has caused numerous problems in the Court's case-law. These cases are being dealt with in the third part of this work ("Domestic immunities").

---

[51] Harris/O'Boyle/Warbrick, *European Convention*, p. 187; Bröhmer, *State Immunity*, p. 179; Grosz/Beatson/Duffy, *Human Rights*, C6-15.

[52] See below, p. 25.

[53] *Fogarty v. the United Kingdom* [GC] (no. 37112/97), Judgment of 21 November 2001, EHRR 2002, para. 25; *McElhinney v. Ireland* [GC] (no. 31253/96), Judgment of 21 November 2001, EHRR 2002, para. 26; *Al-Adsani v. the United Kingdom* [GC] (no. 35763/97), Judgment of 21 November 2001, EHRR 2002, para. 48.

IV. *The "Ashingdane Test"*

Ever since its judgment in *Ashingdane v. the United Kingdom*, the Court applies the following test in the case of immunities (hence it is often referred to as the "Ashingdane test"):

> [The Court] must be satisfied that the limitations applied do not restrict or reduce the access left to the individual in such a way or to such an extent that the very essence of the right is impaired. Furthermore, a limitation will not be compatible with Article 6 § 1 if it does not pursue a legitimate aim and if there is not a reasonable relationship of proportionality between the means employed and the aim sought to be achieved.[54]

The test is therefore a threefold one: the immunity must have a legitimate aim (1), and it must be proportionate (2). Moreover, the very essence of the right of access to court must not be impaired (3). The three criteria will be examined in the following section.

1. *Legitimate Aim*

That an interference with a Convention article needs to serve a legitimate aim is a general rule in the Convention. Many provisions in the Convention, such as Articles 8 to 11, explicitly name certain aims such as the interest of "morals", "public order", "national security", "public safety" or "economic well-being of the country". It is obvious that the Convention does not specify a certain legitimate aim where inherent rights such as the right of access to court are involved.

Whether the measure in question pursues a legitimate aim is usually uncontroversial in the Convention case-law. It has rarely been found that a State is not pursuing the aim it asserted.[55] The cases which involve a conflict between the right of access to court and immunities do not form an exception to this. At this stage of the test the Court usually considers whether the immunity in question is legitimate. For example, it found that the immunity of international organisations "is a long-standing practice established in the interest of good working of these organisations".[56] Moreover, the Court took the view that the immunity of Members of Parliament served "the legitimate

---

[54] *Waite and Kennedy v. Germany*, para. 59; *T.P. and K.M. v. the United Kingdom* [GC] (no. 28945/95), Judgment of 10 May 2001, ECHR 2001-V, para. 98; *Z and Others v. the United Kingdom* [GC] (no. 29392/95), Judgment of 10 May 2001, ECHR 2001-V, para. 93.

[55] Simor/Emmerson, *Human Rights Practice*, 1.068.

[56] *Waite and Kennedy v. Germany*, para. 61 et seq.

aims of protecting free speech in Parliament and maintaining the separation of powers between the legislature and the judiciary".[57]

In fact, the illegitimacy of the aim pursued with the granting of immunities was only invoked on two occasions by applicants. In the case of *Al-Adsani v. the United Kingdom*, the applicant submitted that the granting of State immunity did not serve a legitimate aim in proceedings concerning claims for compensation for torture.[58] Moreover, in *McElhinney v. Ireland*, the applicant argued that to grant State immunity in a situation where international practice was suggesting an exemption from immunity could not be considered as pursuing a legitimate aim.

The Court did not respond to these submissions in the respective judgments. Instead, it discussed the issue when considering whether the restriction on the applicant's right of access to court by the grant of State immunity was proportionate. The Court's approach is therefore to consider whether the immunity in question *generally* serves a legitimate aim. For example, the fact that States are entitled to immunity in certain civil proceedings generally serves the legitimate aim of comity and an exchange of good offices between States. The particular facts of the applications (e.g. whether the proceedings in question concerned claims for serious human rights violations) are brought into play when assessing whether the application of the general rules of State immunity was proportionate. This approach by the Court is to be welcomed as it prevents the danger of having to consider the question at two different stages ("legitimate aim" and "proportionality"), thereby blurring the line between two different criteria of the *Ashingdane* test.

However, there are cases conceivable in which only a specific situation will justify a restriction on the right of access to court. In those cases the Court will look at the specific context to decide on the "legitimate aim". In *Prince Hans-Adam II von Liechtenstein v. Germany*, the Court considered the exclusion of German jurisdiction concerning claims related to the seizure of German property for the purpose of reparation for the atrocities during the Second World War. The Court regarded this exclusion as a consequence of the particular status of Germany under public international law after 1945:

> *In these unique circumstances*, the limitation on access to a German court (...) had a legitimate objective.[59]

---

[57] *A v. the United Kingdom* (no. 35373/97), Judgment of 17 December 2002, RJD 2002-X, para. 77.

[58] See admissibility decision of *Al-Adsani v. the United Kingdom*, EHRR 2000 CD, p. 103.

[59] *Prince Hans-Adam II of Liechtenstein v. Germany* [GC] (no. 42527/98), Judgment of 12 July 2001, RJD 2001-VIII, para. 59 (Emphasis added).

What can be concluded from the above is that the Court is usually prepared to consider the granting of immunity as legitimate. If the criterion of "legitimacy" can therefore be said not to be causing much controversy, the emphasis of the *Ashingdane* test is put on the criterion of proportionality.

2. *Proportionality*

Although the principle of proportionality is not mentioned in the text of the Convention itself, it has become a dominant theme in the case-law under the Convention.[60] Some even suggest that proportionality has acquired the status of a general Convention principle.[61] In the classic sense, proportionality is the technique by which the Court determines whether an interference with one of the qualified rights (Articles 8 to 11) is necessary in a democratic society, or whether there is a reasonable justification for difference in treatment under Article 14.[62] For the purpose of determining the scope of limitations on implied rights (such as the right of access to court), the principle has occasionally been referred to as "the Court's principal yardstick".[63]

Proportionality requires that a fair balance must be struck between the demands of the general interests of the community and the requirements of the individual's fundamental rights.[64] Additionally, the extent of a deviation from a right must not be excessive in relation to the legitimate aim which has occasioned it.[65]

This stage of the test usually involves a close scrutiny by the Court of the case at issue. The Court considers, as far as international immunities are concerned, the legal situation under public international law, e.g. whether or not it is widely accepted international practice to grant State immunity in cases of serious human rights violations. Moreover, the Court will also deal with the question whether the applicant had any alternative remedies in order to institute proceedings, even though – as will be seen – the weight of that argument varies depending on what kind of immunity is at issue. The burden of proof that the interference is proportionate lies on the government.[66]

---

60 Reid, *Practitioner's Guide*, p. 45; Harris/O'Boyle/Warwick, *European Convention*, p. 11.

61 Van Dijk/van Hoof, *Theory and Practice*, p. 81.

62 Simor/Emmerson, *Human Rights Practice*, 1.070; Grabenwarter, *Europäische Menschenrechts-konvention*, § 17, 14; Reid, *Practitioner's Guide*, p. 45.

63 Simor/Emmerson, *Human Rights Practice*, 1.070.

64 *Sporrong and Loenroth v. Sweden* (7151/75 and 7152/75), Judgment of 23 September 1982, Series A 52, para. 73.

65 Van Dijk/van Hoof, *Theory and Practice*, p. 80.

66 Simor/Emmerson, *Human Rights Practice*, 1.071.

a) *The margin of appreciation*

When determining the proportionality of an interference with the right of access to court, the Court allows the State a certain "margin of appreciation" but subject to its supervision.[67] The doctrine of a margin of appreciation reflects the principle of subsidiarity, which basically holds that a central authority should not perform functions which can be performed more suitably and effectively at a lower (local) level. The doctrine allows a State a certain measure of discretion when it takes legislative, administrative or judicial action in the area of a Convention right.[68] This is particularly the case regarding issues of moral, social or economic policy on which there is no clear European consensus.[69] An exact formula of the scope of the margin of appreciation does not exist. The scope however varies between the different aims that legitimise interference in the exercise of a right.[70] Those notions which are "more objective" than the concept of morals leave less scope for a broad margin of appreciation.

b) *A margin of appreciation regarding the application of public international law?*

Especially with regard to international immunities, it is interesting that the Court grants the Contracting States a margin of appreciation in determining what is ultimately a legal question (e.g. "Is there an obligation under public international law to grant State immunity in a particular situation?"). One might argue that to grant a margin of appreciation makes perfect sense where social or economical issues are involved with which the domestic authorities are much more familiar, but not as far as questions of interpretation of public international law are concerned. A district court judge might not be in a better situation than, say, seventeen judges in a Grand Chamber of the European Court of Human Rights (partly composed of distinguished professors of public international law) to consider whether State immunity is still accepted under international law in a certain situation. However, that view fails to take into account that the doctrine of margin of appreciation is an expression of the subsidiarity principle which the Court also applies in view

---

[67] *Handyside v. the United Kingdom* (no. 5493/72), Judgment of 7 December 1976, Series A 24, para. 49.

[68] Harris/O'Boyle/Warwick, *European Convention*, p. 12; see generally on the margin of appreciation doctrine: Yourow, *The Margin of Appreciation Doctrine*; Arai-Takahashi, *The Margin of Appreciation Doctrine and the Principle of Proportionality in the Jurisprudence of the ECHR*.

[69] Simor/Emmerson, *Human Rights Practice*, 1.083.

[70] *The Sunday Times v. the United Kingdom* (no. 6538/74), Judgment of 26 April 1979, Series A 30, para. 59.

of the scope of its legal review.[71] According to the "fourth-instance doctrine", the Court leaves the domestic courts a margin of appreciation in applying the relevant law.[72] That is first and foremost the domestic law, but this may also include the application of norms of public international law (other than the Convention itself). In the case of *Melchior v. Germany*, which involved the domestic courts' interpretation of an international treaty under the Vienna Convention on the Law of Treaties, the Court stated:

> [T]he Court recalls the fundamental principle, established by its case-law on the interpretation and application of domestic law, that it is not its function to deal with errors of fact or law allegedly committed by a national court unless and in so far as they may have infringed rights and freedoms protected by the Convention (see, among many other authorities, *Streletz, Kessler and Krenz v. Germany* [GC], nos. 34044/96/01, 35532/97 and 44801/98, *Reports of Judgments and Decisions* 2001–II, § 49, and *Schenk v. Switzerland*, judgment of 12 July 1988, Series A no. 140, p. 29, § 45). It is primarily for the national authorities, notably the courts, to interpret and apply domestic law (see, *mutatis mutandis*, *Kopp v. Switzerland*, judgment of 25 March 1998, *Reports of Judgments and Decisions* 1998–II, p. 541, § 59).[73]

Especially where the rules of public international law form part of the legal system of a Member State[74], it becomes plain that the Court grants the same margin of appreciation to domestic courts when applying international law as it does with regard to the application and interpretation of domestic law. A similar approach, which also has its basis in the principle of subsidiarity, has been taken by the German Federal Constitutional Court, which equally leaves a margin of appreciation to the German ordinary courts when interpreting and applying public international law.[75] This approach has of course not been uncontroversial. In the second part of this work, which deals with international immunities, the question of the extent of that margin of appreciation and alternative suggestions to the Court's jurisprudence in this respect will be discussed in more detail.

3. *The very essence of the right*

Even if a restriction of the right to access to court because of the operation of immunity pursued a legitimate aim and was proportionate, it might

---

71 See also Maierhöfer, *Der EGMR als Modernisierer des Völkerrechts?*, EuGRZ 2002, p. 393.

72 See generally Peters, *Europäische Menschenrechtskonvention*, p. 11; Jacobs and White, *European Convention*, p. 140.

73 *Melchior v. Germany* (no. 66783/01), Decision of 2 February 2006.

74 This is for instance the case in Germany (see Articles 25 and 59 of the Basic Law).

75 BVerfGE 55, p. 367; BVerfGE 77, p. 167; see also Maierhöfer, *Der EGMR als Modernisierer des Völkerrechts?*, EuGRZ 2002, p. 393.

not be permissible if the restriction impairs the essence of the right.[76] In other contexts, the Court finds this to be the case if the right in question has been effectively destroyed by the restriction; thus, Contracting Parties have to ensure that an acceptable scope for its exercise remains.[77] Given the effect that the operation of immunity has on the right of access to court, it is surprising that the criterion has so far not played a crucial role in the case-law on immunities and Article 6 (1).

Occasionally, the Court's approach with regard to immunities and the "very essence of the right" is a "relative one".[78] It will first consider the criteria "legitimate aim" and "proportionality" and, after having found that these two conditions have been satisfied, conclude that *therefore* the "very essence of the right to access to court" was not impaired by the immunity.[79] According to the Court, the assessment of the third criterion thereby depends on the assessment of the first two criteria. This approach has been rightly criticised as being "unorthodox and illogical" by Judge Costa in the decision *Prince Hans-Adam II von Liechtenstein v. Germany*.[80] Indeed, the "relative approach" the Court is taking is in danger of mixing up the three different criteria of the test. If the outcome of the third criterion entirely depends on the assessment of the other two, it does not add anything to the test.

There is, however, something even more disturbing about the "very essence" criterion as such in the case of immunities. It is a distinguishing feature of immunities from suit that they bar any action. Therefore, to put it with Judge Ress in *Prince Hans-Adam II von Liechtenstein v. Germany*, they ultimately render the right of access "illusory and theoretical".[81] In other words, immunities totally eliminate the right of access to court, not leaving any scope for its exercise. What, if not the essence of the right of access, is then being affected? Strictly speaking, it is hardly conceivable that an absolute immunity would not impair the very essence of the right to access. Judge Loucaides observed in his dissenting opinion in the case of *McElhinney v. Ireland*: "It is correct that Article 6 may be subject to inherent limitations, but these limitations should not affect the core of the right. Procedural conditions such as time-limits, the need for leave to appeal etc. do not affect the

[76] See *Ashingdane v. the United Kingdom* (no. 8225/78), Judgment of 28 May 1985, Series A 93, para. 57.

[77] Reid, *Practitioner's Guide*, p. 35.

[78] See also Peters, *Europäische Menschenrechtskonvention*, p. 119.

[79] See *Prince Hans-Adam II of Liechtenstein v. Germany* [GC] (no. 42527/98), Judgment of 12 July 2001, RJD 2001-VIII, para. 69.

[80] Ibid., concurring opinion of Judge Costa.

[81] Ibid., concurring opinion of Judge Ress joined by Judge Zupancic.

substance of the right."[82] Judge Loucaides rightly observed that immunity completely prevents "somebody from having his case determined by a court, without any fault on his part".[83]

It appears that the Court itself is not at ease discussing this criterion in the context of immunities, as an analysis of its case-law shows. In its numerous judgments on immunities, the Court usually lists the three criteria of the *Ashingdane* test, just to continue to discuss the first two criteria in great detail. After having found whether or not the criteria of "legitimate aim" and "proportionality" have been met, the Court usually circumvents the discussion of the "very essence" criterion. The latter is simply not mentioned any more. After ruled on the "proportionality" criterion, the Court directly moves on to conclude whether or not Article 6 (1) was violated. In fact, there are only three judgments in which the criterion has been discussed at all by the Court. In *Prince Hans-Adam II von Liechtenstein v. Germany*, the Court took the above-mentioned "relative" approach. The other judgments are the cases of *Waite and Kennedy v. Germany* and *Beer and Regan v. Germany*, in which the Court had to rule on the immunity of the international organisation *European Space Agency* (ESA) which had frustrated the applicants' claim before the German labour courts. The Court found that the applicants had alternative means of resolving their dispute, namely the ESA Appeals Board. It held that the "very essence" of the right of access to court was not impaired because the applicants had somewhere else to turn regarding their employment dispute. In the event of alternative means, it is arguable that the right of access has not been completely eliminated. Still, the applicant will not have access to a *court*. However, in most cases concerning immunities and Article 6 (1) – this applies particularly to domestic immunities – alternative means were *de facto* not available to the applicants or did not concern the claims which the applicants pursued. To hold whether or not their claims were barred by immunity therefore amounted to an "all or nothing" situation for them. Perhaps this explains why the Court refrained from discussing the "very essence" criterion in those cases.

4. *Conclusion*

There are certainly examples in the Court's case-law on the right of access to court in which the "very essence" criterion should be applied in a meaningful way. Such cases may concern compulsory legal representation, court

[82] *McElhinney v. Ireland*, dissenting opinion of Judge Loucaides.
[83] Ibid.

costs, time-limits or denial of legal aid.[84] In those cases, the claimant has the opportunity to have his or her case decided on the merits by the domestic courts if the claimant is represented by legal counsel, has paid court fees and lodged the claim in due time. Immunity however completely bars access to court. Therefore, it is impossible to apply the criterion as far as immunities from suit are concerned. In the present author's view, this contradiction can only be resolved if one abandons this criterion from the test. This approach has for instance been taken by the Commission in an earlier decision.[85] In fact, it is exactly what the Court seems to have done in the majority of cases concerning immunities. This becomes particularly obvious in the cases of *Ashingdane v. the United Kingdom* or *Fayed v. the United Kingdom.*[86] In those cases, the Court did not decide on the issue whether or not Article 6 was applicable. It found that the "same central issues of legitimate aim and proportionality" arose also under Article 8 (the right to respect for one's private life which had also been invoked by the applicants) and consequently proceeded to apply the same *twofold* test to both provisions. Hence the Court *de facto* abandoned the "very essence" criterion from the test without explicitly mentioning it.

Consequently, there should be a mere twofold test when considering complaints of an alleged immunity-related violation of the right of access to court: immunities do not amount to a violation of Article 6 (1) if they serve a legitimate aim and if they pose a proportionate restriction on the right of access to court.

---

[84] For further references see Grabenwarter, *Europäische Menschenrechtskonvention*, § 24, 48 et seq., and Reid, *Practitioner's Guide*, p. 76 et seq.

[85] *Dyer v. the United Kingdom* (no. 10475/83), Commission decision of 9 October 1984, D/R 39, p. 246.

[86] *Fayed v. the United Kingdom* (no. 17101/90), Judgment of 21 September 1990, Series A 294–B, para. 67.

Part II

International Immunities

I. *State Immunity*

1. *State Immunity in public international law*

With regard to State immunity, one has to distinguish between the State which benefits from immunity (the foreign State) and the State which grants that immunity (the forum State). State immunity means the legal principles and rules under which a foreign State may claim exemption from the jurisdiction of another State.[1] Therefore, State immunity bars the courts of the forum State from determining the legal responsibility of foreign States for their actions.[2] In times when there did not yet exist a distinction between a State and its ruler, State immunity was explained by the aim of avoiding degrading the dignity of the sovereign and its nation by placing the sovereign within the jurisdiction of another State.[3]

This personalisation has gradually given way to a more abstract concept of State immunity, which today rests on two principles.[4] The first is the maxim *par in parem non habet jurisdictionem*, which considers all States to be of equal legal standing. Hence two States cannot have their disputes settled in the courts of one of them unless the other waives its immunity as an expression of its equality with the other State.[5] The second principle is that of non-intervention in the internal affairs of one State by another. The most often

---

[1] Steinberger, *State Immunity*, EPIL IV, p. 615.

[2] Bröhmer, *State Immunity*, p. 3.

[3] For overviews on the historical development of sovereign immunity see Steinberger, *State Immunity*, EPIL IV, p. 616; Badr, *State Immunity*, p. 9 et seq.; Damian, *Staatenimmunität und Gerichtszwang*, p. 4 et seq.; Fox, *The Concept of State Immunity and the Justification for State Immunity*, The Law of State Immunity, pp. 40–67.

[4] See Shaw, *International Law*, p. 622; Brownlie, *Principles*, p. 327.

[5] See Brownlie, *Principles*, p. 325; Oppenheim/Lauterpacht, *International Law*, Vol. 1, p. 264; Steinberger, *State Immunity*, EPIL IV, p. 619. Other authors refuse to accept this rationale

cited source for this rationale is the United States Supreme Court decision in *The Schooner Exchange*, which stressed that sovereign immunity serves the perfect equality and absolute independence of sovereigns as well as the maintenance of an interchange of good offices with each other.[6]

a) *Absolute and restrictive immunity*

During the eighteenth and for most of the nineteenth century, the doctrine of sovereign immunity was an absolute one.[7] Absolute immunity means that all claims against a State would be barred. As States acted entirely in an official capacity, every act was necessarily governmental in nature and considered suitable for immunity.[8] However, when States started to get involved in international trade and economic activities, it was increasingly considered inappropriate to grant State immunity in this respect. If States were doing business in the same way as any private person, there was no reason why they should enjoy the privilege of immunity from suit in case of legal disputes resulting from their commercial activities.[9] Therefore, the doctrine of restrictive immunity gradually evolved and has become, with some exceptions (most notably China and the former Soviet Union countries), widely accepted. According to this theory, only governmental actions (*acta jure imperii*) remain immune, whereas acts of a private or commercial nature (*acta jure gestionis*) can be judged upon by foreign courts.

Although the distinction can often prove to be a very difficult task, it is not an impossible one.[10] It is widely agreed that it cannot be the opinion of the State claiming immunity which is decisive for the assessment of whether a certain act should fall into the category of either *acta jure imperii* or *acta*

---

since equality between States would also exist if State immunity did not exist at all (Damian, *Staatenimmunität*, p. 15; Bröhmer, *State Immunity*, p. 11).

6 *The Schooner Exchange v. McFaddon* (1812), 7 Cranch 116.

7 Shaw, *International Law*, p. 625. The first court decisions which restricted state immunity to *acta iure gestionis* date back to the end of the 19th century, see Steinberger, *State Immunity*, EPIL IV, p. 616.

8 Therefore, it was unthinkable to even sue a foreign State for *acta iure gestionis* "without striking an intolerable blow to its dignity" (Gaillard/Pingel-Lenuzza, *International Organisations and Immunity from Jurisdiction: To Restrict or To Bypass*, ICLQ 2002, p. 1).

9 For the historical development of the restrictive approach see: Marasinghe, *The Modern Law of Sovereign Immunity*, MLR 1991, p. 664 et seq.; Steinberger, *State Immunity*, EPIL IV, p. 616.

10 However, distinguished authors have argued that the difficulty of distinguishing between *acta iure imperii* and *acta iure gestionis* is the main argument in favour of an absolute immunity approach (Lauterpacht, *The Problem of Jurisdictional Immunities*, BYIL 1951, p. 222; Steinberger, *State Immunity*, EPIL IV, p. 630). See generally Hafner/Kohen/Breau, *The Definition of Commercial Acts*, State Practice Regarding State Immunities, p. 21.

jure gestionis. Otherwise States would be inclined to decide in their favour and thereby undermine the theory of restrictive immunity. Under international law, the characterisation of an act as either *de jure imperii* and *de jure gestionis* is therefore reserved for the national legislature in accordance with the *lex fori*.[11]

b) *State immunity in international and national law*

State immunity is a norm of general customary international law.[12] However, the principle has been embodied both in international and national legislation.

(1) *International Legislation*

At the level of international law, there have been attempts by both the Council of Europe and the United Nations to adopt a uniform approach towards State immunity.[13]

(a) The European Convention on State Immunity

The Council of Europe's European Convention on State Immunity of 16 May 1972[14] has however been ratified by only eight States.[15] For those countries that are both parties to the European Convention on Human Rights and the European Convention on State Immunity, conflicting obligations could arise from the two Council of Europe treaties. Such a conflict would for instance involve the obligation to grant an individual's right to access to a court against a foreign State versus the obligation to recognise that the alleged foreign State enjoys immunity. However, Article 33 of the European Convention on State Immunity contains a saving clause for "existing agreements in special fields" and the European Convention on Human Rights can be considered as such an existing agreement in the special field of human rights.[16]

---

[11] Bantekas, *Case note*, AJIL 1998, p. 766.

[12] For rather extreme views questioning this widely accepted categorisation, see Orakhelashvili, *Restrictive Interpretation of Human Rights in Recent Jurisprudence*, EJIL 2003, p. 553; Caplan, *State Immunity, Human Rights and* Jus Cogens*: A Critique of the Normative Hierarchy Theory*, AJIL 2003, p. 772.

[13] Other attempts to codify the rules on State immunity have been taken by the International Law Association ("Revised Draft Articles for a Convention on State Immunity of August 1994", ILA Reports of its 66th Conference, Buenos Aires 1994, p. 488) and the Institute of International Law (Institute of International Law, *Contemporary Problems Concerning the Immunity of State in Relation to Questions of Jurisdiction and Enforcement*, Annuaire de l'Institut de Droit International, Vol. 64-II, 1992, p. 390).

[14] ILM 11, p. 470.

[15] The States which have ratified are: Austria, Belgium, Cyprus, Germany, Luxembourg, the Netherlands, Switzerland and the United Kingdom.

[16] Bröhmer, *State Immunity*, p. 188.

(b) The United Nations Convention on Jurisdictional Immunities of States and Their Property

In December 2004, the General Assembly of the United Nations adopted the United Nations Convention on Jurisdictional Immunities of States and Their Property (hereafter the UN State Immunity Convention).[17] Like the European Convention on State Immunity, the purpose of the UN State Immunity Convention was to give some guidance to national courts whose development of international law in this respect had become increasingly sporadic and unreliable.[18] That guidance could be especially useful for those States which until recently adhered to an absolute doctrine of State immunity such as China or the former Soviet countries.[19] The preparations for the treaty took twenty-two years, and it is based on a draft proposal by the International Law Commission of 1991.[20] According to its preamble, the State Parties to the Convention consider State immunity a generally accepted principle of customary international law. Diplomatic immunities as well as Head of State immunity *ratione personae* are not covered by the Convention (Article 3). When adopting the Convention, the General Assembly stated its understanding that the Convention does not cover criminal proceedings.[21]

Article 5 of the Convention provides for a general rule of State immunity, subject to exceptions which are enumerated in Articles 10 to 17 of the Convention. Those exceptions will be considered in the following chapter where appropriate. The Convention's relationship with the European Convention on Human Rights can be taken from Article 26 which provides that nothing in the Convention shall affect the rights and obligations of State Parties under existing international agreements (e.g. Article 6 of the European Convention on Human Rights). Article 27 refers, in cases of a dispute between States about the scope of immunity which cannot be settled between those States, to a settlement of the dispute by arbitration or ultimately by the International Court of Justice. Lastly, the Convention does not apply retroactively (Article 4).

---

[17] UNGA Resolution 59/38 of 2 December 2004; see also Denza, *The 2005 UN Convention on State Immunity in Perspective*, ICLQ 2006, p. 395; Fox, *In Defence of State Immunity: why the UN Convention on State Immunity is important*, ICLQ 2006, p. 399; Gardiner, *UN Convention on State Immunity: Form and Function*, ICLQ 2006, p. 407; Hall, *UN Convention on State Immunity: the need for a human rights protocol*, ICLQ 2006, p. 411; Dickinson, *Status of Forces under the UN Convention on State Immunity*, ICLQ 2006, p. 427.

[18] Denza, *The 2005 UN Convention on State Immunity in Perspective*, ICLQ 2006, p. 398.

[19] Fox, *In Defence of State Immunity*, ICLQ 2006, p. 399.

[20] Ibid.

[21] Ibid., p. 401.

The Convention was open for signature until 17 January 2007 (Article 28). It appears that by June 2009 twenty-eight States had ratified the Convention.[22] Given that small number, it remains to be seen whether the Convention will become a forceful international treaty which serves as guidance for national courts when deciding on claims against foreign States, or whether it will simply share the same fate as the European Convention on State Immunity which, as already mentioned, has only been ratified by eight States and is therefore rather insignificant.[23] As Fox has stated, the Convention represents only a partial codification of State immunity, focused solely on immunity from civil jurisdiction and one which by the need for diplomatic compromise can be faulted for lack of clarity.[24]

(2) *National Legislation*

Domestic codification of State immunity mainly occurred in common-law countries in the late 1970s in order to facilitate the national courts' task of distinguishing between commercial and sovereign acts. Two important examples are the United States Foreign Sovereign Immunities Act 1976 and the United Kingdom State Immunity Act 1976. Other countries such as Canada and Australia subsequently adopted similar domestic statutes. Technically, these acts (like the international conventions) provide for a general principle of State immunity, but subject to an enumerated list of exceptions. Numerous (mostly civil-law) countries do not have special legislation on immunities. In order to fulfil their international obligations, those countries either dedicate particular provisions to international immunities or recognise sovereign immunity as customary or judge-made domestic law.[25]

c) *Waiver of State immunity*

A traditionally recognised exception to State immunity is that a State can waive its immunity, either expressly or impliedly.[26] An expressly declared waiver may be made by a unilateral declaration or in a provision of a private contract or international agreement.[27] Implied submission to the jurisdiction

---

22 The Convention will enter into force thirty days following the date of deposit of the thirtieth instrument of ratification, acceptance, approval, or acceptance with the UN Secretary General.

23 See also Gardiner, *UN Convention on State Immunity: Form and Function*, ICLQ 2006, p. 407.

24 Fox, *In Defence of State Immunity*, ICLQ 2006, p. 403.

25 Steinberger, *State Immunity*, EPIL IV, p. 616.

26 See generally Hafner/Kohen/Breau, *Waiver of Immunity*, State Practice Regarding State Immunities, p. 59.

27 Ipsen/Gloria, *Völkerrecht*, p. 337.

of the forum State has to be interpreted narrowly.[28] States which have instituted proceedings impliedly submit themselves to any counterclaim arising out of the same legal relationship or facts that are the subject-matter of the claim.[29] The intervention or taking of any steps in the proceedings may be regarded as an implied waiver of immunity, unless the intervention only served the aim of claiming immunity in the proceedings.[30] Passive reaction by the foreign State, such as failure to attend a court hearing, cannot be deemed an implied waiver; neither can a provision in a contract which specifies that the law of the forum State is applicable.[31] A waiver will only be valid if the competent organs of the foreign State (at least impliedly) declare the waiver and the declaration is received by the competent authorities in the forum State.

d) *Immunity from attachment and execution*

The jurisdictional aspect of State immunity which was considered above has to be distinguished from immunity from attachment and execution.[32] This concerns the property of the foreign State which is located within the territory of the forum State and is considered below (pp. 88–126).

2. *State immunity and the jurisdiction of the forum State (Article 1 of the Convention)*

As regards State immunity (and in fact this would concern other international immunities too), there exists a particular problem concerning the applicability of Article 6. Arguably, in cases where public international law requires the forum State to grant immunity to a foreign State or an international organisation, the forum State lacks jurisdiction. Consequently, a complaint under Article 6 about a violation of the right of access to court could be considered as incompatible *ratione materiae* with the Convention, in particular in view of its Article 1, which holds:

> The High Contracting Parties shall secure to everyone *within their jurisdiction* the rights and freedoms defined in Section I of the Convention.[33]

---

[28] Ipsen/Gloria, *Völkerrecht*, p. 337.

[29] Shaw, *International Law*, p. 660.

[30] Doehring, *Völkerrecht*, p. 282.

[31] Steinberger, *State Immunity*, EPIL IV, p. 622. For references of whether and under which circumstances agreements to submit disputes to arbitration can be considered as an implied waiver: see Brownlie, *Principles*, p. 340.

[32] A detailed analysis on this topic has been given by Damian, *Staatenimmunität*, pp. 167–188.

[33] Emphasis added.

The first commentator to have implied this argument with regard to State immunity was Damian.[34] Arguing that the procedural guarantees contained in Article 6 are only effective within the given scope of national jurisdiction, he suggests that these guarantees do not extend the scope of jurisdiction into the area traditionally covered by the rules of State immunity.[35] Hence the granting of State immunity in cases which are recognised by public international law is compatible with the right of access to court.[36]

It appears that the Commission took a similar path in the case of *Spaans v. the Netherlands*.[37] There an employee of the Iran-United States Claims Tribunal complained that his claim against the termination of his labour contract was dismissed by the Dutch courts because of that international organisation's immunity. The Commission found that:

> Because of the immunity enjoyed by the Tribunal, the administrative decisions of the Tribunal are not acts which occur within the jurisdiction of the Netherlands within the meaning of Article 1 of the Convention and thus do not engage the responsibility of the Netherlands under the Convention.[38]

It is interesting to note that the Convention organs have never again addressed this problem since this decision was taken in 1988, even though a Commission member took the same view in his concurring opinion in the case of *Waite and Kennedy v. Germany*.[39] However, the argument had its "renaissance" in the House of Lord's judgment in *Holland v. Lampen-Wolfe*,[40] in which Lord Millett found:

> At first sight [Article 6] may appear to be inconsistent with a doctrine of comprehensive and unqualified State immunity in those cases where it is applicable.

[34] Damian, *Staatenimmunität*, pp. 16–17.

[35] Damian, *Staatenimmunität*, p. 17.

[36] Damian, *Staatenimmunität*, p. 17. This passage suggests that a violation could be found if a State would grant immunity in the absence of a duty under international law to do so (e.g. for *acta jure gestionis*).

[37] *Spaans v. the Netherlands* (no. 12516/86), Commission decision of 12 December 1988, D/R 58, p. 119.

[38] Ibid., p. 122.

[39] Concurring opinion by Mr K. Herndl, para. 2: "(...) as regards private law disputes with ESA, the parties to such disputes might not fall under German jurisdiction in the sense of Article 1 of the Convention, because German jurisdiction over those kinds of disputes simply does not exist under international law. The situation can be regarded as similar to a situation where, owing to the total lack of any link with the territorial jurisdiction, courts have to decline to adjudicate a dispute as they have legally no jurisdiction." Moreover, the Commission appears to have taken a similar reasoning in *N, C, F and AG v. Italy* (no. 24236/94, Commission decision of 4 December 1995, ILR 111, p. 154) without however bringing into play Article 1.

[40] *Holland v. Lampen-Wolfe* [2000] 3 All ER, p. 808.

> But in fact there is no inconsistency. This is not because the right guaranteed by art 6 is not absolute but subject to limitations, nor is it because the doctrine of State immunity serves a legitimate aim. It is because art 6 forbids a contracting State from denying individuals the benefit of its powers of adjudication; it does not extent the scope of those powers. Art 6 requires contracting States to maintain fair and public judicial processes and forbids them to deny individual access to those processes for the determination of their civil rights. It presupposes that the contracting States have the powers of adjudication necessary to resolve the issues in dispute. But it does not confer on contracting States adjudicative powers that they do not possess. State immunity, as I have explained, is a creature of customary international law and derives from the equality of sovereign States. It is not a self-imposed restriction on the jurisdiction of its courts that the United Kingdom had chosen to adopt. It is a limitation imposed from without upon the sovereignty of the United Kingdom itself.[41]

Lord Millett's argument has found much support amongst other members of the House of Lords and British academics alike.[42] In the *Jones* case,[43] the House of Lords recently disagreed with the Strasbourg Court's approach that Article 6 was engaged with regard to State immunity. In particular, Lord Hoffmann, by referring to the above statement by Lord Millett, made this argument very accessible by saying:

> I do not understand how a state can be said to deny access to its court if it has no access to give.[44]

To hold that Article 6 does not apply with regard to international immunities is however objectionable for both legal and practical reasons. First, as Yang has rightly pointed out,[45] the word "immunity" presupposes jurisdiction from which the defendant is immune, *i.e.* the courts would have jurisdiction under normal circumstances, but the fact that the defendant is a foreign State

---

[41] Ibid., pp. 846–847.

[42] See Jones, *Article 6 ECHR and Immunities arising in Public International Law*, ICLQ 2003, pp. 464–465; by agreeing with Lord Millett, Voyakis suggests to distinguish between immunities which pose internal limitations (such as parliamentary immunity) and external limitations (such as State immunity) on a State's jurisdiction. The latter consequently would not raise an issue under the Convention (*Access to Court v State Immunity*, ICLQ 2003, pp. 307–310). Note however that other British courts proceeded on the basis that Article 6 (1) applies to cases concerning State immunity (see England and Wales High Court (Queen's Bench Division), *Grovit v. De Nederlandsche Bank & Ors* [2005] EWHC 2944 (QB), para. 75; *Ronald Grant Jones v. the Ministry of the Interior Al-Mamlaka Al-Arabiya as Saudiya (The Kingdom of Saudi Arabia) & Anor, Sandy Mitchell & Ors v. Ibrahim Al-Dali & Ors*, judgment of the Court of Appeal of 28 October 2004).

[43] *Jones v. Ministry of Interiro Al-Mamlaka Al-Arabiya AS Saudiya (the Kingdom of Saudi Arabia)*, [2006] UKHL 26, judgment of 14 June 2006.

[44] Ibid., para. 14.

[45] Yang, *State Immunity in the European Court of Human Rights*, BYIL 2003, p. 340.

precludes the exercise of that jurisdiction. Nevertheless, even if the decision not to exercise its adjudicatory jurisdiction over a foreign State is being taken in order to comply with international obligations, it does not mean that the forum State would not have had jurisdiction in the first place. The forum State merely *refrains* from exercising its jurisdiction, but this must be in conformity with other international obligations such as the European Convention on Human Rights.[46] Those who support the view that the Convention does not apply because the Contracting States lack jurisdiction in cases involving State immunity, also fail to take into account that the forum State has jurisdiction in the case that State immunity is waived. This view might also find some support in the joint separate opinion of three judges of the International Court of Justice in the *Arrest Warrant* case, who held that:

> (...) the impression is created that immunity has value *per se*, whereas in reality it is an exception to a normative rule which would otherwise apply. It reflects, therefore, an interest which in certain circumstances prevails over an otherwise predominant interest, it is an exception to jurisdiction which normally can be exercised and *it can only be invoked when the latter exists*. It represents an interest of its own that must always be balanced, however, against the interest of that norm to which it is an exception.[47]

Moreover, that view is supported by Article 6 of the United Convention on State Immunity which requires State parties to "give effect to State immunity (...) by refraining *from exercising jurisdiction* in a proceeding before its court against another State (...)".[48] It seems odd that, say, a British claimant who files a civil suit for damages in an English court would not come "within the jurisdiction" of the United Kingdom within the meaning of Article 1 of the Convention by the mere fact that the defendant is a foreign State. This would also deprive that claimant of other guarantees under the Convention besides the right of access to court. For example, in the case of *N, C, F and AG v. Italy*,[49] the applicants complained about the length of proceedings before the Italian courts which had found that the applicants' right to execute a decision against the Albanian embassy was barred by State immunity.[50] Although the

---

[46] For a detailed overview of the discussion, see Fox, *The Law of State Immunity*, pp. 74 et seq. ("The relationship of immunity to jurisdiction"). Fox's conclusion, however, remains rather open: "But whether [State immunity] is merely an exception to jurisdiction or a principle of law in its own right, so forming part of, rather than an exception to, jurisdiction, remains uncertain." (Ibid., p. 75).

[47] *Democratic Republic of Congo v. Belgium*, ICJ Reports 2002, Joint Separate Opinion of Judges Higgins, Kooijmans and Buergenthal, para. 71 (emphasis added).

[48] Emphasis added.

[49] *N, C, F and AG v. Italy*, ILR 111, p. 154.

[50] See above, p. 121.

complaint about the length of the proceedings might have raised an issue under the Convention, the Commission did not consider this complaint because it found that Article 6 (1) did not apply.[51] Such a result is clearly unsatisfactory.

Moreover, to distinguish between "external" and "self-imposed" limitations is somewhat artificial. From the claimant's perspective, there is no difference whether the limitation on the forum State's jurisdiction is self-imposed or imposed from outside. In any event, the claimant will have had no access to court.[52]

Second, there are practical reasons for the applicability of Article 6. If a contracting State (erroneously) granted State immunity in a case where international law does not demand that it do so (e.g. in the case of *acta jure gestionis*), the claimant would come within the Contracting State's jurisdiction, because no restriction has been imposed from without upon the forum State's sovereignty. On the contrary, it would constitute a self-imposed restriction. In order to qualify the restriction as "external" or "internal" (in order to decide whether or not the Convention applies), the European Court of Human Rights would have to determine precisely at the admissibility stage whether or not the granting of immunity was required under public international law. This can be a very complicated and tricky task in areas in which international law is far from clear, such as employment issues in embassies. It would not be a very convincing approach by the Court to discuss the current state of public international law at the admissibility stage, and then to proceed with the merits of the case by granting contracting States a margin of appreciation in determining exactly the same question. Lastly, there is no need to interpret the applicability of Article 6 as narrowly as this, as Court takes into account the applicable public international law anyway when applying the *Ashingdane* criteria.[53] A balancing test would certainly do the two conflicting interests more justice.[54]

It is to be regretted that the Court has not yet addressed this problem in its jurisprudence on international immunities, even though the submissions

---

[51] Moreover, in the case of *Hirschhorn v. Romania* (no. 29294/02, Judgment of 26 July 2007), the Court found a violation of Article 6 (1) in proceedings concerning diplomatic immunity because the tribunal concerned had not been independent and impartial. The finding of that violation would not have been possible had the Court followed the above argument that the case did not come within Article 1 of the Convention because of the operation of an international immunity.

[52] Tams, *Schwierigkeiten mit dem Ius Cogens*, Archiv des Völkerrechts 2002, pp. 336–337.

[53] Ibid., p. 337.

[54] See also Yang, *State Immunity in the European Court of Human Rights*, BYIL 2003, p. 340.

of the United Kingdom Government in the case of *Al-Adsani v. the United Kingdom* strongly pointed in the direction of the above-mentioned argument.[55] The fact that the Court nevertheless found Article 6 to apply might indicate that the Court did not consider it as a very strong argument.

3. *State immunity in the recent Convention case-law*

In November 2001, the Grand Chamber of the Strasbourg Court delivered three judgments in which it held that State immunity as granted by the jurisdictions of Ireland and the United Kingdom was compatible with Article 6 (1): *Fogarty v. the United Kingdom*, *McElhinney v. Ireland* and *Al-Adsani v. the United Kingdom*.[56] It was the first time the Court had to rule on this issue.[57] In all three cases, the Court proceeded on the basis that State immunity was compatible with Article 6 (1) if the *Ashingdane* test would have been complied with. The Court held that the limitation on the right to access by the granting of State immunity served a legitimate aim. It noted that State immunity is a concept of international law which developed out of the principle *par in parem non habet imperium*, by virtue of which one State shall not be subject to the jurisdiction of another State. The Court found that State immunity serves to promote comity and to maintain an interchange of good relations between States.[58] Regarding the question of proportionality, the Court reiterated:

> (...) that the Convention has to be interpreted in the light of the rules set out in the Vienna Convention on the Law of Treaties of 23 May 1969, and that Article 31 § 3 (c) of that treaty indicates that account is to be taken of "any relevant rules of international law applicable in the relations between the parties". The Convention, including Article 6, cannot be interpreted in a vacuum. The Court must be mindful of the Convention's special character as a human rights treaty, and it must also take the relevant rules of international law into account (see, *mutatis mutandis*, *Loizidou v. Turkey* (merits), judgment of 18 December 1996,

---

[55] The Government claimed that Article 6 was not applicable because the provision could not extend to matters outside the State's jurisdiction. Due to the State immunity which was required by an international law obligation in the *Al-Adsani* case, the Government argued that the facts fell outside the jurisdiction of the national courts (see *Al-Adsani v. the United Kingdom* [GC] (no. 35763/97), Decision of 1 March 2000).

[56] *Fogarty v. the United Kingdom* [GC] (no. 37112/97), Judgment of 21 November 2001, EHRR 2002; *McElhinney v. Ireland* [GC] (no. 31253/96), Judgment of 21 November 2001, EHRR 2002; *Al-Adsani v. the United Kingdom* [GC] (no. 35763/97), Judgment of 21 November 2001, EHRR 2002.

[57] Before the three decisions by the European Court of Human Rights, the House of Lords had found that State immunity was compatible with Article 6: *Holland v. Lampen-Wolfe* ([2000] 3 All ER, p. 833).

[58] *Al-Adsani v. the United Kingdom*, para. 54.

> *Reports* 1996-VI, p. 2231, § 43). The Convention should so far as possible be interpreted in harmony with other rules of international law of which it forms part, including those relating to the grant of State immunity.[59]

Therefore, the Court opined that State immunity could not in principle be regarded as a disproportionate restriction on Article 6 (1). It supervised the domestic courts' application of the principle of State immunity: if it reflected generally recognised rules of public international law (the domestic courts having a margin of appreciation in that respect), the granting of State immunity was a disproportionate restriction of Article 6 (1). To settle this question, the Court undertook an in-depth assessment and analysis of the applicable public international law. Therefore, it is necessary to look at the particular facts of each case. Before this study will turn to those cases, some thoughts on the Court's general approach on State immunity and Article 6 (1) will be expressed in the following.

The case-law on State immunity and Article 6 (1) is a vivid example of the increasingly important relationship between the Convention and general international law.[60] The Court's approach that the Convention cannot be interpreted in a vacuum and that it must take into account relevant rules of international law does not only have its basis in Article 31 (3) (c) of the Vienna Convention on the Law of Treaties, but also in the Court's case-law itself. The above quote from the State immunity-judgments had been taken from the judgment of *Loizidou v. Turkey* (concerning the applicant's access to her property in northern Cyprus) in which the concept of "jurisdiction" within the meaning of Article 1 of the Convention and the question of reservations of States when ratifying the Convention had to be interpreted in the light of the Vienna Convention on the Law of Treaties.[61] The approach has

---

[59] *Fogarty v. the United Kingdom*, para. 35; *Al-Adsani v. the United Kingdom*, para. 55; *McElhinney v. Ireland*, para. 36.

[60] See generally on the relationship between the Convention and public international law: Ziemele, *Case-Law of the European Court of Human Rights and Integrity of International Law*, p. 187; Villiger, *Articles 31 and 32 of the Vienna Convention on the Law of Treaties in the Case-law of the European Court of Human Rights*, p. 317; Caflisch/Cancado Trindade, *Les Conventions américaine et européenne des droits de l'homme et le droit international general*, Revue Générale de Droit International Public 2004, p. 5; Wildhaber, *The ECHR and International Law*, ICLQ 2007, p. 217; Orakhelashvili, *Restrictive Interpretation of Human Rights in Recent Jurisprudence*, EJIL 2003, p. 529; de Wet, *The Role of European Courts in Reviewing Conflicting Obligations under International Law*, IOLR 2008, p. 359.

[61] *Loizidou v. Turkey* (preliminary objections) [GC], (no. 15318/89), Judgment of 23 March 1995, Series A 310; *Loizidou v. Turkey* (merits) [GC], Judgment of 18 December 1996, Reports 1996 VI, p. 2215; see also the case of *Bankovic and Others v. Belgium and 16 Other Nato States* [GC] (no. 52207/99), Decision of 12 December 2001, ECHR 2001-XI) regarding a "primarily territorial" interpretation of the term "jurisdiction".

been used in other contexts as well, for example in the case of *Mamatkulov and Abdurasulovic v. Turkey*[62] in which the Court decided that any State Party to which interim measures under Article 39 of the Rules of the Court had been indicated in order to avoid irreparable harm being caused to the victim of an alleged violation must comply with those measures. In *Selmouni v. France*, the Court applied Article 31 (3) (c) in order to refer to the definition of "torture" in the United Nations Torture Convention 1984 to affirm that the applicant suffered from torture while being in police custody.[63]

In the present context, the applicability of the Vienna Convention on the Law of Treaties is however interesting because the Court – unlike in the above examples – does not apply Article 31 (3) (c) in order to interpret a certain right in the Convention, but its limitation.[64] There is however nothing in the Vienna Convention on the Law of Treaties which would contradict the applicability of that provision with regard to the limitations of Article 6 (1).

The Court's general approach seems to be correct because it takes into account that the Contracting Parties do not only have obligations towards individuals, but also towards other States which have not ratified the Convention. While it is difficult to find parallel approaches in the jurisprudence of other international tribunals or bodies in this respect (*i.e.* there is no case-law of other international tribunals which would contradict the Court's approach), Clapham has suggested that it is conceivable that the WTO Dispute Settlement Body would take into account conflicting obligations of States under human rights treaties when considering their obligations under the General Agreement on Tariffs and Trade (GATT).[65] However, the above quote from the Court's case-law may well be interpreted differently. The Vienna Convention on the Law of Treaties requires the "taking into account" of other rules of international law. The language therefore appears less strong

[62] *Mamatkulov and Abdurasulovic v. Turkey* [GC] (nos. 46827/99 and 46951/99), Judgment of 6 February 2003. The Court also referred to Article 31 of the Vienna Convention on the Law of Treaties in the cases of *Golder v. the United Kingdom* (regarding the right of access to court, see above, pp. 3–6) and *Johnston and Others v. Ireland* (no. 9697/82), Judgment of 24 January 1986, Series A 112, regarding the interpretation of the term "right to marry"). See also Villiger, *Articles 31 and 32 of the Vienna Convention on the Law of Treaties in the Case-law of the European Court of Human Rights*, pp. 318–320.

[63] *Selmouni v. France* [GC] (no. 25802/94), Judgment of 28 July 1999, EHRR 2000, para. 97.

[64] Orakhelashvili, *Restrictive Interpretation of Human Rights in Recent Jurisprudence*, EJIL 2003, p. 553.

[65] Clapham, *The* Jus Cogens *Prohibition of Torture and the Importance of Sovereign State Immunity*, Liber Amicorum Lucius Caflisch, p. 156; see also McRae, *Approaches to the Interpretation of Treaties: the European Court of Human Rights and the WTO Appellate Body*, Liber Amicorum Lucius Caflisch, p. 1407.

than the Court's finding that the Convention should be "so far as possible interpreted in harmony" with other rules of international law.

Secondly, the question arises whether the "special character" of the Convention which the Court has explicitly mentioned in its judgments on State immunity might allow deviations from general international law. It was deplored that the Court in the *Al-Adsani* case did not bring the concept of the "special character" of the Convention any further.[66] That question must however be answered in the negative. The "special character" of the Convention as a human rights treaty cannot go as far as to generally oblige Contracting States to violate other obligations under public international law. The Court explained the Convention's "special character" in the inter-State case *Ireland v. the United Kingdom* as follows:

> (...) unlike international treaties of the classic kind, the Convention comprises more than mere reciprocal engagements between Contracting States. It creates (...) objective obligations which, in the words of the Preamble, benefit from a 'collective enforcement'.[67]

The "special character" therefore can be characterised by the fact that the Convention is not merely "reciprocal".[68] For example, Contracting Parties may bring "inter-State cases" under Article 24 without having to show that one of their nationals is affected, and individuals have a right under Article 34 to lodge an effective application to claim their human rights, even though the Convention was concluded amongst States as the traditional subjects of public international law. In that respect, the Convention indeed remains "special" amongst other international treaties. However, its "special character" cannot be understood as trumping *per se* other rules of public international law.

4. *Alternative approaches to the conflict between State immunity and Article 6 (1) of the Convention*

When the Court decided on the above cases on State immunity and the right of access to court, the conflict had previously been discussed by legal scholars who took the view that either State immunity should always trump the right to access or *vice versa*.[69] Some of the arguments that have been consid-

---

[66] Ziemele, *Case-Law of the European Court of Human Rights and Integrity of International Law*, p. 198.

[67] *Ireland v. the United Kingdom* (no. 5310/71), Judgment of 18 January 1978, Series A 25, para. 239.

[68] McRae, *Approaches to the Interpretation of Treaties: the European Court of Human Rights and the WTO Appellate Body*, Liber Amicorum Lucius Caflisch, p. 1417.

[69] For an overview see also Bröhmer, *State Immunity*, p. 163 et seq.

ered will be discussed in the following as well as the opinions of two judges (Judge Loucaides and Judge Ress) who expressed different thoughts on the conflict.

a) *The equality of arms-argument and the role of alternative remedies*
In the 1960s, Pahr argued that State immunity could never be compatible with the right of access to court.[70] Since the Convention would not differentiate between the status of procedural parties, the fact that one party is a State could not put a limitation on Article 6 (1). Otherwise the injured individual would be forced to sue the foreign State before its own courts. This could be hardly brought into accordance with the *equality of arms*-principle as an integral part of Article 6 (1). The principle goes back to the case *Neumeister v. Austria*[71] and is applied by the Court so "that each party must be afforded a reasonable opportunity to present his case (…) under conditions that do not place him at a substantial disadvantage *vis-à-vis* his opponent".[72] If the foreign State could only be sued before its own courts, its position would be considerably more advantageous than the one of the individual, and hence contrary to the principles of *fair trial* and *equality of arms*.[73] Such disadvantages might involve a different official language before the foreign courts, difficulties to contact a lawyer or the lack of a territorial link with the foreign State. Pahr's concern for the individual's position is as such not erroneous. Alternative means to institute proceedings before the courts of the foreign State should not be overstated in order not to turn the right of access to court into a "right of access to a court in another State". The application of the *equality of arms*-principle is however somewhat circular: the question of State immunity is a preliminary question at a procedural stage during which the question of *equality of arms* does not yet arise. After all, one is dealing with an access to court-issue.

It should be noted that the Convention will only apply to "alternative remedies", *i.e.* to procedural conditions before the courts of the foreign State which invokes State immunity and to which an applicant might turn to as an alternative, if the foreign State itself has ratified the Convention. Hess has suggested a distinction on account of alternative possibilities for the claimant to obtain redress: if there is no other forum to which the individual can

70 Pahr, *Staatenimmunität und Artikel 6 (1) EMRK*, FS Modinos, p. 222.

71 *Neumeister v. Austria* (no. 1936/63), Judgment of 27 June 1968, Series A 8.

72 *Dombo Beheer BV v. the Netherlands* (no. 14448/88), Judgment of 27 October 1993, Series A 274, para. 33. See generally on the principle of procedural equality: Jakobs and White, *European Convention*, p. 156.

73 Pahr, *Staatenimmunität und Artikel 6 (1) EMRK*, pp. 231–232.

revert to, or if the forum available cannot be regarded as satisfying the *fair trial*-guarantees under Article 6 (1), Hess would suggest to find a violation of the right of access to court.[74] On the other hand, if the individual is able to institute proceedings before the courts of the foreign State which invokes immunity with a prospect that he or she will receive a fair trial, the matter does not raise any issue under Article 6 (1). To support his approach, Hess has argued that Article 6 (1) lays down *fair trial*-obligations without reference to where they must be observed and where the proceedings should take place.[75] Bröhmer has rightly objected to that view that it is not in conformity with the Convention which confers obligations to the Contracting States which they (and not a third party) have to fulfil.[76] It cannot be argued that there is no interference with Article 6 (1) of the Convention if the claimant has the (alternative) possibility of bringing proceedings in the courts of the foreign State.

b) *The comments of Judge Ress in his concurring opinion in the case of* "Bosphorus Airways" v. Ireland

For present purposes, it is also interesting to note the comments by Judge Ress on the relationship of Article 6 (1) and State immunity. Having been a very influential Commission member in the cases of *Waite and Kennedy v. Germany* and *Beer and Regan v. Germany* (which involved the immunity of international organisations), he did however not sit in the Grand Chamber of the Court which decided on the three judgments on State immunity. Nevertheless, he took the opportunity to comment on those cases (in particular the *Al-Adsani* judgment) in his concurring opinion in the case of *"Bosphorus Airways" v. Ireland*:[77]

> (...) international treaties like the Convention may depart from rules and principles of international law normally applicable to relations between the Contracting Parties. Therefore, in the case of *Al-Adsani v. the United Kingdom* (...), the Court's approach to the relationship between different sources of public international law was not the right one. The correct question should have been whether, and to what extent, the Convention guarantees individual access to tribunals in the sense of Article 6 § 1 and whether the parties could and should have been seen as nevertheless reserving the rule on state immunity. Since the Contracting Parties could have waived their right to invoke State immunity by agreeing to Article 6 § 1 of the Convention, the starting point should have

[74] Hess, *Staatenimmunität bei Distanzdelikten*, p. 318.

[75] Ibid., p. 318.

[76] Bröhmer, *State Immunity*, p. 165.

[77] *Bosphorus Hava Yollari Turizm Ve Ticaret Anonim Sirketi v. Ireland* [GC] (no. 45036/98), Judgment of 30 June 2005.

been the interpretation of Article 6 § 1 alone. Unfortunately this question was never asked.[78]

The "waiver"-argument (*i.e.* that the Contracting Parties have waived their right to invoke State immunity when agreeing to the right of access to court under the Convention) is however questionable. A waiver of State immunity was not declared explicitly.[79] There is nothing in the *travaux préparatoires* (preparatory materials) of the Convention that states explicitly that the Contracting Parties wished to waive their entitlement to State immunity when agreeing on Article 6 (1). In any event, Article 32 of the Vienna Convention on the Law of Treaties states that preparatory work of an international treaty is merely a supplementary means of interpretation, as opposed to Article 31 (3) (c) which is among the primary means of treaty interpretation. It can therefore only serve as a means to aid the process of interpretation.[80] To hold that there was an implicit waiver would be erroneous as it was unpredictable for the Contracting Parties when agreeing on the Convention in 1950 that there was a conflict between the two principles, given that it was only in 1975 (in the case of *Golder v. the United Kingdom*) that the right of access of court was "read" by the Court into Article 6 (1).[81] Hence the argument loses a lot of its weight.

But even assuming that the Contracting Parties intended to waive their entitlement to State immunity, such a waiver would have only been declared by themselves. Consequently, the argument does not work when the foreign State is a non-European State. In cases like *Al-Adsani* or *Fogarty*, the immunity was invoked by States such as Saudi Arabia or the United States of America which are not Parties to the Convention. It would not make sense to distinguish between States that invoke State immunity and have ratified the Convention and those which did not, as there would be a danger to create an asymmetry in the applicability of the rules of State immunity.[82]

---

78 *Bosphorus Hava Yollari Turizm Ve Ticaret Anonim Sirketi v. Ireland*, concurring opinion of Judge Ress.

79 See above, pp. 25–26.

80 Villiger, *Articles 31 and 32 of the Vienna Convention on the Law of Treaties in the Case-law of the European Court of Human Rights*, p. 328; see also the 1966 ILC Report, YBILC 1966 II, p. 223.

81 The earliest document which mentions the conflict between State immunity and Article 6 (1) appears to be the article by Pahr (*Staatenimmunität und Artikel 6 (1) EMRK*, FS Modinos, p. 222) published in 1968.

82 See also Bröhmer, *Die völkerrechtliche Immunität von der staatlichen Gerichtsbarkeit*, p. 93.

c) *Judge Loucaides' approach: every blanket immunity is a disproportionate restriction on Article 6 (1) of the Convention*

As a dissenting judge in all three cases on State immunity, Judge Loucaides has developed his own position on the conflict between immunities and Article 6 (1). His position is not solely confined to State immunity, but it was given in the context of these judgments:

> (...) [A] blanket immunity which is applied by a court in order to block completely the judicial determination of a civil right without balancing the competing interests, namely those connected with the particular immunity and those relating to the nature of the specific claim which is the subject matter of the proceedings, amounts to a disproportionate restriction on the right of access to court. In this respect I would like to underline the following points. In present democratic society an absolute immunity from judicial proceedings appears to be an anachronistic doctrine incompatible with the demands of justice and the rule of law. The international law immunities originated at a time when individual rights were practically non-existent and when States needed greater protection from possible harassment through abusive judicial proceedings. The doctrine of State immunity has in modern times been subjected to an increasing number of restrictions, the trend being to reduce its application in view of developments in the field of human rights which strengthen the position of the individual.[83]

(1) *Discussion of the approach*

Judge Loucaides is right when observing that the trends of State immunity on the one hand and individual rights on the other have developed contrarily. Whereas State immunity is being increasingly restricted, the position of the individual in international law (and in particular regarding fair trial guarantees) has been more and more strengthened. It seems appropriate to take this into account when weighing up competing interests under the criterion of "proportionality". As Reinisch put it:

> It may well be that the exclusion of a certain class of potential defendants (...) was acceptable in the 1950s; this concept, however, may have changed. The expansive interpretation of the rights protected under the European Convention on Human Rights in general is a clear evidence for this trend.[84]

That argument mirrors an approach of the Convention organs which have, in other contexts, frequently used a dynamic method to interpret the Convention for the proper fulfillment of the protection of individual rights.[85]

[83] *McElhinney v. Ireland*, dissenting opinion of Judge Loucaides. See also Loucaides, *ECHR – Collected Essays*, pp. 211–214.

[84] Reinisch, *International Organisations before National Courts*, p. 286.

[85] See generally Matscher, *Methods of Interpretation of the Convention*, p. 68.

For example, the Court stated in the case of *Tyrer v. the United Kingdom* (regarding corporal punishment in a British school):

> (…) [T]he Convention is a living instrument which (…) must be interpreted in the light of present-day conditions.[86]

This dynamic approach was used by the Convention organs with regards to concepts which change over time such as "moral standards" and "scientific expertise".[87] Similarly, the term "necessary in a democratic society" – a requirement for lawful interference in qualified rights such as Articles 8 to 11 – necessarily alters with changes in what society tolerates and with scientific advancements.[88] However, the Court has used its "living instrument"-doctrine in order to respond to changes in society which had already taken place in the past. Therefore, it is more questionable to use that doctrine in order to overcome conflicting obligations under public international law which are still ongoing. Perhaps this explains why the Court, in the cases of *Fogarty v. the United Kingdom* and *Al-Adsani v. the United Kingdom*, observed a recent trend to restrict State immunity, but refrained from using the "living instrument"-doctrine to disregard existing obligations under the law of State immunity.

Judge Loucaides' approach is problematic when it comes to the relationship between the Convention and other norms of public international law. His approach is basically based on the premise that the Convention operates as a *lex specialis*, *i.e.* the Court's task is in the first place to apply the Convention articles. General principles of public international law (such as international immunities) have to be disregarded unless where they are expressly referred to in the Convention (e.g. in Article 1 of Protocol No. 1 and Articles 15, 35 (1) or 53).[89]

This view is questionable because it contravenes Article 31 (3) (c) of the Vienna Convention on the Law of Treaties which, as already mentioned, provides that an international treaty (such as the Convention) shall be

[86] *Tyrer v. the United Kingdom* (5856/72), Judgment of 25 April 1978, Series A 26, para. 31.

[87] In *Winterwerp v. the Netherlands*, the Court considered the term "person of unsound mind" in Article 5 (1) (e) as continually evolving due to research progress in psychiatry ((no. 6301/73), Judgment of 24 October 1979, Series A 33).

[88] Simor/Emmerson, *Human Rights Practice*, 1.049. In *Dudgeon v. the United Kingdom*, the Court found that prohibition of homosexual acts by criminal law could no longer be considered as a measure which was "necessary in a democratic society" ((no. 7525/76), Judgment of 24 February 1983, Series A 59). "In the light of modern developments", the Court reconsidered its case-law on the compatibility of a difference in age of consent for homosexuals and heterosexuals with the Convention (*Sutherland v. the United Kingdom* (no. 25186/94), Judgment of 27 March 2001).

[89] *McElhinney v. Ireland*, dissenting opinion of Judge Loucaides.

interpreted while taking into account "any relevant rules of international law applicable in the relations between the parties". Article 31 (3) (c) of the Vienna Convention on the Law of Treaties envisages treaty interpretation against the whole background of international law, including the rules of State immunity.[90] There is nothing in the Convention that would support the view that the right of access to court trumps the rules on State immunity because the former operates as a *lex specialis*. The view also runs into danger of regarding the mechanisms of protection of human rights as separate and self-sufficient legal systems, instead of an integral part of public international law.[91] Because the Convention forms such an integral part, it needs to be interpreted in harmony with other rules of international law. As the former President of the Court, Judge Wildhaber, put it:

> (...) international law remains the foundation on which the Convention operates. Within that framework the relationship of general international law with the Convention is a dynamic and evolutive one, in the sense that the Convention and international law find themselves in a kind of interactive mutual relationship, checking and building on each other. This is probably how it should be, as long as we remain clear about the need to keep the Convention within the general framework of international law (...).[92]

Keeping the Convention within the general framework of international law also means to interpret the latter in harmony with other norms of public international law, and not to give in the first place priority to the Convention rights.[93] Judge Loucaides however suggests the interpretation of the Convention – to use the words of the Court – "in a vacuum". This is particularly difficult because the Convention is an international treaty agreed at a regional level, but the Contracting States do also have obligations under public international law towards non-European States. Having considered the Convention as a *lex specialis*, Loucaides however goes even further by arguing that an immunity which has absolute effect is automatically a violation of the

---

[90] See Villiger, *Articles 31 and 32 of the Vienna Convention on the Law of Treaties in the Case-law of the European Court of Human Rights*, p. 326.

[91] See also Caflisch/Cancado Trindade, *Les Conventions américaine et européenne des droits de l'homme et le droit international general*, Revue Générale de Droit International Public 2004, p. 61.

[92] Wildhaber, *The ECHR and International Law*, ICLQ 2007, p. 230.

[93] See also the *Conclusions of the Work of the Study Group on the Fragmentation of International Law: Difficulties arising from the Diversification and Expansion of International Law* (Adopted by the International Law Commission at its Fifty-Eighth Session in 2006, Yearbook of the International Law Commission 2006, Vol. II, Part Two): "International law is a legal system. Its rules and principles (i.e. its norms) act in relation to and should be interpreted against the background of other rules and principles." (para. 1).

Convention. The application of that principle to international immunities is however problematic. Unlike domestic immunities, national courts grant State immunity because the forum State is seeking to comply with an international obligation. No such obligation exists with regard to parliamentary immunity or immunity of the police, social services or domestic judges. The latter immunities are granted because the State regards them as appropriate, but not in order to comply with public international law. While the premise that absolute immunities are in violation of Article 6 (1) might have some weight as regards domestic immunities, it is less practicable with regard to State immunity.

(2) *Conclusion*

As far as State immunity is concerned, the particular facts of a case are thus only relevant for the Court to establish whether the case falls into one of the categories for which State immunity is recognised under public international law. Approaches that the right of access to court always trumps State immunity or *vice versa* do not have a sufficient basis in international law. Therefore, the conflict between Article 6 (1) of the Convention and State immunity needs to be solved by balancing the competing interests. The following chapters will however demonstrate that this is a very complicated task. The present study will now turn to the case-law of the Court in more detail, starting with employment-related proceedings and State immunity.

5. *State immunity in employment-related proceedings and Article 6 (1) of the Convention*

An area which has not attracted much attention yet is the field of State immunity in employment disputes. Such disputes usually involve recruitment or employment matters in a foreign mission or embassy, military base or in foreign State-owned enterprises, schools and cultural institutions. Originally an area in which State immunity was considered to be absolute,[94] the theory of restrictive immunity is now widely recognised to apply here as well. The exact scope of State immunity in this area is however somewhat unclear. The problem arose in the case of *Fogarty v. the United Kingdom* which concerned alleged discrimination in the recruitment process in a foreign embassy.

a) *The case of* Fogarty v. the United Kingdom

The applicant, Mrs Fogarty, had worked in a secretarial post in the United States Embassy in London. Following alleged sexual harassment resulting in

[94] Sucharitkul, *State Immunities*, p. 242.

her dismissal, she brought a successful claim under the Sex Discrimination Act 1975 before the British Industrial Tribunal. The United States did not claim State immunity in the proceedings. Subsequently, her new applications for similar jobs at the embassy were rejected. Alleging that the application refusals were due to the successful claim before the Industrial Tribunal, the applicant instituted further proceedings against the United States for new breaches of the Sex Discrimination Act 1975. This time, the United States successfully invoked their entitlement to immunity before the British courts; hence the applicant complained about a violation of her right of access to court.

Before the Court, the United Kingdom government argued that international practice regarding State immunity in disputes with employees at embassies and consulates was divided. It relied on an article by Garnett titled "State Immunity in Employment Matters",[95] which gives the most exhaustive available survey of State immunity-practice in this area.

(1) *International practice regarding State immunity in employment disputes*
Garnett identifies four main approaches.[96] A number of common[97] and civil law[98] countries make the distinction on account of the place of employment. Plaintiffs employed at embassies or military bases at whatever level can never sue their employer State before a foreign court because an inquiry into the affairs of these institutions would be illegitimate. Under this approach immunity would however not be granted for employment disputes brought by staff members of a foreign State-owned school or trading corporation.

Other countries distinguish according to the level or position of employment. Claims of senior employees would be barred by State immunity, whereas plaintiffs employed for lower posts would not face a bar to jurisdiction since their tasks are comparable with those of employees in the private sector.[99]

[95] Garnett, *State Immunity in Employment Matters*, ICLQ 1997, p. 81; cited in the judgment at para. 29.

[96] For similar overviews on the applicable international practice, see Fox, *Employment contracts as an exception in respect of employment disputes*, BYIL 1997, p. 97; Yang, *State Immunity in the European Court of Human Rights*, BYIL 2003, p. 386; Hafner/Kohen/Breau, *State Immunity Regarding Employment Contracts*, State Practice Regarding State Immunities, p. 69.

[97] Ireland and New Zealand; the United Kingdom regards the place of employment as a "significant factor".

[98] Germany and – until recently – Italy.

[99] Garnett, *State Immunity in Employment Matters*, ICLQ 1997, p. 84. See e.g. *S v. Republic of India* (1984) 82 ILR, p. 13 (Swiss Federal Tribunal); *Landano v. the United States* (1988), *Jahrbuch des Schweizerischen Arbeitsrechts*, p. 424.

As a third approach, Garnett names legal systems which recognise State immunity on the basis of the nature of the claim.[100] Claims requiring investigations into matters of State security and the organisation of the foreign State's offices are barred by State immunity, whereas actions which do not so (e.g. a claim for unpaid wages) are not.

According to a fourth approach, a nexus based on territorial or national aspects between the forum State and the employee is required in order to proceed with the claim. The existence of such a nexus increases the forum State's interest to consider the claim. For example, both the European Convention on State Immunity and the United Kingdom State Immunity Act 1978 provide for a general exception from State immunity in employment matters. A counter-exception exists for nationals of the foreign State or a third State (unless the nationals of the latter are resident in the forum State).[101] From a human rights perspective, such provisions are not only problematic because they conflict with the right to a court, but also because they discriminate on ground of nationality. Their consistency with Article 14 the Convention (prohibition of discrimination) is being considered below.[102]

The above approaches are not mutually exclusive and often combined in national legislation. The United Kingdom State Immunity Act 1978 serves as a good example. The Act generally excludes State immunity in employment matters, unless a case lacks a territorial nexus. Additionally, there exists a further counter-exception based on the place of employment.

(2) *The decision of the Court*

It was exactly this combination between the first and the fourth approach in the United Kingdom State Immunity Act 1978 which frustrated the applicant's claim in *Fogarty v. the United Kingdom*. The applicant was able to prove a territorial nexus. Although her nationality was Irish, she was resident within the United Kingdom. Hence her action fell under the immunity-exception for employment matters provided for by Section 4 (2) of the State Immunity Act 1978. But Section 16 (1) (a) of the Act recognises a counter-exception concerning the employment of the "member of a mission" within the meaning of the Diplomatic Privileges Act 1964. The latter refers to the Vienna Convention on Diplomatic Relations 1969 which defines the term "member of a mission" broadly speaking as comprising all levels of employment at an embassy or consulate. This arguably includes employees at the administrative and technical service of a mission. The secretarial jobs for

---

[100] Garnett, *State Immunity in Employment Matters*, ICLQ 1997, p. 85.

[101] Similar regulations can be found under the domestic legislation of Australia and Singapore.

[102] See below, p. 49.

which Mrs Fogarty had unsuccessfully applied came within this broad definition and consequently under the counter-exception in Section 16 (1) (a). Thus, the United States were entitled to immunity under the State Immunity Act 1978. However, if the forum State had not been the United Kingdom but a country which grants or denies immunity on account of the position of the (future) employee in an embassy, the result might have been different since the job vacancies for which the applicant had applied did not concern senior posts.[103]

In its judgment, the Grand Chamber of the Court observed a general trend towards limiting State immunity in respect of employment-related disputes, but noted that there was no uniform international practice as to whether, and if so to what extent, State immunity would apply to employment issues in a foreign embassy.[104] It found that, by granting immunity to the foreign State in employment matters, the United Kingdom neither stood alone nor fell outside any currently accepted international standard.[105] The judges in the Grand Chamber also put great emphasis on the fact that the present case involved the recruitment process of staff to an embassy which by its very nature involved sensitive and confidential issues such as the diplomatic or organisational policy of a foreign State.[106] A trend towards relaxation in recruitment proceedings could not be identified. Hence the majority of sixteen (out of seventeen) judges voted against a violation of the right of access to court.[107]

(3) *Discussion of the judgment*

The judgment was widely approved by legal academics.[108] However, it also received some criticism. It has been said that the Court was wrong to hold

[103] The United States would presumably not have been granted immunity under the Australian Foreign States Immunity Act 1985 which makes an exception for employees in routine administrative positions and with permanent residence in Australia (section 12 (6) of the Act).

[104] *Fogarty v. the United Kingdom*, para. 37.

[105] Ibid.

[106] Ibid., para. 38. This argument was put forward by the United Kingdom government which argued that selection of embassy staff constituted an *acta jure imperii*. Proceedings against the decision to refuse a job application would further involve an investigation into the internal organisation of the embassy and would interfere with the foreign State's sovereignty (para. 30).

[107] Note that the Court left open the question of whether or not there existed a "civil right" – which is necessary for Article 6 (1) to apply – since it found that there had not been a violation of that provision anyway. See below, page 161.

[108] Maierhöfer, *Der EGMR als Modernisierer des Völkerrechts?*, EuGRZ 2002, p. 394; Voyakis, *Access to Court v State Immunity*, ICLQ 2003, p. 313; it appears that the judgment was

that the United Kingdom courts' granting of State immunity to the United States in the present case did not fall outside "currently accepted international standards" because those standards were, given the many different approaches explained above, practically non-existent, if by "international standards" one means definite rules that dictate uniform results.[109] Thus it was alleged that any decision by any court could be regarded as not exceeding the margin of appreciation given to national courts of Contracting States in this respect.[110] Moreover, international practice mainly concerned existing employment relationships as opposed to the issue of recruitment in the present case.[111] However, the Court was correct to assume that the granting of immunity did not amount to a disproportionate interference with Article 6. This can be shown by the following analysis of existing international instruments.

At the European level, the European Convention on State Immunity reflects the above discussed approach under United Kingdom law. Article 5 (1) of European Convention on State Immunity excludes immunity in employment proceedings, subject to the counter-exceptions in the second paragraph which require a territorial nexus, just as the United Kingdom State Immunity Act 1978 does. But Article 32 provides that "[n]othing in the present Convention shall affect privileges and immunities relating to the exercise of the functions of diplomatic missions and consular posts and of persons connected with them." The wording of Article 32 is wide enough to cover recruitment decisions in embassies, especially since those acts form part of the official functions of an embassy and are by nature governmental.

Article 11 of the United Nations Convention on Jurisdictional Immunities of States and their Property regulates immunity in respect of contracts of employment between a foreign State and an individual as follows. While as a general rule Article 11 (1) provides that a foreign State cannot invoke immunity in "a proceeding which relates to a contract of employment between the State and an individual for work performed or to be performed", Article 11 (2) provides for a wide range of exceptions which *de facto* renders the granting of State immunity as the general rule in that matter. Article 11 (2) for example covers situations in which the employee has either been recruited to perform particular functions in the exercise of governmental authority, or in which the employee is a diplomatic agent, a consular officer or a member

also approved by Jones, *Article 6 and Immunities arising in Public International Law*, ICLQ 2006, p. 469.

[109] Yang, *State Immunity in the European Court of Human Rights*, BYIL 2003, p. 386.

[110] Ibid.

[111] Ibid.

of the diplomatic staff of a permanent mission to an international organisation. Most importantly in the present context however is the exception in Article 11 (2) (c) which grants State immunity where "*the subject matter of the proceedings is the recruitment*, renewal of employment or reinstatement *of an individual*".[112]

The International Law Association's "Draft Convention on State Immunity" provides in Article IIIC for an "employment matters"-exception from immunity similar to the ones contained in the European Convention on State Immunity and the United Nations Convention on Jurisdictional Immunities of States and their Property, subject to an amendment with a counter-exception where "the employee was appointed under the public (administrative) law of the foreign state such as, inter alia, members of the mission, diplomatic, consular or military staff". The International Law Association's Committee on State Immunity commented that it intended to clarify that "the employment relationship of any and all diplomatic and consular staff and other members of the mission should be immune from the jurisdiction of the courts of the forum state."[113] Into the same direction points the resolution on State immunity by the Institute of International Law.[114] Providing for an "employment dispute"-exception from State immunity in Article 2 (2) (c), it lays down in Article 2 (3) (d) that the forum State should not "assume competence to inquire into the content of implementation of the foreign security and defence policies of the foreign state". Although not explicitly mentioned in the resolution, the formulation is wide enough to cover recruitment processes at embassies and consulates.[115]

(4) *Conclusion*

Taking all these references together, it is possible to conclude that there exists a duty under public international law to grant State immunity in employment proceedings relating to the recruitment at embassies and consulates of staff members at all levels. The existing European Convention on State Immunity, the United Nations Convention on Jurisdictional Immunities of States and their Property and the draft Conventions of the International Law Association and the Institute of International Law arguably provide for immunity regarding the recruitment of an employee for the position for which Mrs Fogarty had applied for. Given the consistency of the international con-

[112] Emphasis added.

[113] Explanatory commentary on the amendment to Article IIIC as cited in *Fogarty v. the United Kingdom*, para. 20.

[114] AIDR 1991, Vol. 64 II, p. 276.

[115] See also Garnett, *State Immunity in Employment Matters*, ICLQ 1997, p. 102.

ventions in this respect, the argument that there did not exist international standards because of the diverging approaches taken by national courts loses a lot of weight. To find a violation of the right of access to court in the case of *Fogarty v. the United Kingdom* had ultimately meant that the United Kingdom could not become a party to the United Nations Convention on State Immunity without being in conflict with Article 6 (1). The United Kingdom would have to change the State Immunity Act accordingly, although the present state is in line with existing international instruments. To hold otherwise would have meant that the Court had found a violation of the Convention for compliance with another Council of Europe treaty, namely the European Convention of State Immunity (which the United Kingdom has ratified). This is hardly a satisfying result.

Moreover, the selection process of employees who represent a State abroad clearly amounts to conduct *jure imperii* which is traditionally covered by State immunity. If the selection of diplomats and staff members of an embassy would be submitted to the jurisdiction of the host State, the equality between States and relations between each other would be far more challenged than in proceedings concerning, say, commercial activities.[116]

(5) *The dissenting opinion by Judge Loucaides*

Only Judge Loucaides did not agree with the remaining judges in the Grand Chamber. This is mostly due to the special approach he developed for the conflict between immunity and Article 6 (1). As a dissenting judge in all three judgments on State immunity, Judge Loucaides suggested that all blanket immunities should be incompatible with the right of access to court whenever their application is automatic without a balancing of competing interests. This approach has been discussed above.[117]

But Judge Loucaides also put forward some arguments which are special to the present case. In his opinion, the fact that the United States had not considered it necessary to invoke immunity in the first proceedings indicated that an intrusion into the internal affairs of the United States was not felt.[118] Be that as it may, the earlier proceedings did not concern a decision in a recruitment process, but a claim under the United Kingdom Sex Discrimination Act 1975. Hence it cannot be said that both proceedings brought by

116 See the concurring opinion of Judges Caflisch, Costa and Vajic in *Fogarty v. the United Kingdom*.

117 See above, p. 38.

118 Dissenting opinion of Judge Loucaides in *Fogarty v. the United Kingdom*. See also the applicant's submissions, para. 31.

Mrs Fogarty were similar because they concerned in the first place discriminatory acts based on sex.

Another argument put forward by Judge Loucaides is that the applicant lacked any alternative means of redress.[119] In *Fogarty v. the United Kingdom*, it is however not plain that alternative means did not exist. Although the applicants submitted that "the United States was clearly not prepared to exercise jurisdiction",[120] the accessible materials on the case do not reveal that the applicant was prevented from filing a lawsuit in the United States for the alleged discrimination. The invoking of immunity does not make the foreign State unwilling to consider the action before its own domestic courts. To have to institute proceedings abroad is clearly inconvenient for the plaintiff. However, the plaintiff will have to cope with this inconvenience as a consequence of having applied for or consented to an employment relationship with a foreign State.[121] The above arguments therefore do not prove wrong the outcome of the case.

b) *Discriminatory immunity rules in employment-related disputes*

Since the applicant in *Fogarty v. the United Kingdom* had tried to bring proceedings against the United States for a violation of the provisions in the United Kingdom Sex Discrimination Act 1975, she also complained under Article 14 (in conjunction with the right of access to court) that she was unlawfully discriminated against by the operating of State immunity in her case.

It should however be noted that the Convention does not recognise yet a provision which prohibits all kinds of discrimination.[122] The prohibition of discrimination under Article 14 has no independent existence and may only be invoked in conjunction with any substantive right under the Convention.[123] Article 14 provides that:

> The enjoyment of the rights and freedoms set forth in [the] Convention shall be secured without discrimination on any ground such as sex, race, colour, language, religion, political or other opinion, national or social origin, association with a national minority, property, birth or other status.

---

119 See also the applicant's submissions in *Fogarty v. the United Kingdom*, para. 31.

120 Ibid.

121 This argument was made by Habscheid (IPrax 2001, p. 398) regarding employment disputes involving international organisations.

122 See however Protocol No. 12 to the Convention of 4 November 2000 which provides in Article 1 for a general prohibition of discrimination.

123 Jacobs and White, *European Convention*, p. 348 et seq.

Providing a complaint falls within the broad ambit of a Convention right, Article 14 is engaged no matter whether or not the measure in question violates the respective substantive right.[124] Therefore, it did not matter that the Court had not previously found a violation of Mrs Fogarty's right of access to court; to bring into play Article 14, it was sufficient that the Court considered Article 6 (1) to apply to the present case. The applicant's submissions nevertheless did not disclose a violation of Article 14. The judges in the Grand Chamber noticed that the United Kingdom State Immunity Act 1978 granted State immunity in relation to all employment-related disputes within the staff of an embassy, irrespective of their subject-matter and of the sex, nationality, place of residence or other attributes of the complainant.[125] Mrs Fogarty was not treated differently from any other person wishing to bring an employment-related suit against a foreign embassy. The decision that Article 14 (read in conjunction Article 6) had not been violated was therefore taken unanimously.

This part of the complaint nevertheless raises an interesting aspect. There are other provisions which might be more problematic with regard to Article 14. Especially counter-exceptions to the "employment dispute"-exception from State immunity for cases in which the individual is not a national of the forum State might come under scrutiny as to its compliance with Article 14. For example, Section 4 (2) of the United Kingdom State Immunity Act 1978 (which basically adopts the approach taken by the European Convention on State Immunity) provides for such a counter-exception: State immunity is granted in employment-related proceedings if the plaintiff is a national of the defendant State (at the time the proceedings are instituted) or a national of a third State who is not resident in the United Kingdom (at the time the contract was made). Hence this provision denies the right of access to court to a certain class of plaintiffs because of their national origin.

Different treatment on account of nationality violates Article 14 unless the State can prove that it was "objectively and reasonably" justified.[126] This requirement is satisfied if the difference in treatment pursues a legitimate aim and is proportionate.[127] The legitimate aim of provisions similar to the above section in the British State Immunity Act 1978 could lie in the lack of interest on behalf of the forum State to provide a forum to employees

---

124 Simor/Emmerson, *Human Rights Practice*, 1.020; *Rasmussen v. Denmark* (no. 8777/79), Judgment of 28 November 1984, Series A 87; *Botta v. Italy* (no. 153/96), Judgment of 24 February 1998, Reports 1998-I.

125 *Fogarty v. the United Kingdom*, para. 42.

126 *Belgian Linguistic Case* (No. 2), Judgment of 23 July 1968, Series A, para. 9.

127 Ibid.; *Darby v. Sweden* (no. 11581/85), Judgment of 23 October 1990, Series A 187, para. 31.

with only a negligible connection to the forum.[128] The forum State might argue that under these circumstances, keeping good relationships with the foreign State takes priority over the individual's interest to institute proceedings. However, as Ress has pointed out, differential treatment on the basis of nationality can hardly be justified "in a world of increased mobility of labour"[129]. Before the Court, there is for example currently an application pending regarding a Russian who obtained her law degree in Greece but was refused to be registered with the Athens Bar Association for not having Greek nationality.[130] Moreover, in the context of the freedom of movement of workers under European Community Law, Article 39 (2) of the EC Treaty grants the right to non-discrimination of workers irrespective of their nationality or place of residence. In the light of this provision, immunity-provisions in employment proceedings which distinguish on nationality might raise an issue under Article 14 read in conjunction with the right of access to court.

c) *The case of* Cudak v. Lithuania

The Court will soon have another occasion to consider State immunity in employment disputes and Article 6 (1). In *Cudak v. Lithuania*,[131] the applicant (a Lithuanian national) had been recruited to the post of a receptionist at the call desk of the Polish Embassy in Vilnius. Her contract of employment included a clause stating that a dispute arising therefrom was to be resolved in accordance with Lithuanian law. After she had successfully lodged a complaint for sexual harassment by a diplomat at the Embassy, she was (after a period during which she had fallen ill because of the tension involving her complaint) refused to enter the Embassy several times and subsequently notified by the Ambassador that she had been dismissed because of her absence on those days on which she had been refused entry (!). When she lodged a claim for compensation for the dismissal, the Lithuanian courts found that they lacked jurisdiction because of the Polish Embassy's immunity.[132] A Chamber of the Court, finding that the application raised complex

[128] Garnett, *State Immunity in Employment Matters*, ICLQ 1997, p. 122, with further references.

[129] Ibid.; Proceedings of the 65th Conference of the ILA (1992), p. 316.

[130] *Bigaeva v. Greece* (no. 26713/05), pending before the Court.

[131] *Cudak v. Lithuania* (no. 15869/02), admissibility decision of 2 March 2006.

[132] There is no special law regulating the issue of State immunity in Lithuania; hence the courts refer to the relevant international provisions on a case-by-case basis (Ibid.); for a summary of the *Cudak* case before the Lithuanian Supreme Court, see Sundikas/Goldammer, *The Restrictive Theory of State Immunity in Lithuania: Reality or Illusion*, BalYbIL 2005, p. 122.

issues of fact and law, declared it admissible in March 2006 and relinquished jurisdiction in favour of the Grand Chamber. A hearing was held on 1 July 2009.[133]

Even though the facts of the case as summarised in the admissibility decision are very brief, one can determine several issues that might arise in *Cudak v. Lithuania*. First, the Court will have to deal with the issue whether or not there is a "civil right" involved in order to engage Article 6 (1). The Lithuanian government argued that the employment dispute concerned the predominantly public-law links between the Polish Embassy and the applicant. In the light of recent changes in its jurisprudence since the Grand Chamber judgment of *Vilho Eskelinen and Others v. Finland*, Article 6 (1) will probably apply to the present case.[134] The merits of the case are more interesting. The Court will probably find that the fact that the parties had agreed that Lithuanian law should apply in the case of a dispute does not amount to a waiver of State immunity by the Polish Embassy. Under international law, a provision in a contract which specifies that the law of the forum State is applicable does not contain an implied waiver of State immunity.[135]

As to the question whether or not the Lithuanian courts violated Article 6 (1) by granting State immunity to Poland in the present application, *Cudak v. Lithuania* appears to differ significantly from *Fogarty v. the United Kingdom* in two aspects. Unlike Mrs Fogarty, Mrs Cudak had already been employed with the foreign State's embassy, and she did not seek reinstatement but wanted compensation for the allegedly unlawful dismissal. This is crucial because, at the material time, Article 11 (1) of the International Law Commission's Draft Articles on Jurisdictional Immunities of States and their Property provided for an exception from State immunity in employment disputes unless "the subject of the proceedings is the recruitment, renewal of employment or reinstatement of the individual" and unless "the employee has been recruited to perform functions closely related to the exercise of governmental authority".[136] As Mrs Cudak complained about the dismissal from her position as a receptionist at the call desk of the Polish embassy, the above counter-exception to the general exception from State immunity in that article did arguably not apply. It appears that Article 11 of the United Nations Convention on Jurisdictional Immunities of States and their Property, which provides for a more detailed list of counter-exceptions, does also

---

[133] A webcast of that hearing can be seen under: http://www.echr.coe.int/ECHR/EN/Header/Press/Multimedia/Webcasts+of+public+hearings/

[134] See above, pp. 7–11.

[135] Steinberger, *State Immunity*, EPIL IV, p. 622. See above, p. 26.

[136] Draft Articles on Jurisdictional Immunities of States and Their Property (1991), II (2) YBILC 13.

not provide for State immunity in the present case. The most relevant counter-exception to the present case would be Article 11 (2) (d) which basically states that a State may invoke immunity from jurisdiction in a proceeding if "the subject-matter of the proceeding is the dismissal or termination of employment of an individual and (...) such a proceeding would interfere with the security interests of that state." Therefore, the counter-exception would only apply if the foreign State (*i.e.* Poland) could prove the existence of a security interest, which is rather unlikely with regard to the dismissal of a receptionist at an embassy's call desk. On the other hand, regardless whether the case would fall within the relevant exception from State immunity, the European Convention on State Immunity states in Article 32 that "[n]othing in the present Convention shall affect privileges and immunities relating to the exercise of the functions of diplomatic missions and consular posts and of persons connected with them." If, as already stated above, that provision is wide enough to cover recruitment proceedings, it might also cover the dismissal of an embassy's employee. Neither Lithuania nor Poland are however parties to that Convention.

Lastly, it will be interesting to see whether the Court gives any weight to the fact that there existed an alternative remedy for the applicant as she could have sued before the Polish courts. Because of the clause in the contract that Lithuanian law applies, the applicant argued that her options to bring a claim before the Polish courts were unrealistic. Given that the Court has usually stressed the existence of alternative remedies as a rather supporting argument in cases involving State immunity, it can be assumed that that argument will not be decisive in the case.

Finally, it should be noted that a Chamber of the Court has relinquished its jurisdiction in favour of the Grand Chamber in another case on employment proceedings in embassies. In *Sabeh El Leil v. France*,[137] the applicant (a French national and chief accountant at the Kuwaiti embassy in Paris) had been dismissed for economic reasons. His claim for damages and compensation against the State of Kuwait had initially been successful as the competent court considered the dismissal as having been "without real and serious cause". When the applicant appealed in order to challenge the amounts awarded to him, the Court of Appeal found that Kuwait enjoyed State immunity in the proceedings, given the applicant's level of responsibility and the general nature of his duties in the Embassy. The applicant's appeal with the Court of Cassation was to no avail. As this book went to press, no hearing has yet been held in that case.

[137] *Sabeh El Leil v. France* (no. 34869/05), admissibility decision of 21 October 2008.

6. *The "personal injury exception" and Article 6 (1) of the Convention: the case of* McElhinney v. Ireland

The international rules on State immunity are in flux. This is not only the case regarding commercial activities or employment disputes, but applies also to personal injuries inflicted on an individual by a State official abroad, that is on the territory of the forum State (the so-called "tort exception" or "personal injury exception"). If there existed a trend towards denying State immunity in such cases, an individual might argue that the forum State, by adhering to an increasingly out-dated traditional approach to grant State immunity while numerous countries already provide for such an exception, restricts the right of access to court in a disproportionate manner. This problem arose in the case of *McElhinney v. Ireland*. The Court had to decide whether the granting of State immunity violated Article 6 in proceedings regarding injury and damage inflicted by State agents on individuals on the territory of another country.

The slightly bizarre facts of *McElhinney v. Ireland* involved a British soldier at a checkpoint barrier at the border of Northern Ireland who unsuccessfully tried to stop the car of the applicant, an Irish citizen. By accident, the soldier was hit by the vehicle being towed to the car and was carried over to Ireland on the tow bar. The applicant claimed that he was unaware of the incident, despite numerous shots fired by the soldier while he was standing on the tow bar, some of which were fired while he was still on Northern Irish territory. The car stopped in a nearby village in Ireland where the soldier allegedly panicked and tried again to shoot twice at the applicant. Because the gun jammed, the applicant survived and subsequently sued the United Kingdom government for damages for the assault by the soldier.

The applicant's attempt to receive compensation for the assault failed before the Irish courts. The High Court found in April 1994 that the United Kingdom was entitled to State immunity. The applicant's appeal was rejected by the Irish Supreme Court in December 1995 which held that the act concerned had to be categorised as an *acta jure imperii*. It further found that it was not established that, as a principle of public international law, immunity no longer applied in respect of personal injuries caused by the tortious act of a foreign State's servant or agent within the sphere of sovereign activity.[138]

[138] *John McElhinney v. Anthony Ivor John Williams and Her Majesty's Secretary of State for Northern Ireland* (hereafter *McElhinney v. Williams*), [1995] 3 The Irish Reports, p. 382. Although the domestic proceedings mainly dealt with the current state of international law regarding the "personal injury exception", a human rights aspect was also being discussed. The plaintiff unsuccessfully claimed that Ireland had violated the right to bodily integrity

As the matter was brought to Strasbourg, a Grand Chamber of the Court referred, as in the *Fogarty* judgment, to a general trend in international and comparative law towards limiting State immunity in respect of the matter concerned.[139] This, however, was not seen as being enough to violate Article 6 (1) as the granting of State immunity by Ireland could not be seen as falling "outside any currently accepted international standards".[140] As an additional element, the Court noted that the applicant had alternative means as he could have pursued an action against the United Kingdom in Northern Ireland.[141] Therefore, the Court held by twelve votes to five that the restriction was proportionate. The separate opinions of the five dissenting judges suggest that the current state of international law regarding the personal injury exception was wrongly assessed by the majority in the Grand Chamber. This should be the starting point in the analysis of the judgment.

a) *Domestic legislation and State practice regarding the personal injury exception*

In the domestic proceedings as well as before the Strasbourg Court, the applicant had submitted that the immunity invoked by the United Kingdom no longer existed under public international law. The United Kingdom government disputed this. To support his view, the applicant referred to both

by refusing to allow the suit to proceed because of State immunity (see pp. 390, 405). Although not invoked by the plaintiff, the High Court considered the constitutional right to claim redress in court but found that it was regulated by the principles of international law as permitted by the Constitution (*McElhinney v. Williams*, p. 390). Article 6 (1) was not considered by the Irish courts. That aspect was not relied on by the applicant before the Strasbourg Court, but it is similar to the complaints under Article 3 in *Al-Adsani v. the United Kingdom* (see below, p. 80). Instead, the applicant invoked Article 5 (in conjunction with Article 13) against both Ireland and the United Kingdom. The Court considered this part of the application as being manifestly ill-founded (and therefore inadmissible) as the application neither concerned the applicant's detention nor his "security of person" (*McElhinney v. Ireland and the United Kingdom* (no. 31253/96), admissibility decision of 9 February 2000, 29 EHRR CD 216).

139 *McElhinney v. Ireland*, para. 38.

140 Ibid., para. 38.

141 Ibid., para. 39. Note however that, in his dissenting opinion, Judge Rozakis rightly identified that (apart from practicable difficulties for the applicant to bring a claim before the courts of the United Kingdom) the "alternative remedies" argument was rather ill-placed in *McElhinney*. Whereas applicants which had been involved in employment disputes with States or international organisations could be expected to have been aware of their (future) employee's immunity, the same could not be said for applicants who had suffered from injuries by a body which enjoyed immunity from a foreign jurisdiction (dissenting opinion of Judge Rozakis in *McElhinney v. Ireland*, para. 4).

national and international legislation. At the national level, the legislation in the United States, the United Kingdom, Australia and Canada were given as examples that countries had ceased to grant immunity for "personal injuries". Section 5 of the United Kingdom State Immunity Act 1978 for instance provides that:

> A State is not immune as respect proceedings in respect of:
> (a) death or personal injury; or
> (b) damage to or loss of tangible property,
> caused by an act or omission in the United Kingdom.[142]

The relevant provisions in the United States Foreign Sovereign Immunities Act 1976,[143] the Canadian State Immunity Act 1985[144] and the Australian Foreign States Immunities Act 1985[145] provide for similar exceptions. So does Article 11 of the European Convention on State Immunity 1972. It should be noted that the above national and international instruments make an exception from State immunity, regardless of whether or not the respective governmental act is to be considered private or official. Thus the traditional *jure imperii/jure gestionis* distinction is no longer applied in this respect. For those countries that have no special legislation on State immunity and which therefore leave the issue to be determined by their courts (which, as the dissenting judges in *McElhinney* rightly observed, are paradoxically civil-law countries),[146] the traditional *jure imperii/jure gestionis* distinction still applies. However, even if one would expect a greater restriction of the jurisdiction of those countries, the sparse case-law on the matter suggests that the above

---

[142] It should be noted that the United Kingdom invoked immunity before the Irish courts which its own law would probably have denied to other countries in the same situation. This circumstance was used by the applicant to claim the principle of "reciprocity": immunity should only be granted where the State invoking it granted reciprocal immunity to other countries (*McElhinney v. Ireland and United Kingdom*; see also *USA v. Dollfus Mieg et Compagnie SA* [1952] A.C., p. 613). The Court did not address this argument. The Irish High Court, the Supreme Court as well as both the United Kingdom and the Irish government rightly observed that the assumption that State immunity operates on the basis of reciprocity lacked any authority in international law (*McElhinney v. Ireland and United Kingdom*, pp. 216, 218; *McElhinney v. Williams*, pp. 392 and 404).

[143] Section 1605 (a) (5) FSIA.

[144] Section 6 of that Act.

[145] Section 13 of that Act. Similar provisions also exist in Singapore and South Africa (see Badr, *State Immunity*, p. 119).

[146] *McElhinney v. Ireland*, dissenting opinion of Judges Caflisch, Cabral Barreto and Vajic.

distinction is very often drawn with great flexibility.[147] In *McElhinney*, it was however obvious that the soldier had been acting in an official capacity.[148]

Having regard only to the above domestic statutes that explicitly provide for a personal injury exception, the question arises whether they reflect international law as it stands or (as was the opinion of the majority of judges in the Grand Chamber) whether one can only make out a trend in international and comparative law towards limiting State immunity in this respect.[149] The Irish Supreme Court was convinced that the above-mentioned domestic statutes did not reflect current international law.[150] It derived from the case *I Congresso del Partido*[151] that national statutes could only be seen as evidence of domestic law and not evidence of international law generally.[152] The Supreme Court also put great emphasis on a comment by Steinberger in the Encyclopedia of Public International Law in which he found that the above-mentioned national exceptions:

> (…) [I]f applied to conduct *jure imperii* of the foreign state will meet objections under general international law. So far, despite lower court decisions under the United States Act (…), such application does not have the support of State practice sufficiently universal to allow derogation from general international law.[153]

---

[147] Yang (*State Immunity in the European Court of Human Rights*, BYIL 2003, p. 369) cites as an example the Austrian Supreme Court which, when deciding on a claim against the United States for damages caused by negligent driving of an embassy car, found that the decisive criterion was the act itself (driving a vehicle) instead of its purpose (in that case, delivering diplomatic mail); hence the act in question was considered a private act and the United States was consequently not granted immunity (*Collision with Foreign-Government Owned Motor Car (Austria) Case*, (1961) 40 ILR, p. 73).

[148] See also Voyakis, *Access to Court v. State Immunity*, ICLQ 2003, p. 314.

[149] The Irish government had argued that the limited number of ratifications of the European Convention on State Immunity indicated the unwillingness of many States to subscribe to the exceptions contained therein (*McElhinney v. Ireland*, para. 27). In the light of both the numerous examples of domestic legislation and attempts to codify the law of State immunity at the international level which provide for similar exceptions), this argument however remains mere speculation (See also *McElhinney v. Ireland*, dissenting opinion of Judges Caflisch, Cabral Barreto and Vajic).

[150] *McElhinney v. Williams* [1995] 3 Irish Reports, p. 403. The applicant had relied on the Supreme Court's judgment in *Government of Canada v. the Employment Appeals Tribunal* ([1992] 2 Irish Reports, p. 484). However, the Supreme Court stressed that this decision concerned only an exception from State immunity in respect of commercial activity. The acts complained of by the applicant were clearly unrelated to any commercial activity ([1995] 3 I.R., p. 399).

[151] [1983] 1 A.C., p. 244; the relevant passage is from Lord Wilberforce's speech at p. 260.

[152] [1995] 3 I.R., p. 402.

[153] Steinberger, *State Immunity*, EPIL IV, pp. 626–627. Steinberger suggests that claims relating to traffic accidents can be met by qualifying participation in traffic as conduct *jure*

The Supreme Court further found that Article 11 of the European Convention on State Immunity, if applied to tortious conduct *jure imperii*, would constitute a deviation from current international law.[154] The majority of judges of the Strasbourg Court agreed:

> (...) with the Supreme Court in the present case (...) that it is not possible, given the present state of development of international law, to conclude that Irish law conflicts with its general principles.[155]

However, one might get the opposite impression if one were to look at various attempts at codifying the current position of international law with regard to State immunity.[156] All existing draft proposals for multilateral conventions were already accessible in the period under consideration (which was the period between 1994 and 1995). They will be considered in the following section.

b) *International instruments and the personal injury exception*
As has already been said, Article 11 of the European Convention on State Immunity provides for a personal injury exception. Moreover, the United Nations Convention on Jurisdictional Immunities of States and Their Property provides in its Article 12 that:

> Unless otherwise agreed between the States concerned, a State cannot invoke immunity from jurisdiction before a court of another State which is otherwise competent in a proceeding which relates to pecuniary compensation for death or injury to the person, or damage to or loss of tangible property, caused by an act or omission which is alleged to be attributable to the State, if the act or omission occurred in whole or in part in the territory of that other State and if the author of the act or omission was present in that territory at the time of the act or omission.[157]

---

gestionis for which State immunity is not available (p. 627). For a similar approach: Damian, *Staatenimmunität*, p. 114; von Schönfeld, *Staatenimmunität*, p. 97.

154 3 IR, p. 403. See also the reasoning of the Dutch District Court of Haarlem in *LF & HMHK v. Germany* (94 ILR, p. 342; cited by Voyakis, *Access to Court v State Immunity*, ICLQ 2003, p. 316): "It is not reasonable to assume that an opinion on jurisdiction must be formed by reference to Article 11 of the European Convention. It is evident (...) that the practice adopted by members of the Council of Europe (...) on this point is far from uniform; this in itself is not a reason for accepting this Convention as a source of unwritten international law (regional customary law)."

155 *McElhinney v. Ireland*, para. 38.

156 For a detailed discussion of these draft proposals see Bröhmer, *State Immunity*, pp. 125–141.

157 Since the Convention which was adopted by the General Assembly in 2004 had been submitted by the International law Commission to the General Assembly of the United

In the resolution adopted by the Institute of International Law named "Contemporary Problems Concerning the Immunity of States in Relation to Questions of Jurisdiction and Enforcement",[158] Article III (e) also provides for a personal injury exception:

> The organs of the forum state are competent in respect of proceedings concerning the death of, or personal injury to, a person, or loss of or damage to tangible property, which are attributable to activities of a foreign state and its agents within the national jurisdiction of the forum state.

Lastly, the International Law Association's "Revised Articles for a Convention on State Immunity" of 1994 denies in Article III (F) State immunity:

> "[W]here the cause of action relates to: 1. Death or personal injury; or 2. Damage to or loss of property, and the act or omission which caused the death, injury or damage either occurred wholly or partly in the forum state or if that act or omission had a direct effect in the forum state.

The 1994 Buenos Aires Conference of the International Law Association confirmed the approach taken in the draft proposal "in the light of the extensive survey of state practice conducted by the Committee".[159]

One can therefore conclude that all international instruments have abolished the distinction between *acta jure gestionis* and *acta jure imperii* regarding personal injury committed by a foreign State on the territory of the forum State.[160] Admittedly, the above formulations vary in a certain respect. Whereas the International Law Commission's proposal requires the occurrence of the tortious act and the presence of the State official in the territory of the forum State, the International Law Association regarded it as sufficient that the tortious act had a direct effect only there. The latter formulation is far wider, and would have encompassed the first shots by the British soldier on Mr. McElhinney if they were (the matter was disputed) fired on Northern Irish territory.[161] Nevertheless, all instruments would have denied immunity to the United Kingdom for those acts which occurred on Irish territory and which formed the basis for the applicant's compensation claim.[162]

Nations in 1991, it very likely also reflects the situation of 1994–1995, *i.e.* the relevant period in *McElhinney*.

[158] *Annuaire de l'Institut de droit international*, Vol. 64-II, p. 393.

[159] Bröhmer, *State Immunity*, p. 133.

[160] Bröhmer, after a detailed analysis of the relevant materials, observed that "all domestic immunity statutes and most of the international immunity instruments contain clauses allowing the exercise of jurisdiction for certain torts without regard to the sovereign or private nature of the tortious act" (*State Immunity*, p. 140).

[161] This was also remarked by the dissenting judges in *McElhinney v. Ireland.*

[162] See also Schreuer, *State Immunity*, p. 44.

c) *The restrictive interpretation of the personal injury exception ("insurable" personal injury)*

An objection might arise at this stage that those exceptions were originally intended to cover road accidents only, the reason being that insurance companies should not be able to shield behind the principle of State immunity. The Court noted this in *McElhinney* when finding that the trend towards limiting State immunity in respect of the tort exception primarily referred to "insurable" personal injury.[163]

As the International Law Commission however pointed out, the above formulations are wide enough to also cover intentional personal injuries.[164] The most famous example for such an interpretation beyond the scope of "insurable" personal injury is the *Letelier* case in which a US court found that section 1605 of the FSIA also covered political assassinations, in that case the killing of the former Chilean Ambassador and Foreign Minister Orlando Letelier with a car bomb on US territory.[165] The personal injury exception was also applied by the Greek Supreme Court (*Areopag*) when refusing to grant State immunity to Germany in tort proceedings brought by Greek citizens for a Nazi massacre in the village of Distomo during the German occupation in 1944.[166] Therefore, the restriction of the tort exception to "insurable injury" is rather questionable.

d) *Acts of the armed forces of the foreign State and the personal injury exception*

In *McElhinney*, the Court also took note of the fact that the case concerned "matters relating to the core area of State sovereignty, such as the acts of a soldier on foreign territory, which, of their very nature, may involve sensitive issues affecting diplomatic relations between states and national security."[167] Article 31 of the European Convention on State Immunity, for example, provides: "Nothing in this Convention shall affect any immunities or privileges enjoyed by a Contracting Party in respect of anything done or omitted to be done by or in relation to its armed forces on the territory of another Contracting State."

Since the assault was committed by a British soldier, the Irish Supreme Court had found that the European Convention on State Immunity took account of a counter-exception in international law from the personal injury

---

163 *McElhinney v. Ireland*, para. 38.

164 Yang, *State Immunity in the European Court of Human Rights*, BYIL 2003, p. 366; Yearbook of the International Law Commission, 1991, Vol. II, Part Two, p. 12.

165 *Letelier v. Republic of Chile*, ILR 63, p. 378.

166 See below, p. 93.

167 *McElhinney v. Ireland*, para. 38.

exception as far as armed forces of the foreign State were concerned.[168] The dissenting judges in *McElhinney* however stated that the "armed forces" exception was not provided for in any other national or international instrument and therefore appeared to be rather specific to the European Convention on State Immunity.[169] Although this argument is not entirely correct (Section 16 (2) of the United Kingdom State Immunity Act 1978 provides for a similar exception[170]), the wording of Article 31 suggests a narrow interpretation.[171] In their explanatory report, the drafters of the European Convention on State Immunity only mentioned special agreements and visits by naval forces of a foreign State, but do not seem to have had in mind a case of an unauthorised entry of a foreign soldier into the territory of the forum State in order to cause injury (as happened in *McElhinney*).[172] Moreover, it has been argued that the new United Nations Convention on Jurisdictional Immunities of States and Their Property does apply to military activities, although it remains subject to the provisions of existing international agreements, including Status of Forces Agreements.[173] Consequently, the fact that the injury in *McElhinney* was caused by a foreign soldier should arguably not have had an impact on the case.

e) *Discussion of the judgment*

Considering that that all existing domestic statutes on State immunity and all international conventions on State immunity (plus the draft proposals by the International Law Association and the Institute of International Law) provide for an personal injury exception, there exists a considerable list of sources according to which State immunity should not have been granted to the United Kingdom in *McElhinney*. That list is arguably more than "just a trend" towards restricting immunity (as the Court put it), and this might be the decisive difference in comparison with the *Fogarty* judgment, in which all international instruments would have provided for immunity.[174] Three of the

---

168 [1995] 3 Irish Reports, p. 402.

169 *McElhinney v. Ireland*, dissenting opinion of Judges Caflisch, Cabral Barreto and Vajic. See also Voyakis, *Access to Court v State Immunity*, ICLQ 2003, p. 314.

170 See also *Holland v. Lampen-Wolfe* [2000] 3 All ER p. 808, pp. 837–840 and 843–845.

171 See also the applicant's submissions in *McElhinney v. Ireland*, para. 30.

172 Yang, *State Immunity in the European Court of Human Rights*, BYIL 2003, pp. 371–372, citing the Council of Europe's *Explanatory Reports on the European Convention on State Immunity and the Additional Protocol*, Strasbourg 1972, p. 39.

173 Dickinson, *Status of Forces under the UN Convention on State Immunity*, ICLQ 2006, p. 427.

174 See also Rozakis (*The ECHR and the Law on State Immunity*, p. 398, as well as his dissenting opinion in *McElhinney*), who stressed that the tort at issue (even though indisputably of a governmental nature) did not suffice to justify the plea of immunity because the

five dissenting judges in *McElhinney v. Ireland* considered that the approach taken by Article 12 of the United Nations Convention on Jurisdictional Immunities of States and Their Property (then the proposal by the International Law Commission) was "at the very least, the expression of a remarkable convergence of tendencies in contemporary international law".[175]

An argument that was increasingly put forward is that the draft instruments by the Institute of International Law, the International Law Association and particularly the International Law Commission, which were considered above, did not represent international law. It was said that the only explanation as to why they have not entered into force as to date is because States could not agree on some of the provisions in the draft articles.[176] The dissenting judges would respond that, although the draft articles by the International Law Commission (which arguably represents the most influential draft) were sent back to a working group for "possible repairs" of some controversial provisions, the relevant Article 12 was not among them.[177] Consequently, there did not appear to be any significant challenges against the personal injury exception. The adoption of the United Nations Convention on Jurisdictional Immunities of States and Their Property in 2004 by the General Assembly has in any event made that argument obsolete for future cases.

One might also object that customary international law may only be derived from treaties (let alone draft versions of treaties) if they represent a universal *opinio juris* for the existence of customary international law.[178] It has been argued that this is not the case regarding the personal injury exception.[179] But one does not even have to go as far as to state that the exception

exercise of local jurisdiction of the forum State in such cases is an assertion of its right to deal with the consequences of unlawful acts on its territory.

175 *McElhinney v. Ireland*, dissenting opinion of Judges Caflisch, Cabral Barreto and Vajic. See also Yang (*State Immunity in the European Court of Human Rights*, BYIL 2003, p. 380): "This seems to be now a widely accepted rule; (...)".

176 Kempen, *Der Fall Distomo*, p. 185.

177 *McElhinney v. the United Kingdom*, dissenting opinion of Judges Caflisch, Cabral Barreto and Vajic. Voyakis (*Access to Court v State Immunity*, ICLQ 2003, p. 315) has however rejected this by stating that this stands at odds with the position adopted by the Special Rapporteur of the ILC which considered that the personal injury exception "cannot be found in customary international law" (Yearbook of the ILC (1983), Vol. II, Part One, p. 39) and the Second Special Rapporteur in 1990 (Yearbook of the ILC (1990), Vol. II, Part One, p. 14). Given the fact that the UN Convention on State Immunity was nevertheless adopted in 2004 (including the personal injury exception in Article 12), the argument loses a lot of weight.

178 Doehring, *Völkerrecht*, p. 136.

179 Dolzer, *Der Areopag im Abseits*, NJW 2001, p. 3525.

represents current international law. It should be sufficient to point out that State practice was so divided over the issue that there was no duty under international law for Ireland to grant State immunity to the United Kingdom for the acts committed by the British soldier.[180]

It is here that the Court applied the "proportionality" criterion possibly too widely. Proportionality suggests that a fair balance should be struck between the interests of the individual on the one side and the interests of the defendant State on the other. But one could say that in the present case there did not even exist a conflict for Ireland between two international obligations. Ireland is obliged under the Convention to grant every individual in its jurisdiction a right of access to court. It was however not plain that Ireland was under any international law duty to grant State immunity to the United Kingdom. In *McElhinney*, the Court considered that "the Convention cannot be interpreted in a vacuum (...) and should so far as possible be interpreted in harmony with other rules of international law (...) including those of State immunity."[181] There would have been no contradiction between this statement and the finding of a violation of Article 6 (1) in the present case.

The Court runs into the danger of setting the threshold for the proportionality criterion at such a high level that a violation of Article 6 (1) in cases of State immunity is hardly conceivable. When stating that "generally recognised rules (...) on State immunity cannot in principle be regarded as imposing a disproportionate restriction on the right of access to court",[182] it fails to clarify what "in principle" means and what kind of exceptions to that principle would exist. Is the Court prepared to find a disproportionate restriction only if Ireland is the sole country which applies State immunity in a particular situation? This appears to be the case when the Court finds that "it cannot be said that Ireland is alone in holding that immunity attaches to suits in respect of such torts committed by *acta jure imperii*".[183] The Court would probably be willing to find a violation of the right of access to court only when a State which grants immunity does so in obvious contradiction to general public international law rules.[184] A conceivable case would be that a Member State grants State immunity for commercial acts (e.g. in a former communist country where the *doctrine of absolute immunity* was applied

---

180 *McElhinney v. Ireland*, dissenting opinion of Judges Caflisch, Cabral Barreto and Vajic.

181 *McElhinney v. Ireland*, para. 36.

182 Ibid., para. 37.

183 Ibid., para. 38.

184 Schreuer states that a State violates Article 6 (1) when granting State immunity in the obvious absence of an international duty to do so (*Die Durchsetzung zivilrechtlicher Ansprüche gegen ausländische Staaten*, ÖJZ 1991, p. 48). See also Damian, *Staatenimmunität*, pp. 16–17.

much longer due to the absence of competition), although it is widely common practice that *acta jure gestionis* no longer enjoy the privilege of State immunity. If the proportionality criterion is applied in a manner that only these cases would cross the threshold, the right of access to court might be, in the author's opinion, restricted excessively.[185] Regarding the fact that all international instruments provided for an exception from immunity in *McElhinney*, that case differs significantly from *Fogarty* and (as will be seen below) from the *Al-Adsani* case in this respect. The case therefore deserves to be treated differently.

f) *Conclusion*

Even if one was of the opinion that Ireland had still acted within its margin of appreciation, any future applications on the personal injury exception will have to be considered in the light of the adoption by the General Assembly of the United Nations Convention on Jurisdictional Immunities of States and Their Property in 2004, which provides in Article 12 an exemption from State immunity. That Convention will have a considerable impact on the Contracting State's margin of appreciation in restricting the right of access to court. As Professor Greenwood put it:

> One of the things that [the United Nations Convention on Jurisdictional Immunities of States and Their Property] will do is to narrow the scope of that margin of appreciation. It will be more difficult to argue that you are not in violation of your obligations to other states to accord them immunity because the nature of the immunity is more clearly spelt out. Conversely it will be more difficult for a state to defend a case in a body like the European Court of Human Rights where what it is defending is according a degree of immunity that goes significantly beyond what is laid down in this Convention and I think this is a drawback to spelling things out as clearly as perhaps the new Convention does.[186]

While the above statement deserves approval with regard to the future impact of the United Nations Convention on Jurisdictional Immunities of States and Their Property, the present author does not consider it as a drawback that the Convention spells out clearly the nature and scope of State immunity. If the UN Convention is widely accepted, it can strengthen the right of access to court and might prevent Contracting States from exceeding their margin

---

[185] See also Yang, *State Immunity in the European Court of Human Rights*, BYIL 2003, pp. 381 and 407.

[186] Comments by Professor Greenwood on the United Nations Convention on Jurisdictional Immunities of States and Their Property at a conference organised by the Royal Institute of International Affairs (Chatham House) on 5 October 2005 titled "State Immunity and the New UN Convention" (www.chathamhouse.org.uk/pdf/research/il/ILPstateimmunity.pdf).

of appreciation in future cases in areas in which State immunity has not been uniformly applied by national courts.

7. State immunity for serious human rights violations and its compatibility with Article 6 (1) of the Convention

The above decision of *McElhinney v. Ireland* dealt with compensation claims for the personal injury of an individual which had been committed by a State official on the territory of the forum State. Now the question will be considered whether Article 6 (1) could be used as a vehicle for civil actions against foreign States for injuries committed abroad, that is outside the territory of the forum State. In other words: does the Convention require the Contracting States to consider claims brought by individuals aiming to secure redress for serious human rights violations committed in other countries? If answered in the positive, the granting of State immunity to the defendant State in such proceedings would constitute a violation of Article 6 (1).

The resort to civil actions before domestic courts is attractive for several reasons to an individual who has suffered from human rights violations by a foreign State, in particularly violations which at the same time constitute crimes against humanity. The International Criminal Court has no jurisdiction over acts committed prior to the date on which it began to operate (that is 1 July 2002), and the jurisdictions of the international criminal tribunals for Rwanda (ICTR) and the former Yugoslavia (ICTY) are regionally limited. Although there is the possibility to institute criminal proceedings before national courts, criminal liability is in any case only an option to hold accountable individual perpetrators, but not governments or States.[187] If the victim tries to gain redress from the individual perpetrator or the State which is accountable for those acts, the standard of proof in civil proceedings is more convenient for a victim than the one that applies to criminal proceedings.[188] Compensation from civil action might also prove to be more satisfactory to the victim than the institution of criminal proceedings.[189] Alternatives to domestic proceedings are not very promising either. International human rights enforcement mechanisms are of a limited nature, especially since they are not binding on those States which are not a party to the relevant instru-

[187] Murphy, *Civil Liability for the Commission of International Crimes as an Alternative to Criminal Prosecution*, HHRJ 1999, p. 2 and p. 49.

[188] Murphy, *Civil Liability for the Commission of International Crimes as an Alternative to Criminal Prosecution*, HHRJ 1999, p. 47. See also the *Report on Civil Actions in the English Courts for Serious Human Rights Violations abroad, Human Rights Committee*, International Law Association (British Branch), EHRLR 2001, p. 133.

[189] Lüke, *Immunität*, p. 273.

ments.[190] The effectiveness of diplomatic protection by the victim's State of nationality (in cases in which the victim is not a national of the perpetrator State) is equally uncertain. A State is under no obligation to grant diplomatic protection and may prefer to refrain from it due to concerns about diplomatic relations with the violator State.[191] As a legal writer put it: "Domestic civil actions (…) may provide the only realistic means of recovery"[192] for gross human rights violations.

a) *Practice outside of Europe*

Whether or not individuals could sue a foreign State before the courts of another State for fundamental human rights violations committed abroad is not a new legal issue. Despite this, the matter has only recently come under consideration by the Strasbourg judges. Previously, the phenomenon of such transnational human rights litigation had mostly been an American one.[193] The reason for this is that the jurisdiction of the United States is traditionally generous with civil claims in this respect. Under the Alien Tort Claims Act 1789, foreigners may file claims for damages regarding certain acts which are committed outside the territory of the United States.[194]

---

190 See *Report on Civil Actions in the English Courts*, EHRLR 2001, pp. 129–130.

191 Garnett, *The Defence of State Immunity for Acts of Torture*, AYIL 1997, p. 104.

192 Ibid., p. 123.

193 Steiner and Alston, *International Human Rights in Context*, pp. 1061 and 1077; Garnett, *The Defence of State Immunity for Acts of Torture*, AYIL 1997, p. 106, p. 115. See however the case of *Controller and Auditor General v. Sir Ronald Davidson* [1996] 2 NZLR, p. 278.

194 The statutory authority for human rights litigation in US law is the Alien Tort Claims Act 1789 (hereafter: ACTA) and the Torture Victim Protection Act 1992. The ATCA permits a civil action for damages by one alien against another alien based on tort constituting a violation of the law of nations that took place abroad (Steiner and Alston, *International Human Rights in Context*, p. 1069). It further permits suits against foreign States for human rights violations, subject to the jurisdictional limitations of the FSIA (*Argentine Republic v. Amerada Hess Shipping Corp*, 488 US 428, pp. 434–435; Lininger, *Recent Developments: Overcoming Immunity Defences to Human Rights Suits in US Courts*, HHRJ 1994, p. 182). The ATCA was originally introduced to provide victims of piracy with a remedy (Hobe, *Durchbrechung der Staatenimmunität bei schweren Menschenrechtsverletzungen*, IPrax 2001, p. 370, n. 18). Although rarely invoked for most of the time, human rights defenders have made frequent use of it since the 1980s (Lininger, *Recent Developments: Overcoming Immunity Defences to Human Rights Suits in US Courts*, HHRJ 1994, p. 182). Regarding compensation claims for alleged acts of torture, the introduction of the Torture Victim Protection Act 1992 has facilitated the institution of such claims. However, only individuals can be sued under that Act (see generally Stephens/Ratner, *International Human Rights Litigation in US Courts*, p. 129; Gery, *The Torture Victim Protection Act*, GWJILE 1993, p. 597).

However, it is not only the broad jurisdictional approach which attracts such claims.[195]

The previous cases on State immunity which have been discussed above have shown how much the Strasbourg Court is influenced by international practice when assessing compatibility with Article 6 (1). Therefore, the present question cannot be answered in isolation from the existing case-law in this area, which requires consideration of a series of cases brought before United States courts.

The United States Foreign Sovereign Immunities Act 1976 (hereafter FSIA) generally grants State immunity to foreign States subject to specified exceptions. Among those exceptions is the "personal injury exception" for injuries committed in the forum State (which was discussed in *McElhinney v. Ireland*) or the "commercial activity exception" concerning *acta iure gestionis*. A general "human rights exception" denying State immunity for human rights violations committed abroad is not recognised under the FSIA. In numerous cases plaintiffs have sought to overcome this hurdle by arguing that the FSIA had to be interpreted subject to public international law.[196]

The case of *Argentine Republic v. Amerada Hess Shipping Corp.*[197] involved an alleged violation of international law when the plaintiff's ship was damaged by an Argentine attack during the Falkland war. The US Supreme Court drew from the plain wording of the FSIA that "immunity is granted in those cases involving alleged violations of international law that do not come within one of the FSIA's exceptions".

Obviously influenced by the Supreme Court ruling was the judgment in *Siderman de Blake v. Republic of Argentina.*[198] The case concerned alleged acts of torture, the prohibition of which was recognised by the ruling Court of Appeal as amounting to a *jus cogens* norm (that is, a peremptory norm of international law). The Court of Appeal found that "the fact that there has been a violation of *jus cogens* does not confer jurisdiction under the FSIA".

---

[195] Lüke has given a detailed summary of why transnational human rights litigations have mainly occurred before US courts. Apart from the broad jurisdiction granted by US legislation, numerous other reasons were listed such as low legal costs, lawyers who only charge fees on the basis that the lawsuit proves to be successful, the impressive amount of damages usually granted by US courts, the fact that many (Latin American) human rights victims and perpetrators reside in the US and the wide support and assistance given by US-based human rights organisations with the filing of lawsuits (See Lüke, *Immunität*, pp. 290–291).

[196] For an overview see Steiner and Alston, *International Human Rights in Context*, pp. 1061; Bianchi, *Denying State Immunity to Violators of Human Rights*, AJIL 1994, p. 195; Stephens/Ratner, *International Human Rights Litigation in US Courts*, p. 125.

[197] 488 U.S. 428 (1989).

[198] *Siderman de Blake v. Republic of Argentina*, [1992] 965 F.2d 699.

Although the court considered it plausible that a *jus cogens* violation could override the principle of State immunity, it found that it should have been up to Parliament to amend national law accordingly.[199]

The argument that governments which committed *jus cogens* violations had impliedly waived their immunity under the FSIA by becoming a party to an international treaty was rejected in *Smith v. Socialist People's Libyan Arab Jamabiriya*[200] and *Princz v. Federal Republic of Germany.*[201] In the latter case, which involved a compensation claim by a former Auschwitz prisoner against Germany, a dissenting judge however opined that Germany had waived and forfeited its immunity due to the unique cruelty of the acts concerned.[202] A frequent objection against this is that a waiver cannot be construed where the perpetrator State has obviously not consented.[203] In *Saudi Arabia v. Nelson*, the plaintiffs had unsuccessfully argued that the human rights violations committed against them while temporarily working in Saudi Arabia had to be regarded as "commercial acts" so that the acts would fall within the "commercial activity exception" of the FSIA.[204]

---

199 See also the case of *Denegri v. Chile*, 1992 WL 9194 (in a civil claim brought by a torture victim, immunity was granted despite a *jus cogens* violation).

200 Case concerning compensation claims by relatives of the Lockerbie attack victims; 101 F.3d 239 (2nd Circuit 1996). Prior to these decisions, the Supreme Court in *Amerada Hess* had rejected this argument where the treaty in question made no explicit reference to a waiver. See also Murphy, p 34; Garnett, pp. 110–111.

201 26 F.3d 1166 (D.C.Cir. 1994); 103 ILR, p. 601. The case concerned a civil claim against Germany brought by a former detainee of the Auschwitz concentration camp. Whereas the District Court denied immunity ("The Foreign Sovereign Immunities Act has no role to play where the claims alleged involve undisputed acts of barbarism committed by a one-time outlaw nation", 103 ILR, p. 598), the decision was quashed on appeal because the FSIA did not expressly permit a "human rights exception". For a similar case with the same outcome see the decision of the US District Court (New York) in *Hirsch v. State of Israel and State of Germany*, 113 ILR, p. 503. See also Reimann, *A Human Rights Exception to Sovereign Immunity*, MJIL 1995, p. 403 and Zimmermann, *Sovereign Immunity and Violations of Jus Cogens*, MJIL 1995, p. 433.

202 Dissenting opinion by Judge Wald, 103 ILR 103, p. 612.

203 Bröhmer, *State Immunity*, p. 191; Reimann, *A Human Rights Exception to Sovereign Immunity*, MJIL 1995, pp. 409 and 417. On the issue of forfeiture, see Kokott, *Mißbrauch und Verwirkung*, p. 149.

204 *Saudi Arabia v. Nelson*, 100 ILR, p. 544. A further proposal is to deny immunity as a reprisal. This is however based on the assumption that the granting of State immunity would amount to a violation of international law, which is not necessarily the case (Bröhmer, *State Immunity*, pp. 192 et seq.).

b) *Conclusion*

Having regard to these cases, international practice up to 2001 (when the Court had regard to that issue) would suggest that a general "human rights exception" for State immunity did not exist. Although the relationship between a violation of a *jus cogens* norm and the rule of State immunity had been touched upon by various courts, the results had basically always been in favour of State immunity. However, the claims were not necessarily unsuccessful because of arguments involving international law, but rather because domestic law did not expressly provide for an exception to immunity.[205]

In the case of *Al-Adsani v. the United Kingdom*, which was the most controversial of the three Grand Chamber judgments on State immunity, this issue had to be considered by the Strasbourg Court. It is also the first time that State immunity was considered from a "right of access to court" perspective in this type of cases.

c) *The case of* Al-Adsani v. the United Kingdom

In *Al-Adsani v. the United Kingdom*, the applicant (a dual British/Kuwaiti national) had allegedly been tortured by a relative of the Emir of Kuwait after circulating a sexual videotape involving that relative. After initial treatment in a Kuwaiti hospital he returned to England, where he received treatment for burns covering twenty-five percent of his total body surface area.[206] Despite being threatened not to take action he instituted proceedings in England against the Government of Kuwait for compensation for the alleged acts of torture in Kuwait. After the High Court struck out his claim, the applicant appealed to the Court of Appeal, which found that Kuwait was entitled to State immunity due to the unambiguous wording of the United Kingdom State Immunity Act 1978. The Act only allowed for an exception from State immunity if personal injury is inflicted on an individual on the territory of the forum State (which is the exception which was considered in *McElhinney v. Ireland*).[207] Like the United States court in *Siderman de Blake*, the Court

[205] See Rensmann, *Internationale Verbrechen und Befreiung von staatlicher Gerichtsbarkeit*, IPrax 1999, p. 268.

[206] See *Al-Adsani v. the United Kingdom*, para. 13.

[207] *Al Adsani v. Government of Kuwait*, (1996) 107 ILR 536. The applicant also complained that he had suffered personal injury while being in England due to telephone threats from Kuwaiti State officials. As the alleged injury had occurred on the territory of the United Kingdom, the "personal injury exception" in Section 5 of the SIA 1978 would have applied. However, the Court of Appeal in *Al-Adsani* decided that on the balance of probabilities the Kuwaiti government could not be held responsible for the threats.

of Appeal pointed out that it was up to Parliament to amend national law accordingly.[208]

Three years later, in 1999, the House of Lords found in the *Pinochet* case[209] that torture was an international crime and prohibited by *jus cogens*. Some judges in the House of Lords found that the immunity for ex-Heads of State for official acts of torture was overridden by *jus cogens*, irrespective of whether or not the State Immunity Act 1978 did expressly provide for such an exception. Nevertheless, they found no contradiction in holding accountable States or State officials in criminal proceedings while at the same time granting immunity in civil proceedings.[210] The Lordships quoted the Court of Appeal's decision in *Al-Adsani* with approval in this respect. However, the different consequences of a violation of *jus cogens* which the House of Lords had drawn in respect of civil and criminal proceedings were criticised as creating a manifest inconsistency.[211]

In *Al-Adsani v. the United Kingdom*, the Court seemed to have agreed with the distinction between civil and criminal proceedings made by the House of Lords. The Grand Chamber decided by nine votes to eight that the British courts had not violated the applicant's right of access to court when rejecting his claim by applying the principle of State immunity.[212] The Court also found unanimously that the United Kingdom was not under a duty derived from Article 3 (prohibition of torture) to provide one of its citizens with a civil remedy in respect of the alleged acts of torture committed abroad.[213]

---

208 Note however the Court of Appeal's decision of 21 January 1994 to grant leave to serve the proceedings upon the Government of Kuwait out of the jurisdiction (100 ILR, pp. 465 et seq.). On pp. 470–471, Lord Justice Evans considered it at least as conceivable that immunity could be denied to Kuwait: "[I]t is possible to argue that since the intention of the State Immunity Act was to give effect to the European Convention of 1972, and more generally to give effect to the rules of customary international law (...), then the reference to immunity in Section 1 (1) of the Act is a reference to immunity in accordance with public or general international law." The Court of Appeal found that immunity could be denied if reluctance under public international law could be shown to give any legal status to acts of torture (Müller/Wildhaber, *Praxis des Völkerrechts*, p. 468).

209 *Reg. v. Bow Street Magistrate*, Ex p. Pinochet, [1999] 2 WLR, p. 827.

210 Ibid., p. 914.

211 Bianchi, *Immunity versus Human Rights: The Pinochet case*, EJIL 1999, p. 264. Whether the argument of consistency is a compelling reason to reject the Court of Appeal's finding in *Al-Adsani* appears to be questioned by Steiner and Alston, *International Human Rights in Context*, p. 1068.

212 *Al-Adsani v. the United Kingdom*, paras. 50–67.

213 Ibid., paras. 35–40. Orakhelashvili has argued that this finding was contrary to the spirit and intention of Article 3 and the Convention as a whole (*Restrictive Interpretation of Human Rights in Recent Jurisprudence*, EJIL 2003, p. 553). However, in the absence of an international obligation to provide a civil remedy for torture committed abroad (see below,

But the outcome of the Grand Chamber decision with regard to the right of access to court under Article 6 was as close as it could get, leading a legal scholar to describe the result as mere coincidence.[214] Eight judges expressed their different views in three dissenting opinions. The crucial question was whether States should be entitled to immunity where there had been a violation of the prohibition of torture.

Initially, the seventeen judges in the Grand Chamber did not differ in finding that the prohibition of torture had evolved to become *jus cogens*. They referred to numerous international human rights treaties which prohibit torture, the *Pinochet* case and the case-law of the International Criminal Tribunal for the former Yugoslavia (ICTY) in order to support their finding.[215] Subsequently, the Grand Chamber divided itself into two almost equally sized groups of judges which headed in completely different directions, both leaving aside the arguments put forward by the other side. Whereas the majority of nine judges did not draw any conclusion from its finding that the prohibition of torture amounted to a *jus cogens* rule, the group of dissenting judges did not address the fact that international practice did not support a restriction on State immunity.

(1) *The decision of the majority*

The latter was however the main argument of the (albeit very small) majority of the judges, who found that the immunity granted to Kuwait amounted to a proportionate restriction on Article 6 (1). The Court had regard to the above discussed United States jurisprudence and noted that, although some judges had expressed sympathy for the plaintiffs, in most cases the plea of State immunity had been successful.[216] Two expert reports on the issue were referred to but were not regarded as supporting a contrary view.[217] The judges noted recent developments, such as an amendment to the United States Foreign Sovereign Immunities Act 1976, which allows United States citizens to sue for acts of torture those States which are designated as sponsors of ter-

pp. 78–79), the Court rightly decided that there was no positive obligation to do so under Article 3.

214 Sutter, *Fällt nun auch die Staatenimmunität? Von einer 'unbemerkten' Revolution im Völkerrecht*, Jusletter, January 2002.

215 *Al-Adsani v. the United Kingdom*, paras. 30–31 and 60.

216 Ibid., paras. 23 and 62.

217 The reports were the *Report on Jurisdictional Immunities of States and their Property* by the Working Group of the International Law Commission (1999) and the *Report on Civil Actions in the English Courts for Serious Human Rights Violations Abroad*, Human Rights Committee, International Law Association (British Branch), EHRLR 2001, p. 129 (only referred to in the concurring opinion of Judges Bratza and Pellonpää).

rorism.[218] The Court also considered the *Pinochet* judgments by the House of Lords and the *Furundzija* decision by the ICTY[219] but stressed that these decisions concerned the criminal liability of individuals which had to be distinguished from the civil liability of States. None of the materials, judgments and international instruments the Court had looked at were found to provide it with a firm basis on which to conclude that States no longer enjoyed immunity from civil suit concerning alleged acts of torture.[220] In saying that it was not *yet* prepared to find a violation of Article 6, the Court however

---

218 *Al-Adsani v. the United Kingdom*, paras. 24 and 64. The 1996 amendments to the United States Foreign States Immunity Act 1976 allow for certain civil suits by US nationals against those States which are on the Secretary of State's list of State sponsors of terrorism. The amendment was introduced by the "Anti-Terrorism and Effective Death Penalty Act 1996". Claims can be brought for personal injury or death resulting from torture, extra-judicial killing, aircraft sabotage or hostage-taking if the act occurred outside the State's territory (see generally Leigh, *1996 Amendments to the Foreign Sovereign Immunities Act with Respect to Terrorist Activities*, AJIL 1997, p. 187). Initially, the "State-sponsored terrorism exception" amendment to the FSIA did not affect the immunity of a foreign State's public property from attachment and execution. Hence the plaintiff who succeeded in the case of *Flatow v. the Islamic Republic of Iran* (999 F. Supp. 1 [D.D.C. 1998]; 76 F. Supp. 2d 16, 18 [D.D.C. 1999]), one of the first reported cases in which the exception was applied, obtained a "Pyrrhic victory" by obtaining a judgment which could not be executed. The case caused a further amendment to the FSIA which allowed for United States nationals to attach and execute judgments against a foreign State's diplomatic or consular properties, subject to a provision under which the president may exercise a waiver in the national security interest of the United States (see Murphy, *Contemporary Practice of the United States Relating to International Law- State Jurisdiction and Jurisdictional Immunities*, AJIL 1999, p. 185; *Al-Adsani v. the United Kingdom*, concurring opinion of Judges Bratza and Pellonpää). In October 1998, President Clinton exercised this waiver in the *Flatow* case because the attachment and execution "would put at risk the protection [the US enjoys] at every embassy and consulate throughout the world by eroding the principle that diplomatic property must be protected regardless of bilateral relations" (*Statement on Signing the Omnibus Consolidated and Emergency Supplemental Appropriations Act*, 1999 34 Weekly Comp. Pres. Doc., p. 2113; see Murphy, *Contemporary Practice of the United States Relating to International Law- State Jurisdiction and Jurisdictional Immunities*, AJIL 1999, pp. 185–186). As a consequence, the plaintiff remained empty-handed at the end of the day (Zaffuto, *A 'pirate's victory': President Clinton's approach to the new FSIA exception leaves the victor empty-handed*, TLR 1999, pp. 687 and 709).

219 *Prosecutor v. Anto Furundzija*, Judgment of 10 December 1998, 38 ILM 317.

220 *Al-Adsani v. the United Kingdom*, para. 63. Note that the UN Convention on State Immunity, adopted in December 2004, does not provide for an exception from State immunity for serious human rights violations (see Hall, *UN Convention on State Immunity: the Need for a Human Rights Protocol*, ICLQ 2006, pp. 411–426). It appears that, as stated by the Chairman of the UN General Assembly's Sixth Committee ad hoc working group, there would have been no agreement on the Convention's text had the negotiations included any discussion on such an exception (Fox, *In Defence of State Immunity: why the UN Convention on State Immunity is Important*, ICLQ 2006, p. 406).

indicated that it might do so on future occasions once international law has evolved further in this respect.

(2) *The reasoning of the minority*

In their dissenting opinion which was joined by four other judges, Judge Rozakis and Judge Caflisch found that the majority of the judges had failed to draw the consequences of accepting that the prohibition of torture amounted to *jus cogens*. Being hierarchically higher than any other rule of international law, *jus cogens* would take precedent over any other rule of international law such as State immunity. The procedural bar created by the immunity would thus automatically be lifted. These effects would apply irrespective of the nature of proceedings, whether criminal or civil:

> It is not the nature of proceedings which determines the effect that a *jus cogens* rule has upon another rule of international law.[221]

The then President of the Court, Judge Luzius Wildhaber, stated that the majority of judges had decided exactly the opposite by allowing State immunity as a lesser rule to prevail over a superior norm in international law.[222] It becomes plain from the above why the dissenting judges did not draw any conclusions from the lack of supporting domestic decisions. It is because they considered that State immunity as the lower norm is automatically void, independent of international practice.[223] According to this view, it is consequently sufficient to show that there exists international practice with regard to the classification of a norm of international law as *jus cogens* (which all judges in the Grand Chamber had stated in the affirmative with regard to the prohibition of torture).[224]

(3) Jus cogens *v. State Immunity*

At first sight, the argument of the minority that State immunity is void because it conflicts with *jus cogens* appears convincing.[225] According to the

[221] Ibid., Dissenting opinion of Judges Rozakis and Caflisch joined by Judges Wildhaber, Costa, Cabral Barreto and Vajic, para. 4.

[222] Comments on *Al-Adsani* by Judge Luzius Wildhaber, President of the European Court of Human Rights, on the occasion of the Opening of the Judicial Year, Strasbourg, 31 January 2002, in: Wildhaber, *The European Court of Human Rights 1998–2006/History, Achievements, Reform*, p. 32; for see also McGregor, *Torture and State Immunity*, EJIL 2007, pp. 903 et seq.

[223] See also Reimann, *A Human Rights Exception to Sovereign Immunity*, MJIL 1995, p. 195.

[224] Maierhöfer, *Der EGMR als Modernisierer des Völkerrechts*?, EuGRZ 2002, p. 395.

[225] In an article published in 2002, the present author suggested that the view of the minority in *Al-Adsani* was preferable (Kloth, *Immunities and the Right of Access to Court under the European Convention on Human Rights*, ELR, Human Rights Issue, August 2002, p. 42).

supporters of that argument, the interaction of the *erga omnes* character of a *jus cogens* rule and State immunity is that a State cannot avoid the consequences of the illegality of its action by sheltering behind immunity.[226] The argument goes that, according to the principle *ex injuria jus non oritur*, rights and privileges such as immunity from suit cannot be derived from an act of torture, while at the same time the United Nations Torture Convention regards the offenders of the prohibition of torture as "common enemies of all mankind".[227]

However, there are weighty arguments to oppose the view taken by the minority in *Al-Adsani* on the relationship between *jus cogens* and State immunity. Even though the peremptory status of a *jus cogens* norm has so far only been codified with regard to international treaties,[228] it is arguable that a norm of customary international law which conflicts with a *jus cogens* norm is void.[229] Since State immunity can be waived, that norm does not

---

226 *Al-Adsani v. the United Kingdom*, dissenting opinion of Judges Rozakis and Caflisch joined by Judges Wildhaber, Costa, Cabral Barreto and Vajic, para. 3.

227 See Bantekas, *Case note*, AJIL 1998, p. 766. Note that the UN Convention on State Immunity does not address the relationship between State immunity and *jus cogens*. It appears that the Working Group on Jurisdictional Immunities of States and their Property (established by the International Law Commission) noted that the issue did not seem ripe enough to attempt to codify it; the Third and the Sixth Committee of the UN General Assembly also refrained from addressing that issue (McGregor, *State Immunity and Jus Cogens*, ICLQ 2006, p. 437).

228 Commenting on the *Princz* case, Zimmermann (*Sovereign Immunity and the Violations of International Jus Cogens*, MJIL 1994–1995, p. 438) stresses that the relevant provisions in the Vienna Convention on the Law of Treaties (Articles 53 and 64) only render void *treaties* which are incompatible with a *jus cogens* norm. Preparatory material of the International Law Commission prior to the entering into force of the Vienna Convention would not suggest that the same were to be true for conflicting norms of customary international law such as the rules on State immunity (leave aside the UN Convention on State Immunity which had not yet been adopted in 2001 and which has not been ratified by the United Kingdom). Hence the implication of a hierarchy of norms between *jus cogens* and State immunity rules would go beyond the traditionally recognised effects of *jus cogens*. This appears to be a bit over-subtle. Whether the principle of State immunity is (merely) based on customary international law or whether the respective forum State has ratified the UN Convention on State Immunity should not be decisive for the present question. The author itself notes that "leading commentators" find that *jus cogens* is capable of invalidating conflicting norms of customary international law (see for further references: Tams, *Schwierigkeiten mit dem Ius Cogens*, Archiv des Völkerrechts 2002, p. 331; see also *Prosecutor v. Furundzija* 28 ILM, p. 317 and Gaja, *Jus Cogens beyond the Vienna Convention*, RdC 1981, p. 271).

229 This is because Article 53 of the Vienna Convention on the Law of Treaties provides that a treaty (and thus arguably a rule of customary international law) is void if, at the time of conclusion, it conflicts with a peremptory norm of international law, *i.e.* "a norm accepted

have *jus cogens* status and would therefore be trumped by the prohibition of torture.[230] That is, if there exists such a conflict. In the present case, this is far from obvious. The line of argument adopted by the dissenting judges presupposes not only the prohibition of torture to be *jus cogens*, but also the obligation of the forum State to deny immunity in cases of a violation of the prohibition.[231] The minority in *Al-Adsani* however failed to show that the prohibition of torture does not only prohibit the infliction of severe ill-treatment, but also directly entitles the victim to take procedural action in a State which did not inflict that ill-treatment.[232] States may not themselves inflict torture, extradite persons to third countries where those persons might face torture, or refrain from bringing criminal proceedings against or extraditing persons within their jurisdiction who are responsible for torture. But an obligation for States to grant access to their courts in civil proceedings to a person who has been tortured abroad by a third State is arguably not (yet) encompassed in the prohibition of torture.[233] On the other hand, State immunity remains a mere exception from the jurisdiction of the forum State without providing for a material aspect which conflicts with the prohibition of torture. As Fox stated:

> State immunity is a procedural rule going to the jurisdiction of a national court. It does not go to substantive law; it does not contradict a prohibition contained in a *jus cogens* norm but merely diverts any breach of it to a different method of settlement. Arguably, then, there is not substantive content in the procedural plea of state immunity upon which a *jus cogens* mandate can bite.[234]

---

and recognised by the international community of States as a whole as a norm from which no derogation is permitted and which can be modified only by a subsequent norm of general international law having the same character" (Article 53 Vienna Convention).

230 Maierhöfer however suggests that State immunity, since it is based on the principles of sovereignty of States and *par in parem non habet jurisdictionem*, should be at the top of any hierarchy of public international law norms since without State immunity these two fundamental principles would be severely undermined (*EGMR als Modernisierer des Völkerrechts*?, EuGRZ 2002, p. 397). However, this view fails to take into account that State immunity may be waived and therefore cannot be regarded as a peremptory norm of international law.

231 See Zimmermann, *Sovereign Immunity and the Violations of International Jus Cogens*, MJIL 1994–1995, p. 438.

232 See also Bröhmer, *State Immunity*, p. 195.

233 For a discussion on the obligations on States to allow remedies for acts of torture under the UN Torture Convention, see below, p. 91.

234 Fox, *The Law of State Immunity*, p. 525; Zimmermann stated that "(...) it seems to be more appropriate to consider both issues as involving two sets of rules which do not interact which each other", MJIL 1994–1995, p. 438. See also Caplan, *State Immunity, Human Rights and* Jus Cogens: *A Critique of the Normative Hierarchy Theory*, AJIL 2003, p. 772.

Referring to that passage, Lord Hoffmann commented as follows in *Jones*:

> To produce a conflict with State immunity, it is therefore necessary to show that the prohibition of torture has generated an ancillary procedural rule which, by way of exception to state immunity, entitles or perhaps requires states to assume civil jurisdiction over other states in cases in which torture is alleged. Such a rule may be desirable and, since international law changes, may have developed. But, contrary to the assertion of the minority in *Al-Adsani*, it is not *entailed* by the prohibition of torture.[235]

If a procedural rule to grant access to the courts of the forum State to a person who has been tortured in a foreign State was entailed in the prohibition of torture, the forum State would arguably be in violation of the prohibition of torture under Article 3 when granting State immunity to the foreign State under such circumstances.[236] At least that would have to be the logical consequence of the view taken by the minority in *Al-Adsani* if one was to find a conflict between the prohibition of torture and State immunity. Neither the minority nor the majority of judges in *Al-Adsani* were however prepared to find that the United Kingdom had violated Article 3 when granting State immunity to Saudi Arabia.[237] The finding that Article 3 had not been violated in any event reflected the provisions of other international treaties, given that the UN Torture Convention only obliges a Contracting State to provide a remedy for torture inflicted by itself (and not by a third State).[238]

It should be reiterated that the United Kingdom, when granting State immunity to Saudi Arabia, did not sanction the acts of torture inflicted upon the applicant in *Al-Adsani*. Those acts remained a breach of international law, but the claim arising from that breach could not be brought before a British court. Hence immunity does not equal impunity (in particular because in the present context criminal proceedings were not at issue).[239] Maierhöfer rightly pointed out that a material norm of public international law does not automatically guarantee its enforcement in international or foreign courts;

---

235 United Kingdom House of Lords, *Jones v. Ministry of Interior Al-Mamlaka Al-Arabiya as Saudiya and others*, judgment of 14 June 2006, para. 45 (with reference to *Bouzari v. Islamic Republic of Iran*, 124 ILR, p. 443).

236 Maierhöfer, *EGMR als Modernisierer des Völkerrechts?*, EuGRZ 2002, p. 397; Tams, *Schwierigkeiten mit dem Jus Cogens*, Archiv des Völkerrechts 2002, p. 342.

237 *Al-Adsani*, para. 41.

238 See below, p. 80.

239 Yang, *State Immunity in the European Court of Human Rights: Reaffirmations and Misconceptions*, BYIL 2003, p. 343.

hence that material norm cannot conflict with the rule of State immunity which only prevents its enforcement in a foreign court.[240]

Not everybody shares this view. It has been said that every *jus cogens* norm contains a procedural rule which guarantees its judicial enforcement which follows from the lack of a central authority watching over the execution and enforcement of international law.[241] The supporters of this argument state that this lack of a centralised enforcement mechanism has led to the evolution of the concept of *erga omnes* norms (to which norms with a *jus cogens* character usually belong) which are subject to superior means of enforcement.[242] This argument is however questionable. It is for example not yet established in public international law that *erga omnes* norms automatically form the basis for the jurisdiction of the International Court of Justice.[243] The latter reasoned in the *East Timor* case: "The *erga omnes* character of a norm and the rule of consent to jurisdiction are two different things."[244] There is no reason why the same should not apply to national courts.

The approach taken by the minority in *Al-Adsani* would also produce results which might not have been intended by the dissenting judges. While the existence of *jus cogens* in international law is an increasingly accepted proposition, its exact scope and content remains an open question.[245] The concept of *jus cogens* is not confined solely to human rights. Other norms such as the principle to refrain from the threat or use of force in Article 2 (4) of the Charter of the United Nations are recognised as *jus cogens* as well.

---

240 Maierhöfer, *EGMR als Modernisierer des Völkerrechts?*, EuGRZ 2002, p. 397; see also Rau, *After Pinochet: Foreign Sovereign Immunity in Respect of Serious Human Rights Violations – The Decision of the European Court of Human Rights in the* Al-Adsani *Case*, German Law Journal 2002, para. 14; Grabenwarter, *Europäische Menschenrechtskonvention*, § 24, 56; ibid., *Probleme paralleler Rechtsverbürgungen durch Vertrag und Gewohnheit*, p. 166 et seq.

241 Bartsch/Elberling, *Jus Cogens v. State Immunity, Round Two: The Decision of the European Court of Human Rights in the* Kalogeropoulou et al. v. Greece and Germany *Decision*, German Law Journal 2003, p. 486. The argument that there is a conflict between *jus cogens* and State immunity in the present case is also supported by: Parlett, *Immunity in Civil Proceedings for Torture: the Emerging Exception*, EHRLR 2006, p. 50; Orakhelashvili, *Restrictive Interpretation of Human Rights in Recent Jurisprudence*, EJIL 2003, p. 553; Reece Thomas/Small, *Human Rights and State Immunity: Is there Immunity from Civil Liability for Torture?* NILR 2003, p. 1; Clapham, *The* Jus Cogens *Prohibition of Torture and the Importance of Sovereign State Immunity*, Liber Amicorum Lucius Caflisch, p. 151; see also Bianchi, *Human Rights and the Magic of Jus Cogens*, EJIL 2008.

242 Bartsch/Elberling, *Jus Cogens v. State Immunity*, German Law Journal 2003, pp. 486–7; Redress Trust, *Immunity v. Accountability* (2000).

243 Klein, *Menschenrechte und Ius Cogens*, Festschrift für Georg Ress, p. 159.

244 *Case Concerning East Timor*, ICJ Reports 1995, para. 29.

245 Caplan, *State Immunity, Human Rights and* Jus Cogens*: A Critique of the Normative Hierarchy Theory*, AJIL 2003, p. 772.

It could become a very severe problem for international relations if domestic judges would rule on international conflicts.[246] Moreover, a domestic court might not be an appropriate forum to determine whether a particular norm of international law has attained the status of *jus cogens*, a task which international lawyers have tried to solve for decades.[247] Having regard to the above arguments, the minority's argument that a violation of *jus cogens* trumps the rule of State immunity should not be followed.[248]

d) *Does the UN Torture Convention restrict State immunity in civil proceedings?*

In *Al-Adsani*, the majority of judges distinguished between the present case and the *Pinochet* judgments of the House of Lords on the basis that the latter concerned criminal proceedings for acts of torture, whereas the former concerned civil proceedings for damages from torture. This distinction has been widely criticised.[249] A weakness of this passage in the *Al-Adsani* judgment is that the judges failed to elaborate more on the reasoning of the House of Lords in the *Pinochet* case. For example, some judges in *Pinochet* held that an act of torture was so illegal that it could not be considered an official act – it is here that the Court in *Al-Adsani* failed to address this argument which could have equally applied to civil proceedings against foreign States.[250] The remainder of their Lordships who found that the former Chilean dictator had not been protected by immunity based their reasoning on the interpretation of the UN Torture Convention. The following section investigates the impact of that reasoning on the *Al-Adsani* case.

In *Pinochet No. 3*, several members of the House of Lords found that the Contracting States to the UN Torture Convention had implicitly removed the immunity of former Heads of States (and other agents) responsible for

---

246 Maierhöfer gives the example of Israeli and Palestinian courts both allowing individual claims for damages against the other party in the Middle East conflict (*EGMR als Modernisierer des Völkerrechts?*, EuGRZ 2002, p. 398).

247 Caplan, *State Immunity, Human Rights and* Jus Cogens: *A Critique of the Normative Hierarchy Theory*, AJIL 2003, p. 773. Even though Bartsch and Eberling rightly suggest that States may be able to "put the past to rest" by concluding international treaties which grant compensation but at the same time exclude individual claims before domestic courts (*Jus Cogens v. State Immunity*, German Law Journal 2003, p. 489).

248 See also Bates, *The Al-Adsani Case, State Immunity and the International Legal Prohibition of Torture*, HRLR 2003, p. 193.

249 Tams, *Schwierigkeiten mit dem Jus Cogens*, Archiv des Völkerrechts 2002, p. 347. Judge Ferrari Bravo, in his dissenting opinion in *Al-Adsani*, called the distinction "formalistic". See also Yang, *State Immunity in the European Court of Human Rights*, BYIL 2003, p. 354.

250 For a discussion of that argument, see below, pp. 126–131.

inflicting torture.[251] The argument was made that, even though the Convention did not explicitly waive or exclude immunity, torture could *per definitionem* only be committed by persons acting in an official capacity (Article 1 of the Convention). If those officials were immune from prosecution, nobody could ever be prosecuted for torture.[252] This raises the question whether the UN Torture Convention has any impact on the immunities of States or its officials with regard to civil proceedings for torture. Even if one would not go as far as suggesting that any immunity had been implicitly removed by the UN Torture Convention, the obligation for the Contracting States to hear civil claims for torture committed outside its jurisdiction would constitute a strong argument with regard to the "proportionality" criterion of the *Ashingdane* test. In *Al-Adsani*, the Court did however not address whether or not such an obligation existed.

(1) *A historic and systematic interpretation of Article 14 of the United Nations Torture Convention*

The United Nations Torture Convention has the major aim of obliging Contracting Parties to either exercise criminal jurisdiction over torturers or extradite them to a third country which will do so (*aut dedere aut judicare*). It makes reference to civil proceedings in its Article 14, which provides that:

> (1) Each state shall ensure in its legal system that the victim of an act of torture obtains redress and has an enforceable right to fair and adequate compensation, including the means for as full rehabilitation as possible. In the event of the death of the victim as a result of an act of torture, his dependants shall be entitled to compensation.
>
> (2) Nothing in this article shall affect any right of the victim or other persons to compensation which may exist under national law.

The wording of that provision is wide and could arguably include claims for damages before the courts of another (e.g. the forum) State, thereby implicitly removing the immunity of the foreign State that has inflicted torture.[253] Unlike the provisions in the Torture Convention dealing with measures to criminalise an act of torture, Article 14 (1) lacks the words "committed in any territory under its jurisdiction" after the word "torture". One might conclude that the omission of a territorial limitation must have some significance given the express inclusion in other provisions. A historical interpretation of Article 14 however suggests that the provision only intended to

[251] *R. v. Bow Street Metropolitan Stipendiary Magistrates, Ex parte Pinochet Ugarte (No. 3)*, 1 AC 2000, p. 147.

[252] See the discussion below, pp. 126–131.

[253] Fox, *State Immunity and the International Crime of Torture*, EHRLR 2006, p. 153.

compel a State to provide redress for those individuals that were tortured on its own territory (and by its own officials). As Byrnes has pointed out in detail, the *travaux préparatoires* suggest that the territorial limitation was omitted by inadvertence.[254] Originally not introduced in the draft Convention, the words "committed in any territory under its jurisdiction" were later added to Article 14 (1) by express decision of the Working Group of the UN Commission on Human Rights but subsequently removed by it upon the adoption of its final version. As the removal of the territorial limitation was not expressly documented, it is very likely that the omission of it from the text was mistaken.[255] When the United States ratified the Convention, it gave an understanding that Article 14 only required a State to provide a private right of action for damages for acts of torture committed in territory under a State's jurisdiction: in other words, a "McElhinney"-like exception for immunities was tolerated, but not an "Al-Adsani"-like exception. That statement has received no objection from other Contracting States.[256]

A contextual interpretation also suggests that the Contracting States did not intend to remove any existing immunities with regard to civil proceedings. Article 14 was placed in the UN Torture Convention among other provisions which contain a territorial limitation. Moreover, under Article 5 (1) (c) of the Convention, a State is only required to establish criminal jurisdiction when "the victim is a national of that State *if that State considers it appropriate*".[257] In the light of that provision, it would be odd to conclude that the Contracting States had intended to go further with regard to civil proceedings and to compel themselves to waive any State immunity for torture in civil cases. Furthermore, as pointed out by Lord Justice Mance in the *Jones* case, Article 14 (2) suggests that there may be existing national legal provisions for redress against torture which go wider than required by Article 14 (1), which might include provisions removing immunity of a foreign State in civil proceedings for damages.

---

[254] Byrnes, *Civil Remedies for Torture Committed Abroad: an Obligation under the Convention against Torture*, pp. 542 et seq.; see also Parlett, *Universal Jurisdiction for Torture*, EHRLR 2007, p. 395; for the contrary view, see Orakhelashvili, *Restrictive Interpretation of Human Rights in Recent Jurisprudence*, EJIL 2003, p. 554; Hall, *The Duty of States Parties to the Convention against Torture to Provide Procedures Permitting Victims to Recover Reparations for Torture Committed Abroad*, EJIL 2007, p. 921. For a general overview of the discussion, see Nowak/McArthur, *The United Nations Convention Against Torture – A Commentary*, pp. 492 et seq.

[255] Byrnes, *Civil Remedies for Torture Committed Abroad: an Obligation under the Convention against Torture*, p. 546.

[256] Ibid.

[257] Emphasis added.

(2) *Conclusion*

Therefore, the UN Torture Convention in its current form does not provide for a universal civil jurisdiction, nor does it provide for an implied removal of State immunity in civil proceedings. As international treaties are living instruments, it is not inconceivable that it might one day be interpreted differently from the original drafters' intent (the dynamic approach of the Strasbourg Court in its interpretation of some Convention rights, among them the right of access to court, being a good example in this respect).[258] The above interpretation of Article 14 has however been supported by legal scholars[259] as well as both British and Canadian courts, namely the Ontario Court of Appeal in *Bouzari v. the Islamic Republic of Iran* and the House of Lords in the *Jones* case.[260] In any event, that interpretation does not mean that the UN Torture Convention prohibits States to refuse to grant immunity to a foreign State accused of torture.[261] It does not however place an obligation on them to do so, even though that interpretation might change in the future.[262] Therefore, Article 14 of the UN Torture Convention cannot (yet) be invoked when considering the proportionality of any interference with the right of access to court. Even more importantly, it cannot be said that allowing civil remedies for torture against a foreign State has become an *erga omnes* obligation. It is therefore questionable to state that, as one writer put it, "Al-Adsani's failure to obtain remedies for torture has injured the interests of the international community as a whole".[263]

---

[258] Note however the recent recommendation by the UN Committee against Torture for a wider interpretation of Article 14 (see also Lord Bingham of Cornhill's comments in *Jones* (para. 23) and McGregor, *State Immunity and Jus Cogens*, ICLQ 2006, pp. 439 and 442).

[259] Fox, *State Immunity and the International Crime of Torture*, EHRLR 2006, p. 153; Murphy, *Civil Liability for the Commission of International Crimes as an Alternative to Criminal Prosecution*, HHRJ 1999, p. 27.

[260] Ontario Court of Appeal, *Bouzari v. the Islamic Republic of Iran*, 127 ILR, p. 427; Lord Bingham of Cornhill (para. 25) and Lord Hoffmann (para. 46, with further references) in *Jones*.

[261] See also Parlett, *Universal Jurisdiction for Torture*, EHRLR 2007, p. 401.

[262] See Nowak/McArthur, *The United Nations Convention Against Torture – A Commentary*, p. 502: "(…) [A]s international law stands at the time of writing this Commentary, States parties are not yet legally required by Article 14 (1) to ensure universal civil jurisdiction before their domestic courts. However, this provision may be interpreted differently in the near future. In our opinion, nothing in the text of Article 14 (1) would prevent an interpretation which ensures that victims of torture can sue and obtain reparation from perpetrators of torture irrespective of where the act of torture occurred."

[263] Orakhelashvili, *Restrictive Interpretation of Human Rights in Recent Jurisprudence*, EJIL 2003, p. 564).

e) *Developments since the* Al-Adsani *judgment*
Since the Court delivered its judgment in the *Al-Adsani* case, there have been some developments in international law which will be considered in the following.

(1) *Developments at the international level*
Firstly, the United Nations Immunity Convention on State Immunity was adopted in December 2004 by the General Assembly. Article 5 of the Convention provides for a general rule of immunity subject to certain enumerated exceptions. Among those, there is no exception for cases concerning severe human rights violations, such as torture unless they have been committed on the territory of the forum State. The Convention does not address the relationship between the violation of a *jus cogens* norm and State immunity, and it appears that the Working Group concluded that the Convention was not the appropriate context for this question.[264] Nevertheless, there have been supporters for a human rights protocol to the Convention allowing for an exception from immunity in those cases.[265]

Only several weeks after the pronouncement of the *Al-Adsani* judgment, the International Court of Justice found that Belgium had violated the rules on immunities of foreign ministers by circulating an arrest warrant against the then incumbent foreign minister of the Democratic Republic of Congo for war crimes and crimes against humanity.[266] The International Court of Justice did not follow the minority in *Al-Adsani* that State immunity was void in case of a *jus cogens* violation.[267] In this context, it is also worth noting that on 19 February 2009, Belgium instituted proceedings against Senegal in respect of a dispute concerning Senegal's compliance with its obligations under the United Nations Convention against Torture to prosecute the former President of the Republic of Chad (Hissène Habré, who lives in exile in Senegal), or to extradite him to Belgium (which issued an international arrest warrant) for the purposes of criminal proceedings for crimes against humanity. The case will presumably address several important questions on the immunity of a former Head of State.[268] Another important development

---

[264] McGregor, *State Immunity and Jus Cogens*, ICLQ 2006, pp. 437 and 441.

[265] Hall, *UN Convention on State Immunity: the Need for a Human Rights Protocol*, ICLQ 2006, p. 441.

[266] *Democratic Republic of Congo v. Belgium*, ICJ Reports 2002.

[267] For a discussion of the judgment, see below (pp. 140–142) and Maierhöfer, *Weltrechtsprinzip und Immunität: das Völkerstrafrecht vor den Haager Richtern/Urteil des IGH Demokratische Republik Kongo gegen Belgien*, EuGRZ 2003, p. 545.

[268] Case concerning questions relating to the obligation to prosecute or extradite (*Belgium v. Senegal*); see the press release of the International Court of Justice of 19 February 2009.

at the international level, the case of *Germany v. Italy* before the International Court of Justice,[269] is considered below, given that it relates to developments at the domestic level which will be considered first.

(2) *Developments at the domestic level*

While the case of *Al-Adsani* case was pending in Strasbourg, the Greek Supreme Court decided in 2000 in the case of *Prefecture of Voiotia v. Federal Republic of Germany* that Germany's accountability for a massacre in the Greek village of Distomo during its occupation of Greece during the Second World War was not shielded by State immunity.[270] The Greek Supreme Court found that the tort exception (as discussed in *McElhinney*) had become customary international law, but that it could not be applied as the case concerned an armed conflict.[271] However, it also held that, by committing the atrocities, Germany had impliedly waived its immunity. The Court later had the opportunity to deal with this case in the application of *Kalegoropoulou v. Greece and Germany* but confirmed its judgment in *Al-Adsani*. However, the decision rather concerns State immunity from execution and is therefore discussed below.[272] In this regard, it should be added that the Greek Special Highest Court issued a final judgment in September 2002 on civil claims against Germany for human rights violations committed during the occupation period. The Greek Special Highest Court was equally divided over the issue of State immunity and *jus cogens* violations as the Strasbourg Court in *Al-Adsani*, and found by six votes to five that Germany was entitled to State immunity.[273]

In *Ferrini v. Federal Republic of Germany*,[274] the Italian Court of Cassation granted in March 2004 compensation to an Italian who had brought a suit against Germany for deportation and forced labour during the Second World War. It found that Germany could not invoke State immunity for war crimes and crimes against humanity. The Italian Court of Cassation based

---

269 Case concerning jurisdictional immunities of the State (*Germany v. Italy*); see the press release of the International Court of Justice of 23 December 2008; see below, pp. 84 et seq.

270 *Prefecture of Voiotia v. Federal Republic of Germany*, Case No. 137/1997; for a case note on the judgment, see Gavouneli/Bantekas, AJIL 2001, p. 198.

271 Regarding that exception under the European Convention on State Immunity and the UN Convention on State Immunity, see Dickinson, *Status of Forces under the UN Convention on State Immunity*, ICLQ 2006, p. 427.

272 See below, pp. 92–100.

273 *Federal Republic of Germany v. Mitiadis Margellos*, Decision of 17 September 2002.

274 *Ferrini v. Federal Republic of Germany*, Rivista di diritto internazionale 2004, p. 539; see also Bianchi, *State Immunity and Human Rights – The Italian Supreme Court Decision on the* Ferrini *case*, EJIL 2005, p. 89.

its decision on the view that, because such crimes amounted to a violation of *jus cogens*, they would consequently (as stated by the dissenting judges in *Al-Adsani*) prevail over the rule of State immunity.[275] The decision received some approval,[276] but was also criticised as a "deplorable superficiality"[277] and for not being an "accurate statement of international law".[278]

Whereas the decisions of the Greek Supreme Court and the Italian Court of Cassation suggest a slight change in international jurisprudence towards a "human rights"-exception from State immunity, other courts have decided the opposite. In *Bouzari v. the Islamic Republic of Iran*,[279] the Ontario Court of Appeal considered a claim for damages brought by a former prisoner in Iran for torture. Like the Court of Appeal in *Al-Adsani v. Kuwait*,[280] the Ontario Court of Appeal found that the domestic law, in the present case the Canadian State Immunity Act, provided for State immunity unless one of its enumerated exceptions applied, which however was not the case for acts of torture. The Court of Appeal further assumed that there was no principle of customary international law which provided an exception from State immunity where an act of torture had been committed outside the forum, even for acts contrary to *jus cogens*.[281] The evidence of State practice led the Court of Appeal to conclude the existence of an ongoing rule of customary international law providing State immunity for acts of torture committed outside the forum state.[282]

The *Jones and Others* case involved a suit for damages in the United Kingdom by three British and one Canadian citizen against Saudi Arabia and several Saudi State officials for alleged acts of torture. Both the United Kingdom Court of Appeal and the House of Lords considered that Saudi Arabia was protected by State immunity and that the granting of that immunity did not amount to a violation of Article 6.[283] However, the United Kingdom Court

---

[275] *Ferrini v. Federal Republic of Germany*, p. 547.

[276] Bianchi, Case note, AJIL 2005, p. 242; McGregor, *State Immunity and Jus Cogens*, ICLQ 2006, p. 439.

[277] Gattini, *War Crimes and the* Ferrini *Decision*, JICL 2005, p. 231.

[278] United Kingdom House of Lords, *Jones v. Ministry of Interior Al-Mamlaka Al-Arabiya as Saudiya and others*, Lord Bingham of Cornhill, para. 22; see also Fox, *State Immunity and the Crime of Torture*, EHRLR 2006, p. 142.

[279] Ontario Court of Appeal, *Bouzari v. the Islamic Republic of Iran*, ILR 127, p. 427; see also Novogrodsky, *Immunity for Torture: Lessons from Bouzari v. Iran*, EJIL 2007, p. 939.

[280] *Al Adsani v. Government of Kuwait*, ILR 107, p. 536

[281] *Bouzari v. the Islamic Republic of Iran*, ILR 127, p. 443.

[282] Ibid.

[283] *Ronald Grant Jones v. the Ministry of the Interior Al-Mamlaka Al-Arabiya as Saudiya (The Kingdom of Saudi Arabia) & Anor, Sandy Mitchell & Ors v. Ibrahim Al-Dali & Ors*, judgment of the Court of Appeal of 28 October 2004; United Kingdom House of Lords, *Jones*

of Appeal and the House of Lords were divided over the issue of whether or not its officials enjoyed immunity in respect of acts of torture.[284] The case is currently pending before the Court.[285]

(3) *The case of* Germany v. Italy *before the International Court of Justice*
In connection with the above-mentioned judgment in the case of *Ferrini v. Federal Republic of Germany*,[286] Germany instituted proceedings before the International Court of Justice against Italy on 23 December 2008, arguing that "[t]hrough its judicial practice (...) Italy has infringed and continues to infringe its obligations towards Germany under international law".[287] Germany contended that Italian judicial bodies have repeatedly disregarded the jurisdictional immunity of Germany as a sovereign State. It appears that the *Ferrini* judgment (concerning a civil suit against Germany based on violations of international humanitarian law during the Second World War) was confirmed in a series of similar decisions and judgments in 2008 with possibly hundreds of additional cases to follow.[288] Moreover, Germany complained about enforcement measures against German property in Italy in order to enforce such judgments as well as declaring similar Greek judgments (concerning a massacre committed by German military units during the occupation of Greece in 1944) enforceable in Italy.[289] Given that the International Court of Justice's decision in the *Arrest warrant* case seemed to have been a rather conservative statement on the law of immunities, there appears to be a considerable prospect of success for Germany in that case.

The case demonstrates the increasing interdependence between the jurisprudence of the European Court of Human Rights and the International Court Justice regarding questions of general public international law.[290] For

v. Ministry of Interior Al-Mamlaka Al-Arabiya as Saudiya and others, judgment of 14 June 2006.

284 See below, pp. 126–131.

285 *The Independent*, 15 June 2006; see below, p. 132.

286 See above, p. 82.

287 Case concerning jurisdictional immunities of the State (*Germany v. Italy*); see the press release of the International Court of Justice of 23 December 2008.

288 Ibid.

289 Ibid. See also the case of *Kalageropoulou and Others v. Greece and Germany* (pp. 106 et seq.).

290 This topic was also addressed by the then president of the International Court of Justice, Dame Rosalyn Higgins, on the occasion of a conference ("International Courts and Tribunals – the Challenges Ahead") organised by the Council of Europe in London in October 2008; see also Dame Higgins' speech ("The International Court of Justice and the European Court of Human Rights: Partners for the Protection of Human Rights") on the occasion of the Opening of the Judicial Year on 30 January 2009 (*Dialogue between judges – fifty*

a national judge facing a case in which the defendant State invokes jurisdictional immunity, the decision can become increasingly difficult. In case immunity is being granted, the plaintiff will almost certainly file an application with the European Court of Human Rights. In case immunity is denied, there is a certain danger that the defendant country might file a respective case with the International Court of Justice. Whereas in Strasbourg the national judge enjoys a certain margin of appreciation when assessing the applicable international law on State immunity, he will certainly not be granted such a margin in The Hague. That situation might eventually lead to a further reluctance by national judges to deny State immunity in certain cases. One of the possible solutions could be a mechanism encouraging the Strasbourg Court to seek the guidance of the International Court of Justice whenever confronted with issues of general international law such as State immunity to ensure consistency in the jurisprudence of both international courts.[291]

e) *Conclusion*

The above cases reveal another dilemma: domestic courts are bound to apply the rules of State immunity as they stand (otherwise they will be accused of violating international law, as seen in the above case of *Germany v. Italy* before the International Court of Justice), but at the same time the rules of State immunity may only be changed through State practice. As Robertson observed:

> (...) international law has the habit of pulling itself up by its own boot-straps (actions by states which have no precedent in 'state practice' serve in their turn as evidence of a new 'state practice', thereby helping to create a new rule of customary international law which will justify similar state actions in the future) (...).[292]

This dilemma can be shown for example by the comments of Lord Bingham of Cornhill in the *Jones* case who, while considering current State practice, commented on the *Ferrini* case (in which the right of access to court trumped the rules of State immunity) that "one swallow does not make a rule of international law."[293] Even though the majority's decision of the Court in *Al-Adsani* is to be approved, it surely would have served as a motor for State

---

years of the European Court of Human Rights viewed by its fellow international courts, p. 97 et seq.).

291 Caflisch, *The Law – Substantive and Procedural Questions*, The Law and Practice of International Courts and Tribunals 2008, Special Issue on the Conference "International Courts and Tribunals – the Challenges Ahead", p. 299.

292 Robertson, *Crimes against Humanity*, p. 429.

293 United Kingdom House of Lords, *Jones v. Ministry of Interior Al-Mamlaka Al-Arabiya as Saudiya and others*, Lord Bingham of Cornhill, para. 22.

practice had the Court found a violation in that case, since domestic courts in Europe could have referred to the Strasbourg jurisprudence, arguing that the granting of immunity would amount to a violation of the Convention. But if one is to reject the arguments that there is sufficient State practice to deny State immunity for serious human rights violations and that a *jus cogens* violation trumps the rules of State immunity, a real change in State practice ultimately has to come from States which shape international law through their legislation and jurisprudence.

8. *The responsibility under the Convention of the foreign State which successfully invokes immunity in the proceedings before the courts of the forum State*

Provided that the foreign State which successfully invokes its immunity in civil proceedings before the courts of the forum State is a Contracting Party to the Convention, the question arises whether the foreign State has any responsibilities under Article 6 (1) in relation to the claimant. In other words: is it possible that a Contracting State (say State A) violates the right of access to court of a person who instituted proceedings against State A before the courts of another Contracting State (State B) if State A frustrates the action by successfully invoking its immunity? Some academics might answer this in the affirmative. Hess for example has argued that in cases involving State immunity, the right of access to court has a double impact on both the forum and the foreign State.[294]

The question first arose in the admissibility decision of *McElhinney v. Ireland and the United Kingdom.*[295] The applicant's complaint under Article 6 (1) was originally introduced against both the forum State (Ireland) and the foreign State which invoked State immunity (the United Kingdom). Mr McElhinney argued that the United Kingdom bore responsibility for his lack of access to the Irish courts since the United Kingdom could have waived her immunity.[296] The obvious problem with this argument is that the foreign State, being merely a litigant in proceedings before the courts of another State, is rather in the position of a third person. The applicant must however

[294] Hess, *Staatenimmunität bei Distanzdelikten*, p. 317. According to Hess, this double impact applies whether or not the foreign State is a Contracting Party to the Convention because of the universal character of human rights which form part of customary international law. However, applications to the Court against States which are not a Contracting Party would be incompatible *ratione personae* with the provisions of the Convention within the meaning of Article 35 (3).

[295] *McElhinney v. Ireland and the United Kingdom*, admissibility decision of 9 February 2000, EHRR 2000, C.D. p. 214.

[296] Ibid., p. 216.

show that he or she came within the foreign State's jurisdiction when that State invoked immunity. This requirement is necessary because Article 1 of the Convention provides that "the High Contracting Parties shall secure to everyone *within their jurisdiction* the rights and freedoms defined in (...) the Convention."[297] If that requirement is not satisfied, the complaint against the foreign State which invoked immunity is incompatible *ratione personae* with the provisions of the Convention and must therefore be declared inadmissible in accordance with Article 35 (3). It is recognised in the jurisprudence of the Court that the concept of jurisdiction is not entirely restricted to the national territory of a Contracting State.[298] However, the Court has accepted only in exceptional cases that acts of the Contracting States producing effects outside their territory can constitute an exercise of jurisdiction by them within the meaning of Article 1.[299] Such exceptional cases were notably recognised when a Contracting State exercised effective control of a foreign territory and its inhabitants abroad as a consequence of military occupation.[300] This situation is however very different from the situation of a foreign State invoking immunity in proceedings before the courts of the forum State. The foreign State does not exercise any effective control over the applicant, but is a mere party to the proceedings and therefore stands on equal footing with the applicant. Consequently, Mr McElhinney required the United Kingdom to secure his right to a fair trial outside of the latter's jurisdiction.[301] Thus, the Court rightly rejected this part of the application as incompatible *ratione personae* with the provisions of the Convention.[302] The Court said:

---

297 Emphasis added.

298 See generally on Article 1: Peters, *Einführung in die Europäische Menschenrechtskonvention*, p. 234; Grabenwarter, *Europäische Menschenrechtskonvention*, § 13, 43; Villiger, *Handbuch*, p. 75; Loucaides, *Determining the Extra-territorial Effect of the European Convention: Facts, Jurisprudence and the Bankovic Case*, in: EHRLR 2006, p. 1; Matscher, *Bemerkungen zur extraterritorialen oder indirekten Wirkung der EMRK*, FS Trechsel, p. 25. The above view is supported by the fact that the wording of the provision does not introduce a territorial limitation (Jacobs and White, *European Convention*, p. 22).

299 *Bankovic and Others v. Belgium and 16 other Nato States*, para. 67.

300 *Bankovic and Others*, paras. 70–71, *Loizidou v. Turkey* (preliminary objections), para. 71; *Cyprus v. Turkey* (no. 25781/94), Judgment of 10 May 2001, paras. 69–81.

301 See also the submissions by the government of the United Kingdom in *McElhinney v. Ireland and the United Kingdom*, p. 216.

302 Ibid., p. 217. The Court further found that the applicant's complaint under Article 14 (prohibition against discrimination in connection with the enjoyment of the rights and freedoms in the Convention) did not raise any issue. Article 14 has no independent existence and must be related to matters which fall at least within the scope of one of the substantive articles in the Convention (*Belgian Linguistics case No. 2*, para. 9; *Inze v. Austria* (no. 8695/79), Judgment of 28 October 1987, Series A 126, para. 36; see generally Robertson/Merrills, *Human Rights*, p. 177). Since the applicant's complaints under Article

> In so far as the applicant complains under Article 6 (...) about the stance taken by the Government of the United Kingdom in the Irish proceedings, the Court does not consider it necessary to address in the abstract the question of whether the actions of a Government as a litigant before the courts of another Contracting State can engage their responsibility under Article 6 (...). The Court considers that, in the particular circumstances of the case, the fact that the United Kingdom Government raised the defence of sovereign immunity before the Irish courts, where the applicant had decided to sue, does not suffice to bring him within the jurisdiction of the United Kingdom within the meaning of Article 1 of the Convention.

The Court has recently confirmed this approach in the decisions of *Kalogeropoulou and Others v. Greece and Germany*[303] and *Treska v. Albania and Italy*,[304] which will be considered in more detail in the next chapter on the conflict between immunity from execution and Article 6 (1). It can thus be concluded that it is settled Convention case-law that the foreign State, when invoking State immunity as the defendant in proceedings before the courts of the forum State, does not have any responsibility under Article 6 (1) because the claimant does not come within its jurisdiction pursuant to Article 1.

II. *Immunity from execution and the right to enforce a judgment under Article 6(1) of the Convention*

1. *The right to execute a judgment*

As already mentioned earlier, the right of access to court as guaranteed by Article 6 (1) does not only provide for the right to institute civil proceedings before a court, but also includes the right to enforcement of a judgment or a decision. In *Hornsby v. Greece*,[305] the Court found that:

> (...) according to its established case-law, Article 6, paragraph 1 (art. 6-1), secures to everyone the right to have any claim relating to his civil rights and obligations brought before a court or tribunal; in this way it embodies the 'right to a court', of which the right of access, that is the right to institute proceedings before courts in civil matters, constitutes one aspect (...). However, that right would be illusory if a Contracting State's domestic legal system allowed a final, binding judicial decision to remain inoperative to the detriment of one party. It

6 (1) were found incompatible *ratione personae* with the provisions of the Convention, the matter did not fall within the scope of the right of access to court under Article 6 (1). Hence there did not arise any issue under Article 14 either.

[303] *Kalogeropoulou and Others v. Greece and Germany* (no. 59021/00), Decision of 12 December 2002, ECHR 2002-X.

[304] *Treska v. Albania and Italy* (no. 26937/04), Decision of 29 June 2006.

[305] *Hornsby v. Greece* (no. 18357/91), Judgment of 19 March 1997, Reports 1997-II.

> would be inconceivable that Article 6 (...) should describe in detail procedural guarantees afforded to litigants (...) without protecting the implementation of judicial decisions; to construe Article 6 (art. 6) as being concerned exclusively with access to a court and the conduct of proceedings would be likely to lead to situations incompatible with the principle of the rule of law which the Contracting States undertook to respect when they ratified the Convention (...). Execution of a judgment given by any court must therefore be regarded as an integral part of the 'trial' for the purposes of Article 6 (...).[306]

That principle has been confirmed by the Court ever since.[307] The right to enforcement of court decisions includes the right to enforcement within a reasonable time[308] and the obligation of the authorities to comply with a court decision.[309] Moreover, the domestic court ordering enforcement of a foreign judgment must ensure that the earlier proceedings before the foreign courts (if they were not national courts of a Contracting Party) were in accordance with Article 6.[310] As regards the conflict between immunity from execution and the right to enforcement of court decisions, the Court has had to consider it to date on several occasions, which are discussed below.

2. *Immunity from execution*

Immunity from enforcement measures such as execution, arrest or attachment is to be distinguished from immunity from adjudication (jurisdictional immunity). Since measures to secure or realise execution of judgments and decisions more directly affect the foreign State as it involves the seizure of assets, they pose a bigger challenge to the relationships of States than jurisdictional immunity.[311] Consequently, States were less willing in the past to restrict immunity from execution to a comparable degree with jurisdictional immunity.

---

306 Ibid.

307 *Dimitros Georgiadis v. Greece* (no. 41209/98), Judgment of 28 March 2000; *Logothetis v. Greece* (no. 46352/99), Judgment of 12 April 2001, paras. 11–16.

308 *Comingersoll S.A. v. Portugal* [GC] (no. 35382/97), Judgment of 6 April 2000.

309 *Antonakopoulos and Others v. Greece* (no. 37098/97), Judgment of 14 December 1999.

310 *Pellegrini v. Italy* (no. 30882/96), Judgment of 20 July 2001, RJD 2001-VIII, para. 40; for further references, see Dutertre, *Key case-law extracts, European Court of Human Rights*, p. 190; Villiger, *Handbuch EMRK*, para. 428.

311 Brownlie, *Principles*, p. 346; see also Crawford, *Execution of Judgments and Foreign Sovereign Immunity*, AJIL 1981, p. 820; Steinberger, *State Immunity*, EPIL IV, pp. 627–630; Fox, *Enforcement Jurisdiction, Foreign State Property and Diplomatic Immunity*, ICLQ 1985, pp. 115–151; Ibid., *Immunity from Execution*, in: The Law of State Immunity, pp. 368–420; Reinisch, *European Court Practice Concerning State Immunity from Enforcement Measures*, EJIL 2006, p. 803.

State practice since the 19th century has generally been uniform in granting foreign States absolute immunity from enforcement measures even where the forum State had denied immunity from adjudication.[312] It was only until after the Second World War that States ceased to grant absolute immunity from execution but restricted it to property serving public and sovereign purposes of the foreign State.[313] National legislation such as the United States Foreign Sovereign Immunity Act, the United Kingdom State Immunity Act or the State Immunity Acts of Pakistan, Singapore or South Africa provide for immunity from execution.[314] Both the European Convention on State Immunity and the United Nations Convention on Jurisdictional Immunities of States and their Property recognise immunity from execution. Article 23 of the European Convention prohibits any "measures of execution or preventive measures against the property of a Contracting State" outside its territory in the absence of express waiver. Article 19 of the United Nations Convention on Jurisdictional Immunities of States and their Property, as adopted by the General Assembly on 2 December 2004, provides that:

> No post-judgment measures of constraint, such as attachment, arrest or execution, against the property of a State may be taken in connection with a proceeding before a court of another State unless and except to the extent that: (a) the State has expressly consented to the taking of such measures as indicated: (i) by international agreement; (ii) by an arbitration agreement or in a written contract; or (iii) by a declaration before the court or by a written communication after a dispute between the parties has arisen; or (b) the State has allocated or earmarked property for the satisfaction of the claim which is the object of that proceeding; or (c) it has established that the property is specifically in use or intended for use by the State for other than government non-commercial purposes and is in the territory of the State of the forum, provided that post-judgment measures of constraint may only be taken against property that has a connection with the entity against which the proceeding was directed.

When seeking to enforce a judgment or decision against a foreign State, the claimant will often seek execution into the foreign State's mission or embassy in the forum State. According to Article 22 (3) of the Vienna Convention on Diplomatic Relations 1961, the "premises of the mission, their furnishings and other property thereon and the means of transport shall be immune from search, requisition, attachment and execution". As a condition for

---

[312] Steinberger, *State Immunity*, EPIL IV, p. 627, with references to a few exceptions in international treaties and in decisions of domestic courts.

[313] Ibid., p. 627; see also Crawford, *Execution of Judgments and Foreign Sovereign Immunity*, AJIL 1981, pp. 824–825.

[314] Steinberger, *State Immunity*, EPIL IV, p. 627. For a detailed overview of the practice of the United Kingdom, Italy, Austria, Belgium and several other European States, see NYIL 1979.

enforcement, there must exist a decision or judgment of the courts of the forum State capable of being enforced, or a document which is automatically enforceable.[315] However, the adjudicating court of the forum State must not have wrongfully denied the foreign State's jurisdictional immunity in the decision or judgment. In that case, the judgment or decision must not be executed, *i.e.* a writ of execution must not be issued and seizures and attachments may not be ordered by the execution authorities unless the foreign State waives its immunity.[316] As can be seen from the above international treaty provisions, immunity from execution may be waived such as jurisdictional immunity.[317] However, a waiver of jurisdictional immunity does not per se entail a waiver of immunity from execution of any resulting judgment.[318] The latter immunity would therefore require a separate waiver.

"Property" in the context of immunity from execution includes movable and immovable objects (e.g. land or buildings such as embassies), legal interest and rights such as intellectual property or industrial property rights, claims or mortgages. In order to demonstrate that the object of an intended measure of execution serves the public purposes of the foreign State, it has to (a) make credible that the object was used for a particular purpose, and (b) that the purpose qualifies as "public". There appears to be no uniform approach as to whether or not the decisive qualification is subject to the practice of the foreign or the forum State, as long as generally recognised criteria of international law are applied. Objects which are indivisible but both serve public and non-public uses are fully protected from immunity from execution; however, there exist particular problems with regard to mixed bank accounts in which funds are used for both trading purposes and public use.[319] National courts may disregard if a foreign State seeks to evade execution by hitherto turning property into public use.[320] Enforcement measures directed against the property of third persons might be stayed if a foreign State has a right in the property concerned.

---

[315] Steinberger, *State Immunity*, EPIL IV, p. 627.

[316] Ibid., p. 627.

[317] Hafner/Kohen/Breau, *Waiver of Immunity from Execution*, State Practice Regarding State Immunities, p. 158.

[318] Crawford, *Execution of Judgments and Foreign Sovereign Immunity*, AJIL 1981, p. 860.

[319] Ibid., p. 860; Ress, *Entwicklungstendenzen der Immunität ausländischer Staaten*, ZaöRV 1980, p. 271.

[320] Steinberger, *State Immunity*, EPIL IV, p. 629.

3. *Case-law of the Court*

The Court has had to consider the conflict between Article 6 (1) and immunity from execution on several occasions: in various admissibility decisions the Court has found that the respective applicants' complaints under Article 6 (1) were manifestly ill-founded within the meaning of Article 35 (3) and (4) of the Convention.

a) *The case of Kalageropoulou and Others v. Greece and Germany*

(1) *Background to the case*

The case concerns crimes committed by German soldiers in Greece during the Nazi occupation in the Second World War.[321] During the German occupation of Greece between 1941–1945, approximately 125.000 civilians, among them around 50.000 Jews, were killed by German soldiers.[322] With the wrongful excuse of seeking revenge and retaliation for partisan attacks, the German army destroyed numerous villages and killed and raped the inhabitants. On 10 June 1944, a unit of the German Schutzstaffel (SS) associated with the Wehrmacht brutally killed 218 inhabitants of the village of Distomo, (located in the Voiotia region) which was completely destroyed.[323]

In 1995, more than 200 relatives of the victims of the Distomo massacre, all of them of Greek nationality, instituted proceedings against Germany before the Livadia Regional Court in Greece in order to claim compensation for loss of the victims.[324] The German government refused to attend the proceedings. On 30 October 1997, the Livadia Regional Court found that the acts amounted to war crimes and crimes against humanity and Germany's accountability could not be shielded by State immunity.[325] The plaintiffs obtained a default judgment against Germany for compensation of the amount of around 28 million euros. Germany appealed against the decision, claiming its entitlement to State immunity in the proceedings and that the Greek courts lacked jurisdiction.

---

321 "Straßburger Gericht befasst sich mit Distomo", *Berliner Zeitung*, 10 October 2001; "Straßburg soll jetzt helfen", *Frankfurter Allgemeine Zeitung*, 10 May 2002.

322 Ibid.

323 Bartsch/Eberling, *Jus Cogens vs. State Immunity, Round Two: The Decision of the European Court of Human Rights in the* Kalogeropoulou et al. v. Greece and Germany *decision*, in: German Law Journal 2003, p. 477; Kempen, *Der Fall Distomo*, p. 179.

324 The Federal Republic of Germany is the legal successor of the Third Reich and has acknowledged its responsibility for the deeds of Nazi Germany (see Zimmermann, *Sovereign Immunity and Violations of Jus Cogens*, MJIL 1995, p. 436).

325 *Prefecture of Voiotia v. Federal Republic of Germany*, Case No. 137/1997; for a summary of the judgment, see Bantekas, *Case note*, AJIL 1998, p. 765.

In May 2000, the Greek Court of Cassation (*Areios Pagos*) dismissed Germany's appeal and found that the principle of State immunity could not be invoked for serious human rights violations.[326] The decision came to many as a surprise and was taken by a very narrow a majority of six to five (which was therefore as close as the majority of the Grand Chamber in *Al-Adsani*). While the five dissenting judges found that the Anglo-American jurisprudence did not suggest that a "human rights exception" for State immunity could be regarded as forming part of international law, the majority of judges of the *Areios Pagos* had relied on the "personal injury exception" in the European Convention on State Immunity, even though Greece was not a party to it.[327] The dissenting judges however doubted whether the European Convention on State Immunity could give any guidance as to the present state of international law, due to the limited number of ratifications.[328] In any case, the *Areios Pagos* probably erred in applying the European Convention on State Immunity, since it expressly excludes retrospective application in its Article 35 (3) (the events in question occurred in 1944).[329] The *Areios Pagos* also found that the "armed forces" exception in Article 31 of the European Convention on State Immunity (which provides that State immunity cannot be dispensed with for military acts) did not apply to the present case: the provision should apply where the offences for which compensation was sought had targeted civilians generally, but not in the case of specific individuals in a given place who were not connected with military operations (such as the Distomo victims). Moreover, the *Areios Pagos* reasoned that Germany had tacitly waived its immunity when committing the above crimes against humanity which violated *jus cogens*.

It is noteworthy that the case appears to combine both the arguments raised in the cases of *McElhinney v. Ireland* and *Al-Adsani v. the United Kingdom*. The injury inflicted on the victims occurred on the territory of the forum State and therefore engaged the "personal injury exception". At the same time, the case touches upon the relationship of State immunity and *jus cogens* violations which has been discussed above.[330]

The German government refused to accept the judgment due to the alleged incompatibility with current international law. In an official statement on its

[326] *Prefecture of Voiotia v. Federal Republic of Germany*, Case No. 11/2000; see also Kempen, *Der Fall Distomo*, p. 181 and Gavouneli/Bantekas, AJIL 2001, p. 198.

[327] Hobe, *Durchbrechung der Staatenimmunität bei schweren Menschenrechtsverletzungen*, IPrax 2001, p. 368.

[328] Ibid.

[329] Kempen, *Der Fall Distomo*, p. 184.

[330] See above, pp. 72 et seq.

website,[331] the government clarified that the acts committed by the Schutzstaffel (SS) had to be considered as *acta jure imperii* which were protected by State immunity. The decision of the *Areios Pagos* was without precedent, contrary to public international law, and opened the floodgates for countless similar claims against Germany in other countries.[332] Should the question of reparation for World War II-crimes be reopened, an enormous financial burden would be put on Germany. At the time, there were several thousands lawsuits pending against Germany before Greek courts regarding similar crimes.[333] The government stressed that the entering into of a bilateral global compensation treaty with Greece in 1960 which provided for the payment of around 60 million euros by Germany had put an end to compensation requests. It further disputed that individuals were entitled to compensation in domestic proceedings.[334] The judgment was criticised by both the German media and legal scholars.[335]

The case also brought to reality some of the fears expressed by two concurring judges in *Al-Adsani v. the United Kingdom*[336] about possible disruptions in international relations between the forum and the foreign State, *i.e.* in the present case Greece and Germany. Although the Greek government tried to keep at distance from the judgment, the German ambassador protested in Athens. The German government delivered an unusually clear message that

---

331 "Verurteilung der Bundesrepublik Deutschland durch das oberste griechische Gericht zu Schadenersatz wegen eines Massakers im 2. Weltkrieg", Statement by the German government, www.bundesregierung.de.

332 Bröhmer has argued that "Germany would have no alternative but to disregard any judgments of municipal courts awarding damages to victims of these crimes" (*State immunity*, p. 211).

333 The *Berliner Zeitung* of 17 October 2000 and Dolzer (*Der Areopag im Abseits*, NJW 2001, p. 3525) even estimated 60.000–65.000 lawsuits against Germany before Greek courts.

334 For a detailed analysis of claims under international and domestic law for war crimes committed in Greece under Nazi occupation, see Paech, *Der juristische Schatten der Wehrmachtsverbrechen in Griechenland*. For a brief survey, see Hobe, *Durchbrechung der Staatenimmunität bei schweren Menschenrechtsverletzungen*, IPrax 2001, pp. 371–372. The pursuit of such claims might be precluded by Article 5 (2) of the London Agreement concerning German Foreign Debts which suspends the examination of these claims until a final settlement could be reached through a peace treaty (Bantekas, *Case note*, AJIL 1998, p. 767). The 1990 Moscow ("two plus four") Treaty could arguably be seen as such a peace treaty. However, these considerations are to be distinguished from the question whether Greek courts had jurisdiction to consider the merits of such claims.

335 Von Münch: "Ein gefährliches Urteil", *Die Welt*, 24 May 2000; Hobe, *Durchbrechung der Staatenimmunität bei schweren Menschenrechtsverletzungen*, IPrax 2001, p. 368; Dolzer, *Der Aereopag im Abseits*, NJW 2001, p. 3525; Kempen, *Der Fall Distomo*, p. 179; see also Herdegen, *Völkerrecht*, p. 263.

336 *Al-Adsani v. the United Kingdom*, concurring opinion of Judges Bratza and Pellonpäa.

relations between the two EU Member States were in a crisis and could be seriously harmed.[337]

(2) *The enforcement proceedings in Greece*
Since Germany refused to comply with the judgment, the plaintiffs sought to execute the judgment by applying for expropriation of the assets owned by the Federal Republic of Germany in Athens. Among them were the Goethe house, German secondary schools and the German Institute for Archaeology.[338] According to section 923 of the Greek Code for Civil Procedure, this would have required the consent of the Greek Minister of Justice. The provision safeguards against execution of a judgment into property of foreign States. The applicants made the relevant application to the Minister of Justice, but received no reply. Despite not having the required approval, they instituted enforcement proceedings. Germany's objection, relying on the missing requirements of section 923 of the Code of Civil procedure, was dismissed by the Athens Court of First Instance, which found that the provision was incompatible with Article 6 of the Convention.

On appeal by Germany, the Athens Court of Appeal set aside the Court of First Instance's judgment. Applying the "Ashingdane criteria", it held that section 923 of the Code of Civil Procedure pursued a legitimate aim (namely to avoid disturbances in the country's international relations) and was proportionate to that aim: if a private individual were able to have a judicial decision against a foreign State enforced without obtaining the prior consent of the executive, the country's national interests would be compromised and its foreign policy placed in the hands of individuals.[339] The Athens Court of Appeal also took into account that the applicant's right to have their judgment enforced was not completely frustrated as they could exercise that right in another country (presumably Germany) or "subsequently at a more appropriate time".[340] As the applicants' appeal to the Court of Cassation was to no avail (the court referred in its decision to the judgments in *Al-Adsani* and *McElhinney*), they applied to the Strasbourg Court, complaining that

[337] "Gerichtsvollzieher im Goethe-Institut", *Süddeutsche Zeitung*, 13 July 2000; see also *Der Spiegel*, 28/2000; Dolzer, NJW 2001, p. 3525. In this context, see also the case concerning jurisdictional immunities of the State (*Germany v. Italy*) before the International Court of Justice, pp. 84 et seq.
[338] *Kalogeropoulou and Others v. Greece and Germany*; *Süddeutsche Zeitung*, 13 July 2000.
[339] *Kalogeropoulou and Others v. Greece and Germany.*
[340] Ibid.

Article 6 (1) and their right to property (Article 1 of Protocol No. 1) had been violated.[341]

(3) *The decision of the Court*

On 12 December 2000, the Court declared the application inadmissible as manifestly ill-founded. The decision was not only important because it belonged to a series of cases concerning the judicial treatment of crimes committed by the Nazis during the Second World War,[342] but also confirmed the Court's case-law with regard to State immunity for severe human rights violations.[343]

(a) The complaint against Germany

As far as the application was directed against Germany (the applicants claimed that Germany's refusal to comply with the decision of the Livadia Court of First Instance violated their right to enforce a judgment under Article 6 (1) and their right to property under Article 1 of Protocol No. 1), the Court found that this part of the application was incompatible *ratione personae* with the provisions of the Convention within the meaning of Article 35 (3). As Germany had the position of a litigant in the proceedings before the Greek courts and was therefore "on equal footing" with the applicants, the Court held that the applicants did not come within the jurisdiction of Germany within the meaning of Article 1.[344]

(b) The complaint against Greece

Of more interest is the Court's decision on the applicant's complaints under Article 6 (1) and Article 1 of Protocol No. 1 against Greece. Regarding the applicant's right to have a judgment enforced, the Court found that the Greek State's refusal to allow them to bring enforcement proceedings amounted to

---

[341] "Straßburger Gericht befaßt sich mit Distomo", *Berliner Zeitung*, 10 October 2001; "Straßburg soll jetzt helfen", *Frankfurter Allgemeine Zeitung*, 10 May 2002; "Bald Urteil zur Staatenimmunität", *Frankfurter Allgemeine Zeitung*, 30 July 2002.

[342] Bartsch/Eberling, *Jus Cogens vs. State Immunity*, German Law Journal 2003, p. 477; those decisions were notably the cases of *Sawoniuk v. the United Kingdom* (no. 63716/00), Decision of 29 May 2001, RJD 2001-VI; *Papon v. France* (no. 54210/00), Judgment of 25 July 2002, RJD 2002-VIII; and *Priebke v. Italy* (no. 48799/99), Decisions of 5 April 2001 and 7 March 2002. Those cases however concerned the right to a fair trial in criminal proceedings.

[343] See above, pp. 64–77.

[344] See above, pp. 86 et seq., and Bartsch/Eberling, *Jus Cogens vs. State Immunity*, German Law Journal 2003, p. 483. Note that complaints about any acts by Germany which occurred prior to 5 December 1952 (the date of Germany's ratification), including acts committed during the Second World War, would be incompatible *ratione temporis* with the provisions of the Convention.

an interference with Article 6 (1). It then continued to apply the "Ashingdane criteria". The Court reasoned that sovereign immunity served a legitimate aim (*par in parem non habet imperium*) and found that the interference was proportionate:

> (...) the Court considers that although the Greek courts ordered the German State to pay damages to the applicants, this did not necessarily oblige the Greek State to ensure that the applicants could recover their debt through enforcement proceedings in Greece. (...) the applicants appeared to be asserting that international law on crimes against humanity was so fundamental that it amounted to a rule of *jus cogens* that took precedence over all other principles of international law, including the principle of sovereign immunity. The Court does not find it established, however, that there is yet acceptance in international law of the proposition that States are not entitled to immunity in respect of civil claims for damages brought against them in another State for crimes against humanity. The Greek government cannot therefore be required to override the rule of State immunity against their will. (...)[345]

The decision that Greece had not violated Article 6 (1) came to no surprise because the Court had just issued its judgment in *Al-Adsani*. A departure from that finding (if at all) was not to be expected after only fifteen months, even though Judge Rozakis commented on the case that the Chamber could easily have overcome the hurdles of the case-law.[346] Perhaps the case could have also served to further clarify the relationship between *jus cogens* and State immunity, a question which the majority in *Al-Adsani* had avoided answering. However, while the outcome of the case is to be welcomed (of course depending on one's opinion on the *Al-Adsani* judgment), the reasoning lacks some clarity.

The Court failed, at least at this stage of the decision, to clearly elaborate on what exactly constituted the interference with Article 6 (1). It immediately considered the legitimacy of the granting of State immunity by Greece to Germany as the defendant in the execution proceedings. Instead, it should have started by finding that section 923 of the Greek Code of Civil Procedure, which provides that enforcement proceedings cannot be brought against a foreign State unless the Minister of Justice approves, formed the legal basis for the Greek State's refusal to enforce the applicant's judgment against Germany. That refusal constituted the interference in the applicant's right to enforcement of their judgment under Article 6 (1). Since section 923 of the Greek Code of Civil Procedure was intended to avoid disturbances in relations with other States, and the Minister of Justice's refusal was aimed to avoid such disturbances between Germany and Greece, the interference (*i.e.*

[345] *Kalogeropoulou and Others v. Greece and Germany.*

[346] Rozakis, *The ECHR and the Law on State Immunity*, p. 401.

the refusal and the subsequent decisions confirming it, not the rules of State immunity as such) served a legitimate aim. The Court should have continued to consider the proportionality of the interference by finding that the refusal was proportionate. As has been explained above, a prerequisite for the execution of a judgment against a foreign State is that the adjudicating courts did not wrongfully deny jurisdictional immunity to the foreign State. It is here that the Court could have ruled whether or not the Greek State's application of the rules of State immunity in the execution proceedings was compatible with current international law, in particular with its finding in the *Al-Adsani* case and with the judgments of the adjudicating courts in Greece which had found the opposite, *i.e.* that Germany could not be granted State immunity for the crimes committed in 1944.

Since the Livadia Court of First Instance found that section 923 of the Greek Code of Civil Procedure violated the applicants' right to a court, while the Athens Court of Appeal found that the provision constituted a proportionate restriction on Article 6 (1), one would have hoped that the Court would have elaborated more on section 923 of the Greek Code of Civil Procedure and the way the provision was applied by the Greek courts. For example, the Athens Court of Appeal found that the provision was proportionate because the applicants could have exercised their right to enforcement "in another country or subsequently at a more appropriate time". But would the attempt to execute the judgment in Germany really have constituted an alternative remedy, and when is a "more appropriate time" for the execution of a judgment issued in 1997 which grants damages for Second World War atrocities? It is deplorable that the Court did not directly deal with the Greek courts' reasoning but instead considered the rules of State immunity without putting them into the real context of the present case.

Admittedly, the Court had regard to the above when examining the applicants' complaints under Article 1 of Protocol No. 1 (right to property), which however does not change the fact that its approach under Article 6 (1) rather missed the point. The Court found that the applicants' right to property had not been violated, even though their enforceable claim against Germany amounted to a "possession" within the meaning of Article 1 of Protocol No. 1. The fact that the applicants were unable to have their judgment enforced amounted to interference with their right to property. It was here that the Court considered the refusal based on section 923 of the Greek Civil Code to be "in the public interest" because it was intended to avoid disturbances in relations between Greece and Germany. As to the question whether or not the interference was proportionate, the Court again stated that "the Greek Government could not be required to override the principle of State immunity against their will and compromise their good international relations in order to allow the applicants to enforce a judicial decision delivered at the end of judicial proceedings."[347] The Court also found that, since the applicants must have been aware of the risk they were taking in bringing enforcement proceedings against the German State without first obtaining the consent of the Minister of Justice, the situation could not reasonably have founded any legitimate expectation of being able to recover compensation for the atrocities.[348]

(4) *Further developments on the matter*

While the applicants' case was pending before the Strasbourg Court, the Greek Special Highest Court (which is composed of judges of the *Areios Pagos* and the highest administrative court of Greece) issued a final judgment on 17 September 2002 on civil claims against Germany for human rights violation committed during the occupation period: with another very narrow majority of six votes to five, the court found that Germany was entitled to State immunity.[349] It appears that the reasoning of both the majority and the minority of the judges mirrored the different reasonings of the judges in the Grand Chamber of the Strasbourg Court in *Al-Adsani*.[350]

It should be added that some relatives of the Distomo victims also instituted civil proceedings against the Federal Republic of Germany before German courts for damages,[351] the final decision of the ordinary courts being the decision of the Federal Court of Justice of 26 June 2003 (which was initially postponed in order to await the outcome of the proceedings before the Greek Special Highest Court).[352] After their constitutional complaint to the Federal Constitutional Court (*Bundesverfassungsgericht*) was to no avail, four applicants lodged an application with the Court against Germany in June 2006, complaining about a violation of Article 1 of Protocol No. 1 of the Convention (right to property). Their case is still pending (*Sfountouris and Others v. Germany*, no. 24120/06).

Lastly, in a parallel case concerning a massacre of civilians by the German armed forces in the municipality of Kalavrita in 1943, the European Court of

---

347 *Kalogeropoulou and Others v. Greece and Germany.*

348 Ibid.

349 *Federal Republic of Germany v. Mitiadis Margellos*, decision of 17 September 2002 (for further references see Bartsch/Eberling, *Jus Cogens vs. State Immunity*, German Law Journal 2003).

350 See above, pp. 64–77.

351 For an analysis of the claims of the victims under German law, see Paech, *Der juristische Schatten der Wehrmachtsverbrechen in Griechenland.*

352 NJW 2003, p. 3488; for a discussion of the decision see Pittrof, *Compensation Claims for Human Rights Breaches Committed by German Armed Forces Abroad During the Second World War: Federal Court of Justice Hands Down decision in the Distomo Case*, German Law Journal 2004, p. 15.

Justice decided in a judgment of 15 February 2007 that a legal action brought to obtain compensation was not covered by the term "civil matters" within the meaning of the Brussels Convention on Jurisdiction and the Enforcement of Judgments in Civil and Commercial Matters.[353] The applicants had argued before the Patras Court of Appeal (which had referred the matter to the European Court of Justice for a preliminary ruling under Article 234 EC Treaty) that the Brussels Convention created an exception from State immunity in respect of all acts which have been perpetrated during an armed conflict but which affected persons not involved in the fighting. Once the European Court of Justice had found that the Brussels Convention did not apply, it found it no longer necessary to decide whether or not the Convention had created such an exception from the rules of State immunity.

b) *The case of* Treska v. Albania and Italy

The second case in which the Court had to rule on the conflict between the right to execute a judgment and State immunity concerned a plot of land with a villa which had belonged to the applicants' father and which had been confiscated without compensation by the Albanian regime in 1950. Through an inter-state agreement between Italy and Albania, the plot of land was bought by Italy as the Italian Ambassador's private residence in 1991. As the land was not alienable under Albanian law at the time, the Albanian government only transferred the property title to the villa (and not the land) to the Italian government. The relevant property titles were not entered into the Tirana Property Register. The applicants, who had informed the Italian Ambassador about their property claims over the villa prior to the purchase, obtained in 1992 an allocation order regarding the villa by the Tirana District Court, which ordered the Albanian Ministry of Foreign Affairs to make it possible for that the applicants to enter into possession of the villa. They also obtained a decision by the Tirana Commission on Restitution and Compensation of Properties, which found that the confiscation in 1950 had been unlawful and that the properties should be returned.

Proceedings against the Italian Embassy in Albania for restitution of the property were to no avail because the Tirana District Court held that it did not have jurisdiction. However, in April 1997, the Tirana District Court ordered the Italian Embassy to pay a monthly rental fee for the use of the plot of land. After that decision (which was taken in the absence of the Italian Embassy) became final, the Tirana District Court issued a writ for the enforcement of its judgment. The Italian Embassy did not comply with the

---

353 *Irini Lechouritou and Others v. Federal Republic of Germany*, Judgment of the Court of Justice in the Case C-292/05 of 15 February 2007 (EuGRZ 2007, p. 192).

judgment, nor did the Albanian authorities enforce it. An appeal to the Albanian Constitutional Court in 2000 was dismissed, the reason being that the immunity of the Italian Embassy and the inviolability of its premises gave rise to a circumstance where the District's Court decision could not be enforced in practice. The applicants complained under Article 6 (1) of the Convention about the failure of the Albanian authorities to execute the court decisions and to enable them to recover possession of the property allocated to them.[354]

As in the case of *Kalageropoulou and Others v. Greece and Germany*, the Court approached the matter as a problem of the "right of access to court", although – strictly speaking – the applicants had access to an adjudicating court and obtained a decision in their favour which became final. As the Albanian courts however refused to execute the decision because the Italian embassy in Tirana was protected by immunity in accordance with Article 1 of the Vienna Convention on Diplomatic Relations, there was interference with their right to have their judgment enforced (as part of their right to a court). The Court regarded the applicable rules on State immunity as designed to ensure the optimum functioning of diplomatic missions (*ne impediatur legatio*) and to promote good relations between sovereign States.[355] In line with its judgments in the cases of *McElhinney*, *Fogarty* and *Al-Adsani*, the Court found that the Contracting States could not "be required to override against their will the rules of State immunity (…)".[356]

The applicants' complaint under Article 1 of Protocol No. 1 of the Convention was also rejected by the Court as being manifestly ill-founded. The Court found that, even though the final decisions of the Albanian District Court constituted a legitimate expectation for the applicants to recover possession of the property in question, the omission to enforce those decisions was in the public interest in view of the existing rules of State immunity.[357]

---

354 The applicants also submitted complaints directed against Italy. They had brought proceedings in Italy in order to have the judgement of the Tirana District Court enforced. Their claim was dismissed by the Rome District Court and the Court of Appeal in December 2004. The applicant's respective complaint under Article 6 (1) was inadmissible for non-exhaustion of domestic remedies (Article 35 (1) of the Convention) as they failed to lodge a complaint with the Italian Court of Cassation. As far as the applicants complained that the Italian Embassy had violated their right to property (Article 1 of Protocol No. 1 of the Convention) when purchasing the villa from the Albanian government while being aware that the applicant's restitution was in progress, their complaint was incompatible *ratione materiae* with the provisions of the Convention as they did not engage the responsibility of Italy under the Convention (see above, p. 88).

355 *Treska v. Albania and Italy.*

356 Ibid.

357 Ibid.

The Court noted that the applicants' title to the property was not invalidated by the Albanian authorities, but that it could be converted into an entitlement to future compensation from the Albanian government.[358] Even though the applicants had not yet availed themselves of that remedy, it can be assumed that the possibility to obtain redress from the Albanian government was the decisive factor in the "proportionality" issue.

With regard to Article 6 (1), the Court took basically the same approach in the case of *Kirovi v. Bulgaria and Turkey* which concerned the premises on which the Turkish consulate in Burgas (Bulgaria) was located.[359]

c) *The case of Manoilescu and Dobrescu v. Romania and Russia*

The Court appears to accept that interference with the right of access to court may be proportionate even when the national authorities of the forum State did not in general rely on the principle of State immunity, as long as the forum State has made clear that non-enforcement of a final decision stems from a desire not to infringe immunity from execution enjoyed by a foreign State.[360] In *Manoilescu and Dobrescu v. Romania and Russia*, two Romanian applicants had received restitution for property which had meanwhile be assigned to the Russian Federation, which used it as its embassy in Bucharest. The applicants complained under Article 6 (1) that they were unable to execute a final decision regarding their entitlement over the property.[361] While several Romanian authorities and courts were involved in the execution process, it appears that only one Romanian court explicitly reasoned that execution of that decision would breach the immunity enjoyed by the Russian Federation's diplomatic mission in Romania.[362] The remaining decisions at the national level merely mentioned that the applicant's application "had been brought against entities lacking the capacity to take part in the proceedings".[363]

The Court found that the lack of enforcement of the applicant's property title was not disproportionate interference with Article 6 (1), as it considered

[358] Ibid.

[359] *Kirovi v. Bulgaria and Turkey* (no. 58694/00), Decision of 2 October 2006.

[360] *Manoilescu and Dobrescu v. Romania and Russia* (no. 60861/00), Decision of 3 March 2005, para. 71.

[361] The applicants are the heirs of the person who had owned the property in the past. It had been requisitioned by the Romanian State in 1945 and had subsequently become the property of the USSR by means of an exchange between the latter and Romania in 1962. The applicants obtained a decision for restitution of the building in 1997 (ibid., paras. 1–15).

[362] Ibid., para. 24.

[363] Ibid. See the decisions of the Bucharest County Court of 4 October 1999 (para. 28) and the Bucharest Court of Appeal of 25 October 2000 (para. 30).

that the Romanian courts had somewhat tacitly acknowledged and based their decisions on the principle of a foreign State's diplomatic immunity.[364] While the outcome of the case in principle deserves approval, one would have hoped that the Court would have been more critical of the rather weak reasoning of the domestic courts in that case. A mere reference that the entities in question "lacked the capacity to take part in the proceedings", without making reference to the rules of State immunity, can hardly be said to meet the formal requirements to be expected from a national court when interfering with a Convention right. As a minimum requirement for proportionality of an interference with the right of access to court, national courts should explicitly consider in their decisions that a claim is barred by the rules of State immunity.

d) *The case-law of the Commission: the case of* N, C, F and AG v. Italy

It is interesting to note that the Commission had to consider an application with almost symmetrical facts to the above case of *Treska v. Albania and Italy*. In the case of *N, C, F and AG v. Italy*,[365] the applicants (all Italian nationals) had purchased a villa in Rome which had previously been let to Albania and had become the seat of the Albanian mission in Italy. After the applicants had given the Albanian embassy notice to quit, they obtained an eviction order which became final.[366] However, the bailiff refused to evict the Albanian embassy because of the immunity of the Albanian embassy and its premises.[367] The applicants complained under Article 6 about the eviction proceedings. The Commission declared the application inadmissible. Taking note of the principle of State immunity from execution, it found that Article 6 of the Convention should be interpreted with due regard to diplomatic immunity as traditionally recognised, and that that immunity posed a justified a limitation on the applicant's right of access to court.[368]

e) *Immunity from execution and State agencies: the case of* Hirschhorn v. Romania

The right of access to court (and its execution aspect) may also conflict with the immunity of State agencies or enterprises. State immunity *ratione personae* does also cover State-owned enterprises or agencies.[369] Immunity

364 Ibid., para. 72.

365 *N, C, F and AG v. Italy*, ILR 111, p. 154.

366 ILR 111, p. 156.

367 The case is discussed in more detail below, pp. 121–122.

368 ILR 111, p. 158.

369 Steinberger, *State Immunity*, EPIL IV, p. 621; Herdegen, *Völkerrecht*, p. 245; Brownlie, *Principles*, p. 341.

from jurisdiction is thereby determined according to their principal functions, *i.e.* whether the State agency acts *jure imperii* or *jure gestionis*.[370] With regard to immunity from execution, State agencies enjoy such immunity as far as the assets in question serve a public purpose.[371] In the Court's case-law there has so far only been one case which touched upon those issues. The case of *Hirschhorn v. Romania*[372] concerned the immunity of the American agency, *United States – Peace Corps*, an agency specialising in health, agricultural and environmental issues at the international level. The organisation had rented a premise from the Romanian government which the latter had confiscated in 1952 and which had later been returned by judgment of a Romanian court to the heir of its former legitimate owner. The latter's attempt to execute that judgment was to no avail. An important aspect of the case is that *United States – Peace Corps* did not own the property (as did the embassies concerned in the above cases of *Treska v. Albania and Italy*, and *Manoilescu and Dobrescu v. Romania and Russia*). It had merely rented the building from a Romanian State company, and the contract had even expired during the applicant's restitution proceedings. Consequently, it would have been possible for Romania to return the disputed building to the applicant without violating any immunity that *United States – Peace Corps* might have enjoyed.[373]

In a judgment of 26 July 2007 the Court found unanimously that Romania had violated the applicant's right of access to court under Article 6 (1). It did not consider it necessary to establish whether or not *United States Peace Corps* enjoyed any diplomatic immunity (the agency had refused to submit any information about its statute and its functions).[374] The Court however noted that any immunity that might have existed did not oppose a transfer of the property from the Romanian State to the applicant, as *United States-Peace Corps* would have had the opportunity to invoke its immunity had the applicant brought an action for possession.[375] Even though the judgment appears to be a rare case in which the right of access to court took precedence over international immunities, the decisive circumstance of the case was that the agency had only rented (and thus did not own) the premises.

---

370 In case the acts of the State agency can be qualified as both *jure imperii* and *jure gestionis*, the actual centre of activities is decisive (Steinberger, *State Immunity*, EPIL IV, p. 621).

371 Herdegen, *Internationales Wirtschaftsrecht*, p. 71; see also the *National Iranian Oil Company* case (Federal Constitutional Court of Germany, BVerfGE 64, p. 1).

372 *Hirschhorn v. Romania* (no. 29294/02), Judgment of 26 July 2007.

373 Ibid., para. 56.

374 Ibid., para. 53.

375 Ibid., para. 60.

f) *Conclusion*
As it appears that cases such as *Treska v. Albania and Italy*, *Manoilescu and Dobrescu v. Romania and Russia*, *Kirovi v. Bulgaria and Turkey* and *Hirschhorn v. Romania* all concerned plots of land or buildings which had been expropriated by Communist regimes after the Second World War and which had then been sold or rented to foreign States, more cases of this kind can be expected in the Court's future case-law.

4. Jus cogens *and the right to enforcement of a judgment*

Finally, some thoughts on the relationship between the right to execute a judgment and *jus cogens* should be developed in this chapter. The above case of *Kalageropoulou and Others v. Greece and Germany* served as a very good example of how the relationships between States may deteriorate if domestic courts allow claims against foreign States by denying them immunity in situations which have traditionally been covered by State immunity. One further aspect should therefore be mentioned at this stage which touches upon the relationship between the right of access to court and the right to enforce a judgment as well as the relationship between these two aspects of Article 6 (1) and the violation of a *jus cogens* norm.

Let us assume that, as the minority in the *Al-Adsani* judgment has argued, a violation of a *jus cogens* norm such as the prohibition of torture automatically renders void a foreign State's immunity from the consequences which arise from that act (which, as has been discussed above, is a rather questionable view). The concurring judges in *Al-Adsani*, Judges Pellonpää and Bratza, cited the judgment of *Hornsby v. Greece*[376] as a source that a violation of a *jus cogens* norm would not only require an adjudicating court to deny jurisdictional immunity to the foreign State and decide on the merits of the case. The judges inferred from the above that, in case the claim proved to be successful, the domestic authorities would also have to execute the judgment irrespective of the rules of State immunity from execution. The judgment could then be enforced through an attachment of the foreign State's property, even if it served public purposes (e.g. embassies or schools which are run by the foreign State). Judges Pellonpää and Bratza concluded from the above that, if the Court had found a violation of Article 6 (1) in the *Al-Adsani* case, the consequences of such a ruling, in particular the deterioration of good relationships between the States concerned, were unforeseeable. Given the considerable diplomatic distress between Germany and Greece prior to the

---

[376] *Hornsby v. Greece*; see also Maierhöfer, *Der EGMR als 'Modernisierer' des Völkerrechts?*, EuGRZ 2002, p. 391.

case of *Kalageropoulou and Others v. Greece and Germany*,[377] it is difficult to argue that the concurring judges did not have a point.

However, it is questionable whether the *Hornsby v. Greece* judgment really supports the view that the violation of a *jus cogens* norm (assuming that it rendered void the jurisdictional immunity of the foreign State in the proceedings before the courts of the forum State) also requires the execution of such a judgment. As has been explained above, jurisdictional immunity and immunity from execution are two different legal concepts. For example, a waiver of jurisdictional immunity by the foreign State does not affect its immunity from execution. Immunity from execution, which protects the foreign State's property in the forum State, exists independently of the nature of the act for which the foreign State is being held accountable for in the proceedings. Therefore, it would not be inconsistent for States to be held accountable for acts of torture in proceedings before a foreign court, but for the victim to have to execute the judgment in accordance with the generally accepted rules on immunity from execution. This would put the victim in the same situation as any other plaintiff who sued the foreign State for, say, *acta jure gestionis* such as commercial transactions.

As the right to have a judgment enforced has been read into Article 6 (1) in the same way as the right of access to court, the same limitations apply (*i.e.* any interference must serve a legitimate aim and be proportionate). The right to execute a judgment may therefore be restricted by the rules of immunity from execution if such a limitation is proportionate, which is the case if the property concerned was protected by immunity because it serves a public purpose. In the absence of a direct conflict between a violation of a *jus cogens* norm and immunity from execution (which is not connected to the act which caused the violation but rather to the foreign State's property), it is not compelling that the view of the minority in *Al-Adsani* would have opened the floodgates for diplomatic problems between States with regard to the enforcement of future judgments in which jurisdictional immunity is not granted because of a *jus cogens* violation. It appears that the Court of Appeal in the *Jones* case pointed in the same direction.[378] Of course, if one was to hold that Contracting States had an obligation to grant civil remedies for acts of torture committed abroad by another State, they would also have the obligation to disregard immunity from execution. But as has been shown above, international law (in particular the UN Torture Convention) does not yet

---

[377] See above, pp. 92–100.

[378] *Ronald Grant Jones v. the Ministry of the Interior Al-Mamlaka Al-Arabiya as Saudiya (The Kingdom of Saudi Arabia) & Anor, Sandy Mitchell & Ors v. Ibrahim Al-Dali & Ors*, judgment of the Court of Appeal of 28 October 2004, para. 77, ILM 45 [2006].

recognise such an obligation. Therefore, it is important to bear in mind that the argument that the State responsible for an act of torture cannot derive any advantages or privilege from that act is flawed with regard to immunity from execution. The latter does not derive from that act.

III. *Immunities of Heads of State, foreign ministers, diplomats and other State officials*

States can only act through their agents such as Heads of State, foreign ministers or diplomats. In order not to undermine the immunity of States, their agents also enjoy immunities which however vary to a certain degree from State immunity. The following chapter explores those immunities and their relationship with Article 6 of the Convention.

1. *Immunity of incumbent Heads of States*

a) *The legal position under public international law*

In the absence of a specific international treaty regulating this question, the immunity of Heads of State is currently governed only by customary international law. Because a Head of State is seen as embodying the dignity and sovereignty of the State, the office is closely intertwined with State immunity. Historically, the Head of State personified the State; hence there did not even used to be a distinction between the two types of immunity.[379] International law distinguishes between the immunity of incumbent and former Heads of State. While Heads of State hold office, they traditionally enjoy absolute immunity (*ratione personae*), without distinction between criminal or civil proceedings.[380] The immunity covers both their official as well as their personal acts, and is based on the principle *ne impediatur officium*. It was recently confirmed by the International Court of Justice in the case of *Democratic Republic of Congo v. Belgium* (hereafter the *Arrest Warrant* case):

> The Court would observe at the outset that in international law it is firmly established that, as also diplomatic and consular agents, certain holders of high-ranking office in a State, such as the Head of State, Head of Government and Minister for Foreign Affairs, enjoy immunities from jurisdiction in other States, both civil and criminal.[381]

---

[379] Bröhmer, *State immunity*, p. 30.

[380] Watts, *The Legal Position in International Law of Heads of State, Heads of Government and Foreign Ministers,* (1994-III) 247 RdC, p. 57 et seq.

[381] ICJ Reports 2002, para. 51.

Even though the judgment primarily concerned the immunities of a serving foreign minister, the International Court of Justice found that they were similar to those of a serving Head of State. Obviously, the latter could not be more restricted.[382] Moreover, international jurisprudence widely took the approach that Heads of State enjoy absolute immunity.[383]

Some common law countries, however, recognise some exceptions to immunity of incumbent Heads of State in civil and administrative proceedings. Section 20 of the United Kingdom State Immunity Act for example confers the privileges and immunities enjoyed by a head of diplomatic mission on a Head of State. A number of common law countries have enacted legislation on similar lines.[384] As Article 31 of the Vienna Convention on Diplomatic Relations (1961) contains some specific and exclusive exceptions (such as actions in relation to private property in the territory of the receiving State; succession and inheritance disputes; and professional or commercial activity outside their official functions), Heads of State are not entirely immune from civil proceedings under such legislation if the scope of their immunity equals the immunity of heads of diplomatic missions. But even those exceptions suggest that only acts of a purely personal or private character do not attract immunity. For example, the Cour de Cassation de Paris held that President Mobutu of Zaire did not enjoy immunity in relation to his ordering of a tent village to be erected in connection with his sixtieth birthday celebrations.[385] Moreover, the then incumbent king of Egypt was not granted immunity by the French courts for the purchase of a dress for his wife.[386]

---

382 Ibid., paras 51 and 57.

383 Confirming absolute immunity of Heads of State in civil proceedings in US courts: *Lafontant v. Aristide* (District Court of New York), 844 F.Supp. 128; *Alicog v. Kingdom of Saudi Arabia* 860 F.Supp. 379; *Jungquist v. Shaik Sultan* 940 F.Supp.; *Tachiona v. Mugabe* 169 F.Supp. 2d 259. European case-law: *Mobutu v. SA Cotoni* 91 ILR p. 259 (Belgium); *Re Sharon and Yaron* 127 ILR, p. 770 (Belgium); *Mobutu and Republic of Zaire v. Societé Logrine* (1994) ILR, p. 481 (France); *Gaddafi* (2001) 125 ILR, p. 490 (France); *Mellerio v. Isabelle de Bourbon* 33 Dalloz II 1872, DP 1872, p. 124 (France); *Re Honecker* 80 ILR, p. 365 (Germany); *Bank of Credit and Commerce International (Overseas) Ltd (In Liquidation) v. Price Waterhouse* (No. 1), [1997] 4 All ER p. 108 (United Kingdom).

384 Fox, *The Resolution of the Institute of International Law on the Immunities of Heads of State and Government*, ICLQ 2002, p. 124. Note that in the United States, the FSIA does not provide for a provision on Heads of State. Their immunity is consequently governed by common law (Ibid., p. 124).

385 *Mobutu and Republic of Zaire v. Societé Logrine* (1994) 113 ILR, p. 481.

386 *Farouk, ex-King of Egypt v. Christian Dior* (1957) 24 ILR, p. 228.

(1) *International instruments*

The United Nations Convention on the Jurisdictional Immunities of States and Their Property does not give any guidance to the subject. The ILC Commission omitted a Head of State from the scope of its final draft articles on the Convention.[387] Article 3 (2) of the Convention therefore states that the Convention is without prejudice to the immunities accorded under international law to Heads of States *ratione personae.*

In 2001, the Institute of International Law adopted a resolution on "Immunities from Jurisdiction and Execution of Head of States and of Government in International Law".[388] Intended to be a restatement of existing law, the first part of the resolution refers to serving Heads of State. With regard to criminal matters, its Article 2 states that "Heads of State shall enjoy immunity from jurisdiction before the courts of a foreign State for any crime he or she may have committed, regardless of its gravity." Concerning civil and administrative matters, Article 3 provides that:

> (...) the Head of State does not enjoy any immunity from jurisdiction before the courts of a foreign state, unless that suit relates to acts performed in the exercise of his or her official functions.

The resolution therefore restricts the immunity in civil matters to official acts. However, it has been criticised for not being a strict statement of the law in force at the relevant time and, while significant, cannot be said to have authoritative value that would contradict clear jurisprudence of national and international courts.[389]

(2) *Exemptions in the statutes of international criminal tribunals*

It should be noted that absolute immunity for serving Heads of State does apply as far as the jurisdiction of other States is concerned. Incumbent Heads of State do not enjoy immunity in respect of international crimes before international criminal tribunals. The charters of the international military tribunals of Nuremberg (Article 7) and Tokyo (Article 6), the Statutes of the International Criminal Tribunals for the former Yugoslavia (Article 7) and Rwanda (Article 6), and the Statute of the International Criminal Court (Article 27), all provide that immunities which might attach to the official capacity of a Head of State do not bar those international tribunals from exercising jurisdiction over that person.

---

[387] Fox, *The Resolution of the Institute of International Law on the Immunities of Heads of State and Government*, ICLQ 2002, p. 124.

[388] *Annuaire de l'institut*, Vancouver Session, 2001, Vol. II, p. 742.

[389] See Fox, *The Resolution of the Institute of International Law on the Immunities of Heads of State and Government*, ICLQ 2002, p. 124.

b) *The case of* Association SOS Attentats and Beatrix de Boery v. France

To date, the conflict between immunities of incumbent Heads of State and Article 6 have had to be considered by the Court on one occasion. The case concerned the bombing in 1989 of a French aeroplane in flight above the Tenere desert in which 170 people (mostly French citizens) died. After a judicial investigation in France, six Libyan officials (among them the brother-in-law of Colonel Muammar Gaddafi and head of the Libyan secret service) were sentenced in 1999 to life imprisonment *in absentia* by the Paris Assize Court and also ordered to pay compensation for non-pecuniary damage to the victims' families.[390]

The applicants before the Court, the French wife of one of the victims and a French NGO (*Association SOS Attentats, SOS Terrorisme*) composed of members of victims of terrorist attacks and their heirs, lodged a civil-party complaint against Colonel Gaddafi, the incumbent Libyan Head of State, for complicity in murder and destruction of property by use of an explosive substance in furtherance of a conspiracy calculated to disturb public order through intimidation or terror.

An investigating judge ruled that there was a case to answer and the Indictment Division of the Paris Court of Appeal upheld that ruling in a judgment of October 2000, in which it held that although the immunity of foreign Heads of State had always been accepted by the international community (including France), it had been subject to limits since the Second World War, namely the agreements establishing the military tribunals of Nuremberg and Tokyo and the Statutes of the International Criminal Tribunals for the former Yugoslavia and Rwanda as well as the Rome Statute of the International Criminal Court.[391] All these Conventions reflected the will of the international community to prosecute the perpetrators of the most serious crimes, including those committed by a Head of State. Moreover, the Paris Court of Appeal referred to the *Pinochet* ruling by the House of Lords as evidence of a general practice to the effect that immunity covers acts of public authority performed by a Head of State, provided that these are not international crimes. Consequently, the court held that no immunity could cover complicity for a terrorist conspiracy in which a Head of State ordered the destruction by explosives of an airliner in flight carrying 170 civilians.[392]

That decision was quashed by the Court of Cassation in March 2001, which held that "under international law as it stands at present the crime

[390] *Association SOS Attentats and Beatrix de Boery v. France* [GC] (no. 76642/01), Decision of 4 October 2006, para. 9.

[391] Ibid., para. 12.

[392] Ibid.

complained of, whatever its gravity, is not covered by any of the exceptions to the principle of immunity from jurisdiction for foreign heads of State in office".[393] The applicants thus brought an application to the Court, complaining of a violation by the Court of Cassation of their right of access to court. Even though the date of the filing of the application, 11 September 2001, was pure coincidence, it nevertheless had an unintended symbolic meaning.

(1) *The decision of the Court*

After a hearing was held in June 2006, the Grand Chamber of the Court decided to strike the application out of its list in accordance with Article 37 (1) (c) of the Convention as it found it no longer to be justified to continue the examination of the application. The applicants had signed an agreement in 2004 with the "Gaddafi International Foundation for Charity Associations" in which the latter announced that it would make an *ex gratia* payment to the families of the 170 victims. In exchange for the receipt of that compensation the members of the families desisted from any actions or claims against Libya or Libyan citizens and waived the right to bring any kind of civil or criminal proceedings before any French or international court based on the explosion on board the aircraft.[394] The second applicant did not sign the waiver in the agreement but stated that she would take her final decision to accept compensation in the light of the Court's conclusion in the instant case. Therefore, the Court found that the above agreement led it to consider that it was no longer justified in continuing the examination of the application.[395]

(2) *The conflict between immunity of incumbent Heads of State and Article 6 (1) of the Convention in the present case*

Even though the Court did not decide on the merits of the case, it is nevertheless interesting for present purposes to consider how it should have decided had the application not been struck out of its list because of the 2004 Agreement.

As can be seen from the above, the majority of States grant absolute immunity to an incumbent Head of State, independent of the seriousness of the offence (which in the present case was, without doubt, extremely serious). Even taking into account that some countries provide for exceptions from Head of State immunity in accordance with Article 31 of the Vienna Convention on Diplomatic Relations, the present case does not fall into those

[393] Ibid., para. 13.
[394] Ibid., para. 14.
[395] Ibid., para. 39.

categories. The matter concerned neither private property disputes in the territory of the receiving State nor commercial activity outside Gaddafi's official functions. A good argument in favour of the applicants could have been a referral to Article 3 of the Resolution of the Institute of International Law which excludes immunities for acts which are not performed in the exercise of official functions in civil and administrative matters. Arguably, the bombing of an aircraft would fall outside this category. However, it has been already stated that the resolution does not reflect the current state of public international law. Article 3 is rather a *de lege ferenda* provision.[396]

Moreover, the reasoning of the Paris Court of Appeal (which did not grant immunity in the present case) appears rather dubious. First, its reference to the *Pinochet* rulings by the House of Lords is misleading. Those proceedings concerned the immunity of a former Head of State, whereas the present case concerned the immunity of an incumbent. That difference is important because the latter traditionally also enjoys immunity in respect of non-official acts, whereas the former does not.

The Paris Court of Appeal also found that international crimes are an exception to immunity of incumbent Heads of State under customary international law, since the charters of the international military tribunals of Nuremberg (Article 7) and Tokyo (Article 6), the Statutes of the International Criminal Tribunals for the former Yugoslavia (Article 7) and Rwanda (Article 6) as well as the Statute of the International Criminal Court (Article 27) made exceptions for such immunity. However, this view is dubious. The International Court of Justice found in the *Arrest Warrant* case that the above provisions likewise did not enable it to conclude that any such exception existed in customary international law in regard to national courts.[397] The crucial difference is that the principles of immunity are based on the equality of States. In contrast to that, international criminal tribunals do not concern the exercise of national authority of one State over another.[398] This distinction has also been supported by the Special Court for Sierra Leone in its decision of 31 May 2004 on the claim to immunity by Mr Charles Taylor, the former Liberian Head of State. The Special Court for Sierra Leone held that it was because the court possessed an international character that a Head

[396] Fox, *The Resolution of the Institute of International Law on the Immunities of Heads of State and Government*, ICLQ 2002, p. 124.

[397] ICJ Reports 2002, para. 58.

[398] Another good reason in support of that distinction is that the risk that foreign courts may abuse derogations from the rules of immunity does not arise when the judicial body exercising criminal jurisdiction is international in character; see Gaeta, *Ratione Materiae Immunities of Former Heads of State and International Crimes: The Hissène Habré Case*, JICJ 2003, p. 194.

of State was not entitled to immunity in proceedings before it.[399] Moreover, the Court of Appeal of Brussels applied this distinction in a case concerning the criminal responsibility of Ariel Sharon for complicity or failure to intervene in massacres which took place in two Palestinian refugee camps in Lebanon in 1982.[400] The above exceptions in the statutes of the international criminal tribunals therefore cannot be seen as reflecting the current state of public international law with regard to State's obligations to grant immunity to foreign incumbent Heads of State *in their national courts.*

Not everybody shares that view. It has been stated that, if the above provisions in the statutes of the international criminal tribunals were merely treaty stipulations and the irrelevance of official capacity (and consequently the exception from immunity of Heads of States) for international crimes had thus not already become a generally accepted rule of customary international law, the principle *nullum crimen sine lege* would be breached if Heads of States were accused of crimes under those statutes.[401] This view however fails to take into account that the principle *nullum crimen sine lege*, which holds that only the law can define a crime and prescribe a penalty, is limited primarily to substantive criminal law. The principle is, for example, reflected in the Court's case-law on Article 7 of the Convention, which prohibits retroactive criminal legislation. The Court did not see that principle violated in a case in which applicants complained about changes to the statute of limitations and related procedural rules governing criminal prosecutions.[402] The situation is not different with regard to immunities. They neither define the material criminal law, nor do they lay down rules on criminal responsibility as such. Changes in public international law on the scope of immunities for criminal offences do not conflict with the principle *nullum crimen sine lege.*[403]

---

399 See Deen-Racsmany, *Prosecutor v. Taylor: The Status of the Special Court for Sierra Leone and Its Implications for Immunity*, LJIL 2005, p. 299; Nouwen, *The Special Court for Sierra Leone and the Immunity of Taylor: the Arrest Warrant Case Continued*, LJIL 2005, p. 645.

400 *Re Sharon and Yaron*, Court of Appeal of Brussels (Belgium), (2002) 127 ILR, p. 112.

401 Zappalà, *Do Heads of State in Office Enjoy Immunity from Jurisdiction for International Crimes?*, EJIL 2001, p. 603.

402 *Coeme and Others v. Belgium* (no. 32492/96), Judgment of 22 June 2000, RJD 2000-VII, paras. 142–151; Gomien, *Short Guide to the European Convention on Human Rights*, p. 71; see generally on Article 7: Grabenwarter, *Europäische Menschenrechtskonvention*, § 24, 140 et seq.

403 In any event, Article 7 (2) of the Convention states that the principle does not prejudice the punishment of any person for acts which, at the time when they were committed, were criminal according to the general principles of law recognised by civilised nations.

Hence the existence of the above exceptions in the international statutes does not support the conclusion that public international law already recognises such exceptions in domestic proceedings because otherwise the international statutes would violate the principle of *nullum crimen sine lege*.

(3) *Conclusion*

Therefore, the French Court of Cassation arguably did not restrict Article 6 (1) in a disproportionate manner when granting immunity in the present case. The decision also received support from the International Court of Justice, which cited it in the *Arrest Warrant* case.[404] It becomes plain from that passage in the *Arrest Warrant* judgment that the International Court of Justice regarded the decision of the French Court of Cassation as correctly reflecting the legal position of incumbent Heads of State under public international law.

2. *Immunity of former Heads of State*

a) *The legal position under public international law*

Once a Head of State leaves office, he or she is no longer protected by immunity *ratione personae*, but only from immunity *ratione materiae*. Such immunity (also called functional immunity) is determined with reference to the nature of the acts in question. It consequently applies only to official acts, but continues after the Head of State leaves office. For example, Article 13 of the resolution of the Institute of International Law ("Immunities from Jurisdiction and Execution of Head of States and of Government in International Law") states that a former Head of State enjoys no immunity from jurisdiction in criminal, civil or administrative proceedings except for acts performed in the exercise of official functions.[405]

b) *Conflict with Article 6 (1) of the Convention*

There are two situations conceivable in which the immunity of a former Head of State might be challenged under Article 6 (1) before the Court with special reference to international crimes. The first would consist in a civil suit for damages by victims (or their relatives) of human rights abuses which are attributable to a former Head of State and which were committed when he

[404] ICJ Reports 2002, para. 58 (read in conjunction with paras. 56–57).

[405] Note that on 19 February 2009, Belgium instituted proceedings against Senegal with regard to the extradition of the former President of the Republic of Chad for the purposes of criminal proceedings for crimes against humanity. The case will presumably address several questions on the immunity of a former Head of State (Case concerning questions relating to the obligation to prosecute or extradite, *Belgium v. Senegal*; see the press release of the International Court of Justice of 19 February 2009).

or she held office.[406] To date, there has been no application before the Court in which the question arose whether torture committed for State purposes can be categorised as an act performed in exercise of official functions of a former Head of State. If the question would be answered in the negative, a former Head of State would not benefit from immunity *ratione materiae* for these acts. The granting of immunity in such an instance would then arguably violate the right of access to court of the persons seeking to institute civil proceedings. The question is highly debated amongst both legal academics and judges (for instance in the *Pinochet* judgments).[407]

An almost identical problem (with regard to the question whether or not torture can be considered as an official act for the purposes of the UN Torture Convention) has arisen in the *Jones* case, which was decided by both the Court of Appeal of England and Wales and the House of Lords with regard to the immunity of State officials. As the plaintiffs in that case are reported to have lodged an application with the Court, it is more appropriate to deal with this question in the context of that case. It is considered below.[408]

c) *Case-law of the Court*

The second situation in which the immunity of former Heads of State in fact raised an issue under the Convention concerns two applications which were brought to the Court at the time when Augusto Pinochet faced extradition proceedings in the United Kingdom between 1998 and 1999. They involve a rather atypical situation in the present context, as the applicants lodged their complaints with a view to seeking extradition of the former Chilean Head of State to France and Switzerland in order to sue him for compensation in the courts there.

One of these applications, *Jaccard-Veloso and Others v. the United Kingdom*,[409] was brought by victims and relatives of victims of the regime of

---

406 See generally Bröhmer, *Diplomatic Immunity, Head of State Immunity, State Immunity: Misconceptions of a Notorious Human Rights Violator*, LJIL 1999, p. 361.

407 The second sentence of Article 13 of the resolution of the Institute of International Law makes an express reservation on the immunity *ratione materiae* ("Nevertheless, he or she may be prosecuted and tried when the acts alleged constitute a crime under international law, or when they are performed exclusively to satisfy a personal interest, or when they constitute a misappropriation of the State's assets and resources.") The exception is however worded in such a way as to avoid to give an answer on whether or not such acts are to be considered "official" (See Fox, *The Resolution of the Institute of International Law on the Immunities of Heads of State and Government*, ICLQ 2002, p. 121).

408 See below, pp. 125 et seq.

409 *Jaccard-Veloso and Others v. the United Kingdom* (no. 44191/98). The case is unpublished, but has been reported by Clapham, *Revisiting Human Rights in the Private Sphere*, pp. 513 et seq.

General Augusto Pinochet in Chile.[410] Some of the applicants were resident in Switzerland and France at the time when Pinochet was arrested in London in 1998.[411] During the pending extradition proceedings before the House of Lords, the applicants lodged a complaint with the Court. They argued that their right to bring civil proceedings against Pinochet in France and Switzerland would be violated if the United Kingdom refused to extradite the former dictator due to his immunity. The case was brought to Strasbourg before the House of Lords decided that Pinochet did not enjoy Head of State immunity. But since Pinochet was not extradited to Spain because of his state of health, the applicants' complaints remained valid. The release of Pinochet, so the applicants' argument went, would mean that there could be no hearing in the French and Swiss courts. Consequently the applicants would be denied a hearing in France or Switzerland. That denial was allegedly attributable to the United Kingdom. The applicants argued that Head of State immunity for serious human rights violations would put a disproportionate restriction on Article 6.

The remarkable aspect of this application is what Clapham (who was one of the legal counsels for the applicants before the Court) calls "a transnational right to access to justice under Article 6".[412] In other words, if the United Kingdom authorities failed to extradite Pinochet, they would allegedly violate the applicants' right of access to the civil courts in France and Switzerland. While the decision on extradition would take place within the United Kingdom jurisdiction, the violation of Article 6 would take place in France and Switzerland where an available and willing court system would have been precluded from hearing the applicants' case.[413] The applicants relied on the judgment of *Soering v. the United Kingdom*, a case in which the United Kingdom was found to have violated Article 3 if it had extradited a murderer to the United States who would have been subjected to inhuman and degrading treatment while on death row. Whereas the violation in *Soering* would have been the extradition, the violation in *Jaccard-Veloso*

[410] The acts perpetrated against the husband of one of the applicants were the subject of a request by Switzerland to the United Kingdom for the extradition of Pinochet. The other applicants' complaints related to cases of torture and disappearances between 1973 and 1984 (Clapham, *Revisiting Human Rights in the Private Sphere*, p. 524).

[411] For a detailed account of the arrest see Robertson, *Crimes against Humanity*, pp. 393–427; Brody/Ratner, *The Pinochet Papers: The Case of Augusto Pinochet in Spain and Britain*.

[412] Clapham, *Revisiting Human Rights in the Private Sphere*, p. 528.

[413] Ibid., p. 529. Hence Article 6 would apply in the present case, even though extradition proceedings as such do not come within the scope of the provision (*Mamatkutlov and Abdurasulovic v. Turkey*, para. 80; *Maaouia v. France* [GC] (no. 39652/98), Judgment of 5 October 2000, RDJ 2000-X, para. 40; see also Reid, *Practitioner's Guide*, p. 302).

and Others would have been the failure to extradite.[414] Moreover, the applicants relied on the Court's finding in the judgment *Loizidou v. Turkey* that the Convention represents "a constitutional instrument of European public order".[415] They concluded that the case for a judgment which would prevent a future violation would be stronger where the abuse of rights would take place in a Contracting State (as opposed to the United States in *Soering*).

Neither of these arguments is very convincing. First, the Court is generally not easily prepared to stop an extradition in view of future violations if the applicant is to be extradited to another Contracting State. This is because there is a rebuttable presumption that the receiving State will comply with its Convention obligations and, in any event, a future violation would still come within the Court's jurisdiction.[416] Given that, it is hard to see how the case for a judgment which would prevent a violation of Article 6 would be stronger where the lack of access would be in the courts of another Contracting State. Moreover, the two situations are not really comparable, because the Swiss and the French courts would not have denied access: it was rather that the United Kingdom's decision not to extradite Pinochet would have deprived the applicants of the opportunity to have the defendant appear in the court hearings.

The main argument against *Jaccard-Veloso and Others* is that the facts of the case do not come under Article 1 of the Convention, which states that "the High Contracting Parties shall secure to everyone within their jurisdiction the rights and freedoms" of the Convention. The applicants who planned to bring civil proceedings against Pinochet in France and Switzerland where they were resident did not come within the jurisdiction of the United Kingdom by the mere fact that they happened to reside elsewhere in Europe.

It is recognised in the jurisprudence of the Court that the concept of jurisdiction is not entirely restricted to the national territory of a Contracting State.[417] However, the Court has accepted only in exceptional cases that acts of the Contracting States producing effects outside their territory can constitute an exercise of jurisdiction by them within the meaning of Article 1.[418] Such exceptional cases were notably recognised when a Contracting State

---

414 Clapham, *Revisiting Human Rights in the Private Sphere*, p. 529.

415 *Loizidou v. Turkey* (preliminary objections), para. 62.

416 *A.G. v. Sweden* (no. 27776/95), Decision of 26 October 1995; Erdal/Bakirci, *Article 3 of the European Convention on Human Rights, A Practitioner's Handbook*, p. 150; Leach, *Taking a Case to the European Court of Human Rights*, p. 39.

417 See generally on Article 1: Peters, *Einführung in die EMRK*, p. 234; Grabenwarter, *Europäische Menschenrechtskonvention*, § 13, 43; Matscher, *Bemerkungen zur extraterritorialen oder indirekten Wirkung der EMRK*, Festschrift Trechsel, p. 25.

418 *Bankovic and Others v. Belgium and 16 Other Nato States*, para. 67.

exercised effective control of a foreign territory and its inhabitants abroad as a consequence of military occupation.[419] Other exceptions were activities of diplomatic or consular agents abroad[420] and, most importantly in the present context, where the extradition or expulsion of a person by a Contracting State gave rise to an issue under Articles 2 or 3. The latter exception concerns the situation in the *Soering* case. But whereas in *Soering* the applicant was clearly on the territory (and therefore within the jurisdiction) of the United Kingdom at the time of the pending extradition, the applicants in *Jaccard-Veloso and Others* were not within the jurisdiction in a way that could have incurred the liability of the United Kingdom.

The Court decided in the admissibility decision of *McElhinney v. Ireland and the United Kingdom*[421] that the defence of sovereign immunity by the United Kingdom in the Irish courts did not bring the Irish applicant within the United Kingdom's jurisdiction within the meaning of Article 1. Moreover, the Court recently decided in *Ben El Mahi and Others v. Denmark*[422] that the applicants, who were resident in Morocco and who complained that the Danish government had failed to intervene in a Danish newspaper's publication of caricatures of the Islamic prophet Muhammad, did not have a jurisdictional link with Denmark within the meaning of Article 1. The decision not to extradite on the grounds that the extraditable person is protected from immunity concerns a comparable situation to the above cases. There was likewise no jurisdictional link between the applicants and the United Kingdom. As a result, the United Kingdom was not obliged under the Convention to grant the applicants effective access to French or Swiss courts by extraditing the defendant in those proceedings.

The Court did not follow the applicants' arguments and, by a Committee of three judges, declared the application *Jaccard-Veloso and Others v. the United Kingdom* inadmissible as being manifestly ill-founded, without giving further reasons. In a similar case, *Pradenas and Others v. the United Kingdom* (no. 51287/99), a group of victims from Spain who had suffered at the hands of the Chilean military junta between 1973 and 1990 had unsuccessfully asked the Court for interim measures under Rule 39 of the Rules of the Court to prevent the release of General Pinochet by the British authorities.[423]

---

[419] *Bankovic and Others v. Belgium and 16 Other Nato States*, paras. 70–71, *Loizidou v. Turkey* (preliminary objections), para. 62; *Cyprus v. Turkey*, paras. 69–81.

[420] *Bankovic and Others v. Belgium and 16 Other Nato States*, paras. 73; Jacobs and White, *European Convention*, p. 22 (with further references).

[421] See above, p. 86.

[422] *Ben El Mahi and Others v. Denmark*, (no. 5853/06), Decision of 11 December 2006.

[423] See the Press Release of 17 January 2000 issued by the Registrar of the Court.

Their case was also declared inadmissible as being manifestly ill-founded by a Committee of three judges in 2001.[424]

3. *Immunity of diplomats and foreign ministers*

a) *Diplomatic and consular immunities*

In contrast to the principle of State immunity, diplomatic and consular immunity seeks to protect friendly relations among nations as well as the efficient performance of the functions of diplomatic missions as such.[425] The protection of diplomatic relations between States is therefore also aimed at maintaining peace between States.[426] However, these rules also indirectly seek to protect the rules on State immunity which could be circumvented by subjecting the organs and persons acting on the States' behalf to the jurisdiction of the forum State.[427] The rules on diplomatic and consular immunities have been codified in both the Vienna Convention on Diplomatic Relations of 1961 and the Vienna Convention on Consular Relations of 1963.

(1) *Diplomatic immunities*

According to Article 21 of the Vienna Convention, the premises of the mission of the foreign State is inviolable and (together with the furnishing and other property thereon) immune from search, requisition, attachment or execution. Article 29 of the Vienna Convention concerns the personal inviolability of diplomats which comprises two aspects: first, immunity from any form of law enforcement action such as arrest or detention; second, the duty to accord special protection by the receiving State.[428] Diplomatic premises and papers, property and correspondence are also inviolable (Article 30 of the Vienna Convention).

The jurisdictional immunities of diplomats are set out in Articles 31 and 32 of the Vienna Convention on Diplomatic Relations. Diplomats enjoy absolute immunity from the criminal jurisdiction of the receiving State[429] and immunity from civil and administrative jurisdiction except in special cases specified in Article 31 of Vienna Convention. These are actions relating to private immovable property situated in the territory of the receiving State

---

[424] The decision is unpublished.

[425] Buergenthal/Maier, *Public International Law*, p. 215; Dahm, *Völkerrecht I*, p. 317.

[426] Doehring, *Völkerrecht*, p. 277.

[427] Steinberger, *State Immunity*, EPIL IV, p. 615.

[428] See Denza, *Diplomatic Agents and Missions, Privileges and Immunities*, EPIL I, p. 1043.

[429] The receiving State may however draw the attention of any offence to the head of mission in order to ask for a waiver or, in extreme cases, declare the diplomat a *persona non grata* (Denza, *Diplomatic Agents and Missions, Privileges and Immunities*, EPIL I, p. 1043).

(unless the diplomat holds it on behalf of the sending State for the purposes of the mission), inheritance actions and actions relating to any professional or commercial activity exercised by the diplomatic agent in the receiving State outside his official functions.[430] According to Article 32 of the Vienna Convention, immunity may be waived by the sending State.[431] Members of the family of a diplomat forming part of his household (except local nationals) enjoy full diplomatic immunity. Article 37 of the Vienna Convention lays down restricted immunity for administrative and technical staff, service staff and private servants of members of the mission.[432] Article 38 of the Vienna Convention limits the immunity of diplomats who are nationals or permanent residents of the receiving State. The immunity of diplomats who are in transit in third States is regulated by Article 40 of the Vienna Convention.

(2) *Consular immunities*

Consular immunity is addressed in the Vienna Convention on Consular Relations of 1963. The immunities enjoyed by consuls resemble those accorded to diplomats but are more limited in scope.[433] Article 41 of the Vienna Convention provides that consuls are immune from arrest or detention except for serious crimes and following a decision by the competent judicial authorities.[434] Under Article 43 of the Vienna Convention, consular immunity is restricted in both criminal and civil matters to acts done in the official exercise of consular functions.[435]

b) *Case-law of the Convention organs*

The case-law of the Court on diplomatic immunity somewhat overlaps with the cases that have already been discussed above in the chapter on the right to execute a judgment. As applicants sought to enforce their final decisions against a foreign State by attachment of the latter's assets in the forum State, the inviolability of the premises of the foreign State's mission was inevitably concerned. The cases of *Kalageropoulou and Others v. Greece and Germany*,

---

[430] See in general Vicuna, *Diplomatic and Consular Immunities and Human Rights*, ICLQ 1991, p. 34; Denza, *Diplomatic Agents and Missions, Privileges and Immunities*, EPIL I, p. 1040; Brown, *Diplomatic Immunity: State Practice under the Vienna Convention on Diplomatic Relations*, ICLQ 1988, p. 53; McClanahan, *Diplomatic Immunity*.

[431] See further Denza, *Diplomatic Agents and Missions, Privileges and Immunities*, EPIL I, p. 1043; Brownlie, *Principles*, pp. 360–361.

[432] See also Brownlie, *Principles*, p. 363.

[433] Wallace, *International Law*, p. 132.

[434] Buergenthal/Maier, *Public International Law*, p. 218.

[435] Shaw, *International Law*, p. 690.

Treska v. Albania and Italy, *Manoilescu and Dobrescu v. Romania and Russia*, and *Hirschhorn v. Romania*, can therefore also be read as involving diplomatic immunity. The Court however addressed the decisions rather in the context of Article 6 (1) and State immunity from execution.

However, the Commission addressed diplomatic immunity in the case of *N, C, F and AG v. Italy*.[436] The applicants (all Italian nationals) had purchased a villa in Rome which had previously been let to Albania and had become the seat of the Albanian mission in Italy. In 1990, the applicants gave the Albanian embassy notice to quit and summoned it to appear before the Rome magistrate in order to terminate the tenancy; the embassy opposed the eviction on the ground of its immunity.[437] The Rome magistrate provisionally confirmed the eviction on the ground that the Albanian embassy was considered to be acting in the capacity of a private individual. That decision was confirmed by a court in Rome and became final.[438] However, the bailiff refused to evict the Albanian embassy because of the immunity of the latter and its premises. An application against that refusal was dismissed by the Rome magistrate in 1993 because of the inviolability of the premises of a diplomatic mission.

The applicants complained under Article 6 that the eviction proceedings were excessively long, although they acknowledged the principle of inviolability of the premises of diplomatic missions. The Commission declared the application inadmissible. It applied its traditional approach towards immunities and stated that:

> In respect of disputes concerning the seats of diplomatic missions, the Commission notes that customary international law accords sending States immunity, not only from execution, but also from jurisdiction in the receiving state. (...) Article 6 of the Convention should be interpreted with due regard to (...) diplomatic immunity as traditionally recognised. In such cases, the defendant is inaccessible and it is for the domestic court to apply the corresponding limitation of its jurisdiction. Accordingly, the Commission considers that the particular circumstances of the case would have justified a limitation of the applicant's right of access to court.[439]

Admittedly, the application primarily concerned a foreign State's immunity from execution, which has already been considered above.[440] However, it can be taken from the above that the immunities granted under the Vienna Conventions may restrict the right of access to court under Article 6 (1).

---

436 *N, C, F and AG v. Italy*, 111 ILR, p. 154.
437 Ibid., p. 155.
438 Ibid., p. 156.
439 Ibid., p. 158.
440 See above, p. 1034.

However, while the Commission proceeded to consider diplomatic immunity as placing a justified restriction on Article 6, it wrongly assumed that the provision did not apply. As to the length of proceedings, the Commission found that:

> (...) since the applicants were not entitled under Article 6 of the Convention to have access to court in the present case, the Commission considers that they cannot invoke this provision to complain about the length of the proceedings which actually took place, Article 6 (1) not being applicable to those proceedings.[441]

That part of the decision is flawed. Even though immunities may serve as a proportionate restriction on the right of access to court, the Court nowadays rightfully considers Article 6 (1) to apply.[442] In that instance, the Commission should have considered whether or not the period of three years for the execution of the applicant's decision had been excessive, instead of declaring the application incompatible *ratione materiae* with the provisions of the Convention because there was no right to enforce a decision against a foreign mission.[443] It appears that the applicants finally accepted that their claim against the Albanian mission had been unsuccessful, but they complained in the first place before the Commission that this conclusion had taken the Italian authorities and courts three years. That period indeed might have raised an issue under the Convention.[444]

Another question raised by the applicants is interesting in the present context. The applicants claimed that Article 21 of the Vienna Convention on Diplomatic Relations obliged Italy to find suitable alternative premises for the Albanian embassy. That provision provides that the receiving State either shall facilitate the acquisition of its territory by the sending State or assist the latter in obtaining accommodation in some other way. The Commission pointed out correctly that Article 21 of the Vienna Convention clearly refers to relations between States and does not confer any rights on individuals to have such action taken.[445]

---

441 *N, C, F and AG v. Italy*, pp. 158–159.

442 See above, pp. 26–31.

443 *N, C, F and AG v. Italy*, p. 159.

444 Regarding the length of proceedings, see Reid, *Practitioner's Guide*, pp. 144 *et seq*., Jacobs and White, *European Convention*, p. 166 *et seq*. and Grabenwarter, *Europäische Menschenrechtskonvention*, §§ 24, 68 et seq.

445 *N, C, F and AG v. Italy*, p. 158.

c) *Immunity of foreign ministers*

Like the immunity of Heads of State, the immunity of foreign ministers is a matter of customary international law. But unlike the former, there is hardly any State practice on the latter. Hence the judgment of the International Court of Justice in the *Arrest Warrant* case[446] attracted wide attention. In that case, the International Court of Justice found that Belgium had violated the rules on immunities of foreign ministers by circulating an arrest warrant against the then incumbent foreign minister of the Democratic Republic of Congo for war crimes and crimes against humanity. As to the scope of immunity granted to a foreign minister, it found that:

> The Court would observe at the outset that in international law it is firmly established that, as also diplomatic and consular agents, certain holders of high-ranking office in a State, such as the Head of State, Head of Government and Minister for Foreign Affairs, enjoy immunities from jurisdiction in other States, both civil and criminal.[447]

The International Court of Justice reasoned that under customary international law the immunities accorded to foreign ministers were not granted for their personal benefit but to ensure the effective performance of their functions on behalf of their respective States.[448] Neither the very limited State practice (it cited the House of Lords judgments in the *Pinochet* case as well as the French Cour de Cassation's judgment in the *Gaddafi* case) nor national legislation and the relevant provisions in the statutes of international criminal tribunals indicated that there existed an exception under customary international law from a foreign minister's immunity from criminal process for war crimes or crimes against humanity.[449] Thus, Belgium had disregarded that immunity by circulating the arrest warrant.[450]

The judgment has attracted considerable criticism.[451] In her dissenting opinion, Judge van den Wyngaert argued that the reasoning was flawed in two ways. First, the International Court of Justice had erroneously assumed that there was a rule of customary international law granting immunity to incumbent foreign ministers. A rule of customary international law requires two elements, State practice and *opinio iuris* to the effect that that rule exists,

---

[446] *Democratic Republic of Congo v. Belgium*, ICJ Reports 2002.

[447] Ibid., para. 51.

[448] Ibid., para. 53.

[449] Ibid., para. 58.

[450] Ibid., para. 71.

[451] For a discussion of that judgment see Cassese, *When May Senior State Officials Be Tried for International Crimes? Some Comments on the Congo v. Belgium Case*, EJIL 2002, p. 853; Wirth, *Immunity for Core Crimes? The ICJ's Judgment in the Congo v. Belgium Case*, EJIL 2002, p. 877; Van Alebeek, *The Immunity of States and Their Officials*, pp. 195 et seq.

but the International Court of Justice had wrongfully inferred from the "negative State practice" (*i.e.* the abstaining from instituting criminal proceedings against foreign ministers of foreign States) evidence of an *opinio iuris*.[452] The International Court of Justice had merely proceeded from a questionable analogy with immunities for diplomatic agents and Heads of State.[453] Second, she disputed that incumbent foreign ministers were immune from the jurisdiction of other States when charged with war crimes and crimes against humanity.[454]

No case has yet been brought to the Strasbourg Court with regard to the immunity of foreign ministers. However, given the judgment of the International Court of Justice in the *Arrest Warrant* case, it is very likely that the Court would not be prepared to find a violation of Article 6 (1) in the instance that a national court would base its decision on the broad immunity assumed by the International Court of Justice in that case. As far as the immunity of former foreign ministers is concerned, it can be assumed that they will only be protected by immunity *ratione materiae* in the same way as former Heads of State. That could raise the question whether the granting of immunity (no matter whether immunity of former foreign ministers, former Heads of State or other State officials) in civil proceedings for torture violates Article 6 (1). The following part of this chapter provides some guidance in respect of that problem.

4. *Immunity of other State officials*

a) *The legal position under public international law*

It appears that, unless the immunities of State officials are addressed by an international treaty (such as the Vienna Conventions on Diplomatic and Consular Relations) or a higher degree of immunity is specifically provided to officials by customary international law (such as Head of State immunity in comparison with State immunity as such), the same immunity which is accorded to States is accorded to its officials for whom the State is responsible.[455]

---

452 *Democratic Republic of Congo v. Belgium*, ICJ Reports 2002, dissenting opinion of Judge van den Wyngaert, para. 13.

453 Ibid., para. 14. It is however difficult to understand that, while diplomats enjoy immunities under the Vienna Convention on Diplomatic Relations, the person in charge of his or her State's relations with all other States may not benefit from such immunities. One might argue that diplomats are based in a foreign State, whereas a foreign minister is not. However, given the importance of foreign ministers in international relations as well as their frequent travels, that objection does not appear to be very convincing.

454 Ibid., para. 24.

455 For a general overview, see Van Alebeek, *The Immunity of States and Their Officials*, Chapters 5 and 6.

This principle has been stated explicitly in Article 2 (1) (b) (iv) of the United Nations Convention on the Jurisdictional Immunities of States and their Property which defines the term "State" as including "representatives of the State acting in that capacity". Hence immunity is provided for official, but not for private acts. As the Appeals Chamber of the International Criminal Tribunal for the Former Yugoslavia stated in the case of *Prosecutor v. Blaskic*:

> Such officials are mere instruments of a state and their official action can only be attributed to the state. (...) state officials cannot suffer the consequences of wrongful acts which are not attributable to them personally but to the state on whose behalf they act: they enjoy so-called 'functional immunity'. This is a well-established rule of customary international law going back to the 18th and 19th centuries, restated many times since.[456]

That degree of immunity given to State officials is seen as necessary in order not to undermine the immunity of the foreign State by targeting its officials and to eventually subject the foreign State to the jurisdiction of the host State.[457] Given that the decisive criterion is then the classification of a certain act as either "private" or "official", difficulties may arise with immunity for acts which constitute severe human rights violations. This is also because, when it comes to gross human rights violations, it is difficult to maintain the above statement by the Appeals Chamber that "the consequences of wrongful acts are not attributable to [officials] personally".

It appears that the following case, which has so far only been decided by the British courts, will soon have to be considered by the Court. It raises some very important issues under Article 6 in respect to the above matter.

b) *Case-law of the Court: the Jones and Others case*

The case concerned three British nationals and a Canadian who alleged that they had been tortured by Saudi officials.[458] They brought civil proceedings in the United Kingdom for damages for personal injury, both against Saudi Arabia and against its officials. The Court of Appeal found that, while Saudi

---

456 *Prosecutor v. Blaskic* (1997) 110 ILR, p. 707.

457 See the judgment of the German Federal Supreme Court in the *Church of Scientology Case* (1978) 65 ILR, p. 193, at p. 198.

458 Three applicants had been arrested, tortured and forced to confess a series of bombings in the country. They spent two-and-a-half years in prison. The fourth applicant, Mr Jones, was injured in a bomb blast in Riyadh and held for more than two months. All applicants were released in 2003 after an al-Qaida bomb attack in Riyadh which disproved official Saudi claims that the attacks were the result of an alcohol turf war among Westerners (See *The Independent*, "Torture' Britons lose bid to sue Saudis", 15 June 2006).

Arabia itself was protected by State immunity,[459] the officials were not.[460] In June 2006, the House of Lords however allowed the appeal by Saudi Arabia with regard to the denial of immunity for to Saudi officials.[461] The case, which appears to be currently being taken to the Strasbourg Court, raises important questions about the relationship between the immunity of State officials and Article 6 of the Convention. It is all the more important since its outcome would very likely apply also to other categories such as former Heads of State or former foreign ministers.

The main question which arose in the *Jones and Others* case (hereafter *Jones*) with regard to the immunity of the Saudi officials was whether or not the alleged conduct, the infliction of torture, could be seen as an official act. If that could be answered in the affirmative, immunity *ratione materiae* would apply. If however the conduct were held to fall outside the scope of official activity, the applicants could have proceeded with their claim under the condition that the remaining requirements of British jurisdiction were met. Thus, the granting of immunity would have violated their right of access to court.

In order to answer this question, the Court of Appeal judges took as a starting point the House of Lords judgments in the *Pinochet* case. It is therefore useful to summarise the main arguments from those judgments in the following. Augusto Pinochet, former dictator of Chile, was arrested in 1998 in London after Spain had requested his extradition regarding criminal charges (inter alia for torture) brought by former victims throughout his dictatorship between 1973 and 1990.[462] In *Pinochet No. 1*, the House of Lords found by three votes to two that, in a nutshell, Pinochet did not enjoy any immunity as a former Head of State for the alleged crimes because the commission of an international crime like torture fell outside the scope of official activity.[463] After that decision was set aside in *Pinochet No. 2* because of one judge's activities for Amnesty International (which had intervened in the proceedings),[464] the House of Lords decided in *Pinochet No. 3* by six

---

[459] See above, pp. 83–84.

[460] *Ronald Grant Jones v. the Ministry of the Interior Al-Mamlaka Al-Arabiya as Saudiya (The Kingdom of Saudi Arabia) & Anor, Sandy Mitchell & Ors v. Ibrahim Al-Dali & Ors*, judgment of the Court of Appeal of 28 October 2004.

[461] United Kingdom House of Lords, *Jones v. Ministry of Interior Al-Mamlaka Al-Arabiya as Saudiya and Others*, judgment of 14 June 2006 (ILM 45 [2006]). The House of Lords, when considering the appeal of the claimants, also found that the Kingdom itself enjoyed State immunity regarding the alleged acts of torture (see above, pp. 97–98).

[462] See Robertson, *Crimes against Humanity*, p. 393 et seq.

[463] *Ex parte Pinochet (No. 1)* (1998), 4 All ER, p. 897.

[464] *R. v. Bow Street Metropolitan Stipendiary Magistrates, Ex parte Pinochet Ugarte (No. 2)* (2000) 1 AC, p. 6.

votes to one that Pinochet did not enjoy any immunity in respect of the alleged crimes.[465] Whereas some judges followed the reasoning of *Pinochet No. 1*, others found that the acts concerned should be considered as being official. However, those judges found that the Contracting States to the UN Torture Convention had implicitly removed the immunity *ratione materiae* of officials from criminal proceedings. Article 1 of the Torture Convention defines torture as a situation in which "pain or suffering is inflicted by or at the instigation of or with the consent or acquiescence of a public official or other person acting in an official capacity". Given that an act of torture therefore required *per definitionem* to be committed in an official capacity, granting immunity from criminal proceedings to officials would eventually lead to the outcome that nobody could ever be prosecuted for torture. As one of the judges put it: "No rational system of criminal justice can allow an immunity which is coextensive with the offence."[466]

In practice, both reasoning differed in that the latter view would only have allowed Pinochet to be extradited for crimes of torture committed after the United Kingdom had ratified the Torture Convention (which it did in 1987). Since Pinochet was not extradited and was finally allowed to return to Chile because of his alleged poor health, the differing views between the members of the House of Lords did not have any real impact on that case. They probably would as far as the *Jones* case is concerned. Admittedly, some judges in the *Pinochet* case considered their judgment to have no effect on the immunity of former Heads of State in civil proceedings for damages. Lord Phillips for instance stated:

> Were these civil proceedings in which damages in respect of acts committed by Senator Pinochet in the government of Chile, Chile could argue that it was itself indirectly impleaded. That argument does not run where the proceedings are criminal and where the issue is Senator Pinochet's personal responsibility, not that of Chile.[467]

(1) *The decision of the Court of Appeal*

When Lord Phillips had to decide on the *Jones* case while it was before the Court of Appeal which found that the State officials were not entitled to immunity, he however changed his mind with regard to the above statement in *Pinochet*:

---

465 *R. v. Bow Street Metropolitan Stipendiary Magistrates, Ex parte Pinochet Ugarte (No. 3)* (2000) 1 AC, p. 147.

466 Ibid., Lord Millett.

467 Ibid., p. 281.

> On reflection I have concluded that the argument does not run in relation to civil proceedings either. If civil proceedings are brought against individuals for acts of torture in circumstances where the state is immune from suit *ratione personae*, there can be no suggestion that the state is vicariously liable. It is the personal responsibility of the individuals, not that of the state, which is in issue. The state is not directly impleaded in the proceedings.[468]

This constitutes the obvious problem with granting States immunity in civil proceedings, but denying it to their officials: one might argue that the proceedings indirectly implead the State, thereby circumventing State immunity and interfering into that State's internal affairs. The Court of Appeal, in particular Lord Justice Mance, did not share these concerns. It regarded a civil claim as no more impleading into the foreign State's affairs than any criminal proceedings against its officer; the responsibility to institute such proceedings being that of the forum State under the UN Torture Convention.[469] Moreover, the foreign State would not be impleaded in a direct sense as there would be no obligation to indemnify any official found to have committed torture.[470] To support this view, the court examined the relevant jurisprudence of US courts under the Alien Tort Claims Act.[471] Moreover, Lord Justice Mance was convinced that Article 1 of the UN Torture Convention did not define torture as an official act: the "public official requirement" would identify the author of the acts, but it did not lend the acts themselves any official or governmental character. Even if it did, the "public official requirement" was only part of the torture definition "for the purposes of the [UN Torture] Convention" (Article 1 of the Convention) and its scope should not be extended to the context of immunities.[472]

Regarding the execution of any civil judgments obtained by torture victims before the courts of the forum State, the Court of Appeal did not share the doubts of judges Bratza and Pellonpää which they described in their concurring opinion in *Al-Adsani*:[473] claims against individuals officials would not raise problems regarding execution against State property because those individuals' assets could be made object of the execution.[474] It also considered that the granting of immunity to officials would amount to a disproportion-

---

[468] *Ronald Grant Jones v. the Ministry of the Interior Al-Mamlaka Al-Arabiya as Saudiya (The Kingdom of Saudi Arabia) & Anor, Sandy Mitchell & Ors v. Ibrahim Al-Dali & Ors*, judgment of the Court of Appeal of 28 October 2004, para. 128.

[469] Ibid., paras. 71 et seq.

[470] Ibid., para. 84.

[471] Ibid., paras. 58–68.

[472] Ibid., para. 70.

[473] See above, pp. 94 and 105.

[474] Ibid., para. 77.

ate restriction of the victim's right of access to court under Article 6 (1). This was because of the absence of any settled international principle affording the State the right to claim immunity in respect of its officials (in comparison to the State itself or its diplomats or Heads of State). The Court of Appeal found that it was a relevant factor whether or not an adequate remedy was provided by the State where the torture occurred (as required by Article 14 of the UN Torture Convention), thereby bringing into play the "alternative remedy" criterion, which the Strasbourg Court had not applied in the *Al-Adsani*-case.[475] Lastly, the Court of Appeal considered that the applicable domestic law, the United Kingdom State Immunity Act, did not expressly cover the civil liability of State officials for torture. The gap could not be filled by the assertion that the immunity possessed by a State should be mirrored by an immunity possessed by the official whose behaviour has given rise to the State's immunity.[476]

(2) *Criticism of the judgment*

The judgment of the Court of Appeal was criticised by one writer as "a prime example of how radical a court can be in its eagerness to protect human rights".[477] It was alleged that the court had disregarded the relevant legislation and read an extremely liberal understanding into the UN Torture Convention. Such criticism is probably too harsh. The reasoning of the Court of Appeal, while making a courageous attempt to restrict immunity in favour of torture victims, however suffers from two inconsistencies.

First, the Court of Appeal based its finding on the premises that torture cannot be an official act because it is so illegal that it must fall outside the scope of official activity. But to apply this finding in a consequent manner would also require the qualification of torture as an "*acta iure gestionis*" for the purposes of State immunity. This would eventually mean denying immunity not only to State officials, but to States as well. The Court of Appeal was however not willing to do so when finding that Saudi Arabia was protected by State immunity. One might object that international practice widely recognises State-inflicted torture as an official act, whereas there is much less of a consensus about the nature of the act with regard to the immunity of State officials. Nevertheless, there would remain an asymmetry to find that torture is an official act as far as State immunity is concerned, but not for the purposes of the immunity of State officials. This was also noted by Yang, who commented on the *Jones* judgment that "[...] the Court obviously read

[475] Ibid., paras. 85–86.

[476] Ibid., para. 91.

[477] Yang, *Universal Tort Jurisdiction over Torture?*, Cambridge Law Journal 2005, p. 1.

the Torture Convention in different ways depending on whose immunity was in question."[478]

The second inconsistency is closely related to the above. In its Article 1, the UN Torture Convention defines torture as a crime which can only be committed by a person in an official capacity. Nevertheless, the Court of Appeal characterised torture an act which would fall outside official capacity. As Lord Hoffmann has rightly pointed out, it would create an "asymmetry between the Torture Convention and the rules of immunity if it were to be held that the same act was official for the purposes of the definition of torture but not for the purposes of immunity".[479] Because of these inconsistencies, the approach by the House of Lords described below is to be preferred.

(3) *The decision of the House of Lords*

The House of Lords, in a judgment delivered on 14 June 2006, found that the same immunity against suit in a foreign domestic court which protects the State itself also protects the individuals for whom the State is responsible.[480] Lord Hoffmann referred to Article 2 (1) (b) of the UN Immunity Convention which defines "State" to include "representatives of the State acting in that capacity". Even though the applicable domestic law, the United Kingdom State Immunity Act, did not expressly mention officials, the Act had to be read against the background of international law, including the UN Convention on the Jurisdictional Immunities of States and their Property or the UN Torture Convention, which say nothing to remove the immunity of individuals from civil proceedings.[481]

The House of Lords also disagreed with the Court of Appeal upon the nature of the acts in question. Lord Hoffmann considered cases and materials on State liability and concluded that the State is liable for acts done under public authority, whether or not authorised or lawful. In particular, he referred to a draft UN Treaty on the Responsibility of States for Intentional Wrongful Acts. Article 7 of the draft provides that "the conduct of an organ of a state or a person or entity empowered to exercise elements

[478] Ibid., p. 3. For a further discussion of the judgment see Fox, *Where does the buck stop? State Immunity from Civil Jurisdiction and Torture*, LQR 2005, p. 359, ibid., *State Immunity and the International Crime of Torture*, EHRLR 2006, p. 150, Parlett, *Immunity in Civil Proceedings for Torture: the Emerging Exception*, EHRLR 2006, p. 62; Clapham, *The* Jus Cogens *Prohibition of Torture and the Importance of Sovereign State Immunity*, Liber Amicorum Lucius Caflisch, p. 165.

[479] United Kingdom House of Lords, *Jones v. Ministry of Interior Al-Mamlaka Al-Arabiya as Saudiya and others*, judgment of 14 June 2006, para. 79.

[480] Ibid., para. 66.

[481] Ibid., paras. 70–71.

of the government authority shall be considered an act of the state under international law if the organ, person or entity acts in that capacity, *even if it exceeds its authority or contravenes instructions.*"[482] Since there was nothing to suggest that this provision would not apply to acts of torture, the Court of Appeal's finding would produce an asymmetry between the rules of liability and immunity.[483] As to the Court of Appeal's finding that the definition of "torture" in the Torture Convention did not make torture necessarily an official act, Lord Hoffmann reasoned:

> I do not, with respect, find this answer satisfactory. The acts of torture are either official acts or they are not. The Torture Convention does not "lend" them an official character; they must be official to come within the Convention in the first place. And if they are official enough to come within the Convention, I cannot see why they are not official enough to attract immunity.[484]

The House of Lords also pointed to several legal academics who disagreed with the characterisation of torture as a "private act". Whereas some described the argument as "unsound and even preposterous" and stressed that the "artificiality of this legal construct is evident",[485] others regarded it as an argument "which can be easily discarded"[486] or which "was directly contrary to international law".[487] However, it should be added that the opposite view taken by the Court of Appeal also finds support amongst some legal writers.[488]

(4) *The case before the European Court of Human Rights, Conclusion*
The applicants, who were backed by several NGOs such as Amnesty International, brought their case to the Strasbourg Court in 2006.[489] If the Court has to decide upon the application, it can be presumed that this will become another landmark judgment regarding the conflict between immunities and the right of access to court. Given the tiny minority in the *Al-Adsani*-case

482 Emphasis added.

483 Ibid., para. 78.

484 Ibid., para. 83.

485 Cassesse, *When May Senior State Officials be Tried for International Crimes? Some Comments on the Congo v Belgium Case*, EJIL 2002, p. 869.

486 Gattini, *War Crimes and State Immunity in the* Ferrini *Decision*, JICJ 2005, p. 234 at Fn. 41.

487 Fox, *Where does the buck stop? State Immunity from Civil Jurisdiction and Torture*, LQR 2005, p. 355.

488 Robertson, *Crimes Against Humanity*, p. 420; Bianchi, *Denying State Immunity to Violators of Human Rights*, Austrian Journal of Public and International Law 1993/94, p. 227.

489 See *The Independent*, "'Torture' Britons lose bid to sue Saudis", 15 June 2006. The applications are *Jones v. the United Kingdom* (no. 34356/06) and *Mitchell and Others v. the United Kingdom* (no. 40528/06).

concerning the relationship between State immunity and *jus cogens*, the present matter (*i.e.* whether torture can be regarded as an official act for the purposes of the immunity of State officials) could prove no less controversial.[490] If one wants to count numbers: eight Court of Appeal judges and members of the House of Lords in the *Pinochet* and *Jones and Others* cases found that torture could not be considered as an official act, whereas seven held the opposite. When the *Al-Adsani* case was decided in 2001, Judge Ferrari Bravo deplored that the Court had missed "a golden opportunity to issue a clear and forceful condemnation of all acts of torture".[491] It might well be that the Court will consider that this occasion has come in the *Jones and Others* case. In the Court of Appeal judgment in *Jones and Others*, Lord Phillips commented on the *Al-Adsani* judgment as follows:

> Had the Grand Chamber been considering a claim for state immunity in relation to claims brought against individuals, I do not believe that there would have been a majority in favour of the view that this represented a legitimate limitation on the right to access to a court under Article 6 (1).[492]

For the above reasons, however, the reasoning of the House of Lords in the *Jones and Others* case and the conclusion that the granting of immunity was not a disproportionate restriction on the right of access to court is to be preferred.

IV. *Immunity of International Organisations*

The conflict between immunities of international organisations and Article 6 (1) involves a three-party relationship which can be summarised as follows: the first party is the individual who enjoys a right of access to court under the Convention; the second is the international organisation with certain obligations regarding the individual (e.g. contractual liability) and which enjoys immunity from suit; and lastly, there is the Contracting State, which might both be obliged to provide the individual with an opportunity to institute proceedings and at the same time to grant immunity to the organisation.

International organisations first emerged during the second half of the 19th century, but have become significant in number and importance only

---

[490] In this respect, it is interesting to note that two of the Court's most distinguished international lawyers who voted for a violation of Article 6 in *Al-Adsani*, Judges Wildhaber and Caflisch, have meanwhile left the Court.

[491] *Al-Adsani v. the United Kingdom*, dissenting opinion of Judge Bravo.

[492] United Kingdom House of Lords, *Jones v. Ministry of Interior Al-Mamlaka Al-Arabiya as Saudiya and others*, judgment of 14 June 2006, para. 134.

since the end of the Second World War. Just as international organisations are therefore newly-involved entities, so their privileges and immunities have only recently become the subject of negotiations, practical arrangements and academic studies.[493]

1. *Reasons for the immunity of international organisations*

There are several reasons why international organisations enjoy immunity from the jurisdiction of its Member States, especially the ones in which they are temporarily or permanently located. Whereas State immunity finds its basis in the equality and sovereignty of States (*par in parem non habet jurisdictionem*), the immunity of international organisations, which lack such sovereignty, is seen as necessary for the efficient fulfilment of the organisations' purposes.[494] The independence and impartiality of an international organisation has to be protected from the diverging interests and direct influence of its Member States, in particular the host State in which the organisation is located.[495] It is considered unacceptable for individual governments to be able, whether through their executive, legislative or judicial organs, to require an international organisation to take certain actions by commands addressed to the organisation itself or to any of its officials.[496] Hence the argument goes that a national court would not be the appropriate forum for individual claims against such organisations.[497] There exists also the danger that acts performed by an organisation might be judged differently under the various jurisdictions of its Member States.[498] To avoid this requires uniform regulation of those acts.

Immunities for international organisations are usually agreed upon by an international treaty. This can either be the convention creating the organisation,

---

[493] Szasz, *International Organisations*, EPIL II, p. 1325.

[494] See in general Shaw, *International Law*, p. 1205 et seq.; Wenckstern, *Die Immunität internationaler Organisationen* (1994); Council of Europe, *Privileges and Immunities of International Organisations*; Reinisch, *International Organisations before National Courts*; Gaillard/Pingel-Lenuzza, *International Organisations and Immunity from Jurisdiction: To Restrict or To Bypass*, ICLQ 2002, p. 1; Bröhmer, *Die völkerrechtliche Immunität von der staatlichen Gerichtsbarkeit und die Verfahrensgarantien der EMRK- Einige Anmerkungen zu den Urteilen des Europäischen Gerichtshofs für Menschenrechte in den Fällen Waite & Kennedy und Beer & Regan gegen die Bundesrepublik Deutschland*, p. 85; *Mukuro v. European Bank for Reconstruction and Development*, decision of the Employment Appeal Tribunal (1994) ICR 897 (903).

[495] Habscheid, *Die durch Art. 6 I EMRK beschränkte Immunität internationaler Organisationen im Erkenntnisverfahren*, IPrax 2001, p. 397.

[496] Szasz, *International Organisations*, EPIL II, p. 1326.

[497] Wenckstern, *Die Immunität internationaler Organisationen*, p. 18.

[498] Jenks, *International Immunities*, p. 40.

for instance the Charter of the United Nations: according to Article 105 (1) of the Charter, the organisation shall enjoy in the territory of each of its Member States the privileges and immunities as are necessary for the fulfilment of its purposes. However, those rules are usually rather basic. Therefore, Member States of an international organisation can also sign and ratify a special treaty on the immunity of the organisation. This was for instance the case with the "General Convention on the Privileges and Immunities of the United Nations" of 1946 (the so-called "prototype" of immunity treaties for international organisations) or, more recently, the "Agreement on the Privileges and Immunities of the International Criminal Court" of 2002. Thirdly, immunities might be provided for by the headquarters agreement between the organisation and the host State.[499] In many countries, international treaties concerning privileges and immunities of international organisations have been implemented into domestic law by specific legislation, for example the UK International Organisations Act 1968 or the US International Organisations Immunity Act of 1945.[500]

2. *The scope of the immunity of international organisations*

It is not only the international organisation which enjoys immunity. As such organisations can only act through their organs, staff members may also be protected while exercising their functions for all actions taken in their official capacity.[501] For example, Article 105 (2) of the Charter of the United Nations

[499] For example, the UN has concluded headquarters agreements with the United States and Switzerland for its headquarters in New York and Geneva (see Shaw, *International Law*, p. 924).

[500] See Shaw, *International Law*, p. 1211.

[501] Jenks, *International Immunities*, p. 114; see also Koster, *Immunität internationaler Richter*, pp. 75–95. The immunities enjoyed by the members of the Convention organs serve as an illustrative example: Article 40 of the Statute of the Council of Europe and the agreements made there under grant staff members certain privileges and immunities during their discharge and their functions. Article 59 of the Convention declares these immunities applicable to the members of the Commission and the Court. These privileges and immunities are laid down in detail in the Second and Fourth Protocol to the General Agreement on Privileges and Immunities of the Council of Europe (*Collected texts of the Council of Europe*, Strasbourg 1994, pp. 204–207 – Immunity of the Commission members – and pp. 299–301 – Immunity of the judges of the Court –). See further: Frowein/Peukert, *EMRK*, pp. 737–738 (on Article 59); Robertson/Merrils, *Human Rights in Europe*, pp. 297–299; van Dijk/van Hoof, *Theory and Practice*, p. 28 (Commission members) and p. 33 (judges). These rules have rarely been relied on in practice, though. However, in the case of *Zoernsch v. Waldock and McNulty* ([1964] 2 AllER, p. 256), the plaintiff had tried to sue the president of the Commission for having declared inadmissible his application under Article 34 of the European Convention on Human Rights. The British Court which

provides that "Representatives (...) and officials (...) shall similarly enjoy such privileges and immunities as are necessary for the independent exercise of their functions in connexion with the organisation."

There is as yet no general agreement on the precise content and scope of the immunity of international organisations.[502] However, it appears that, unlike States, international organisations still enjoy absolute immunity under current public international law,[503] unless the organisation decides to waive its immunity, which however does not appear to be of much relevance in practice.[504] Absolute immunity also includes immunity for *acta jure gestionis*. The reason for this is that the legal personality of these organisations is limited to its special functions; hence all acts are so deeply connected with the organisation's official function that the situation is comparable to the one of States in the 19th century, when the doctrine of absolute immunity was still applied.[505] Today, judicial decisions which are seeking to limit the immunity of international organisations to *acta jure imperii* (and consequently to the same extent as State immunity) still form a minority. Such a view has been taken by the Italian *Corte di Cassazione* and some Italian legal scholars.[506] The majority of court decisions and legal writers would strongly oppose such a view.[507]

---

decided on the case found that the Commission members were entitled to immunity from suit during their discharge and their functions due to the reference made in Article 59 of the Convention. It appears that the plaintiff did not pursue his claim any further. Hence the case never made its way to the Convention organs in Strasbourg. However, there would have been a certain irony if the Commission had to consider whether the immunity granted to its own members violated the applicant's right of access to court under Article 6 (1).

502 Brownlie, *Principles*, p. 683.

503 On the other hand, the immunity of international organisations is more limited in a geographical sense. With the exception of the United Nations, immunities of international organisations only apply to their Member States (Koster, *Immunität internationaler Richter*, p. 44). However, it is arguable that non-Member States might be obliged to grant immunity under customary international law. The latter is subject to debate, and attempts by the International Law Commission to codify such a rule have so far not suceeded (see Graf Vitzthum/Klein, *Völkerrecht*, p. 313).

504 Graf Vitzthum/Klein, *Völkerrecht*, p. 311.

505 Koster, *Immunität internationaler Richter*, p. 45.

506 E. Habscheid, *Immunität internationaler Organisationen und Art. 6 I EMRK (insbesondere zum Rechtsschutz der Bediensteten)*, p. 263 (with further references). See also the article by Reinisch/Weberm (*In the Shadow of Waite and Kennedy*, IOLR 2004, p. 81) for references to unpublished decisions of both a German and a Greek court.

507 For a general overview, see Council of Europe, *Privileges and Immunities of International Organisations*; Reinisch, *International Organisations before National Courts.*

3. *The conflict between immunity of international organisations and Article 6 (1) of the Convention*

Given the above, it can hardly be said that the immunity of international organisations is in flux compared with the immunity of States. Individuals whose claims against international organisations are barred by immunity still face an international practice which is widely uniform and accepted. That makes it difficult to argue that the right of access to court should trump such immunities without provoking the objection that the Strasbourg Court would abuse its jurisdiction to modernise public international law. Moreover, the majority of disputes in which international organisations are involved are employment disputes. The restriction of immunity would probably not have a favourable effect as it would give the State in which the organisation's headquarters is located considerable power to influence that organisation's internal affairs.

On the other hand, the right of access to court is a human right which represents the rule of law, a fundamental value in a democratic society. Unlike State immunity, the privileges of international organisations are regularly afforded to them by the treaty on which they are founded. Hence these immunities were usually created by States at a time when the Convention was already in force, and its Contracting States were already obliged to grant individuals within their jurisdiction access to their courts.[508] Thus, it is also not consistent to argue that a limitation on Article 6 (1) was taken for granted by the drafters of the Convention with respect to these immunities. Additionally, there is a certain danger that, with the increasing appearance of such organisations in order to face tasks which need to be coordinated at the international level, States may increasingly remove outside the scope of the Convention disputes between those organisations and individuals.

There appear to be two ways to solve that conflict. The first would be to restrict the immunity of international organisations to the same extent as State immunity. Although favoured by some,[509] the difficulties the Court would create by modernising the rules of public international law on a regional basis have already been mentioned.[510] Second, international organisations could provide "alternative means" as compensation for the individual's loss of access to the domestic courts due to the operation of immunities. This is indeed what international organisations often do. With regard to

---

[508] Unless one argues that such rules are in any event granted by customary international law and already existed at the time the Convention went into force.

[509] Gaillard/Pingel-Lenuzza, *International Organisations and Immunity from Jurisdiction: To Restrict or To Bypass*, ICLQ 2002, p. 1.

[510] See also Maierhöfer, *Der EGMR als Modernisierer des Völkerrechts?*, EuGRZ 2002, p. 395.

employment disputes, staff members of an international organisation will usually have recourse to an administrative tribunal. Such tribunals can either be established by the organisation itself, or the organisation submits itself to the administrative tribunal of another organisation. Examples are the United Nations Administrative Tribunal, the International Labour Organisation Administrative Tribunal, the World Bank Administrative Tribunal, or, as far as regional organisations are concerned, the Council of Europe's Administrative Tribunal or the European Union Civil Service Tribunal. Such tribunals have its own statutes in which the procedural rules are laid down. For example, the United Nations Administrative Tribunal is the independent organ competent to hear and pass judgment upon applications alleging non-observance of contracts of employment of UN staff members.[511] The Tribunal is composed of seven members and adopts its judgments by majority vote. There is no appeal, but hearings are held in public (Article 9 of the Statute of the Tribunal). The Council of Europe's Administrative Tribunal has its own Statute, according to which cases are heard by three judges who are not staff members of the Council and who reach their decisions by a majority vote.[512] No appeal lies against decisions (Article 12 of the Staff Regulations). Based on the Treaty of Nice, the Council of the European Union established in 2004 the European Union Civil Service Tribunal which decides on disputes between the European Union and its civil service (a jurisdiction formerly exercised by the Court of First Instance).[513] Its decisions will be subject to appeal on questions of law only to the Court of First Instance and, in exceptional cases, to review by the Court of Justice.

To settle disputes with third parties (such as contractors or persons injured by tortuous acts), some organisations have also provided for resort to their administrative tribunals.[514] Alternatively, persons with no employment relationship with the international organisation can claim their rights in arbitration proceedings which are sometimes included in contracts between the organisation and the third party. Another possibility for the organisation is to procure insurance, and to require the insurance company to defend suits arising under the policy.[515]

---

[511] See the United Nations Administrative Tribunal's website: http://untreaty.un.org/UNAT/main_page.htm.

[512] See Westerdiek, *Le Tribunal Administratif du Conseil de l'Europe: Présentation et Apercu de la Jurisprudence*, Liber Amicorum Lucius Caflisch, p. 951.

[513] See the European Union's press release of 2 November 2004 under: http://curia.europa.eu/en/ actu/communiques/ cp04/info/CP040088EN.pdf.

[514] Szasz, *International Organisations*, EPIL II, p. 1331.

[515] Ibid.

4. *The case-law of the Convention organs*

Case-law of the Convention organs is still very sparse. But the following decisions demonstrate that the Strasbourg organs have considerably developed their approach. Whereas the Commission initially held that the present conflict does not raise any issue under Article 6 (1), the decisions and judgments of the Commission and the Court in the cases of *Waite and Kennedy v. Germany* and *Beer and Regan v. Germany* imply that there is a potential violation of the right of access to court in the absence of sufficient alternative means.

a) *Case-law of the Commission: the case of Spaans v. Netherlands*

In the case of *Spaans v. Netherlands*,[516] a former employee of the *Iran-United States Claims Tribunal*[517] had brought a claim concerning his dismissal from the organisation before the Dutch courts. Although the Hague District Court declared itself competent to deal with the issue, the decision was later quashed on appeal by the Regional Court for lack of jurisdiction due to the immunity enjoyed by the Claims Tribunal as an international organisation. The decision of the Regional Court was confirmed by the Supreme Court which found that "under present international law an international organisation is, in principle, not subject to the jurisdiction of the courts in the host State concerning disputes that have a direct connection with the fulfilment of the organisation's task".[518] Subsequent to these decisions, the applicant made an application to the Commission alleging a violation of Article 6 (1). The application was declared inadmissible by the Commission because the applicant did not come within the jurisdiction of the Netherlands within the meaning of Article 1 of the Convention:

> Because of the immunity enjoyed by the Tribunal, the administrative decisions of the Tribunal are not acts which occur within the jurisdiction of the Netherlands within the meaning of Article 1 of the Convention and thus do not engage the responsibility of the Netherlands under the Convention.[519]

That view, which was also taken by a Commission member in his concurring opinion in the case of *Waite and Kennedy v. Germany*,[520] has already

[516] *Spaans v. Netherlands*, D/R 58, p. 119. The decision was discussed in *Waite and Kennedy v. Germany* (no. 26083/94), Commission Decision of 24 February 1997, EHHR 1999, p. 270, para. 51 and in the concurring opinion of Mr Herndl, (ibid, p. 279).

[517] The Tribunal was established by the Claims Settlement Agreement between the Islamic Republic of Iran and the United States, see *Spaans v. Netherlands*, D/R 58, p. 120.

[518] Ibid., p. 121.

[519] Ibid., p. 122.

[520] Concurring opinion by Mr Herndl, para. 2 (see above, p. 27).

been criticized above: as the forum State merely *refrains* from exercising its jurisdiction as a concession (as opposed to not having jurisdiction at all), this must be in conformity with other international obligations such as the European Convention on Human Rights.[521] A similar approach was also taken by the Civil Tribunal of Brussels in the case of *Manderlier v. Organisation des Nations Unies and Etat Belge*,[522] in which the Tribunal rejected the plaintiff's argument that the United Nation's immunity from suit in Belgium violated Article 6 (1) because "the Convention was concluded between (...) European States only, and cannot be applied to and imposed upon the United Nations". That reasoning however appears to be based on a misconception. It is not the United Nations (or any other international organisation involved in the domestic proceedings before the courts of the forum State) upon which the Convention rights "are being imposed". It is the Contracting Parties which guarantee the right of access under Article 6 (1), but at the same time increasingly hand over powers to international organisations. If such organisations are immune from suit, it is the Contracting States that might violate the Convention, not the international organisation.[523] What the Belgian court perhaps tried to indicate is the problem that Article 6 (1) might be used to impose domestic court proceedings upon an international organisation; an argument which has been considered by the Court in *Waite and Kennedy v. Germany* and which is being discussed below. The Commission in *Spaans* also rejected the application for other reasons:

> (...) it is in accordance with international law that States confer immunities and privileges to international bodies like the Iran-United States Claims Tribunal which are situated in their territory. The Commission does not consider that such a restriction of national sovereignty in order to facilitate the working of an international body gives rise to an issue under the Convention.[524]

The *Spaans v. Netherlands* case was decided in 1988, at a time when the Strasbourg organs were still not very sensitive regarding the conflict between immunities and Article 6. It took almost another decade until the Commission however found that the immunity of an international organisation indeed raises numerous issues as to its compatibility with the right of access to court.

---

[521] See above, pp. 26–31.

[522] Civil Tribunal of Brussels, 11 May 1966; on appeal decided by the Brussels Appeals Court, 15 September 1969; cited by Reinisch, *International Organisations before National Courts*, p. 289.

[523] Any direct complaint against an international organisation with the Strasbourg Court would be incompatible *ratione personae* with the provisions of the Convention, Article 35 (4).

[524] *Spaans v. Netherlands*, D/R 58, p. 122.

b) *The Cases of* Waite and Kennedy v. Germany and Beer and Regan v. Germany

Both cases were decided by the Court at the same time and are identical in their wording. They both involve claims of individuals against an international organisation, the European Space Agency (ESA). All applicants were employed and hired out by private firms to ESA's German office, for which the applicants were then working temporarily ("temporarily" actually meaning periods up to seventeen years). Pursuant to the German Provision of Labour (Temporary Staff) Act, the hiring out of the applicants normally would have required the approval of the respective authorities. In the absence of such approval, the Act provides that such contracts are void, but the Act creates a fictitious employment relationship *ex lege* with the hirer. The applicants therefore sought to obtain a court decision to declare that they had acquired the status of employees of ESA. Before the domestic German labour courts, ESA successfully relied on its immunity from jurisdiction.

(1) *The decisions of the Court*

Whereas the Court unanimously found that the restriction on Article 6 (1) was proportionate, the Commission had earlier come to the same conclusion, albeit with the much narrower margin of seventeen votes to fifteen. As to the question whether the immunity of ESA pursued a legitimate aim, the Court followed the German government and the Commission in holding that immunities of international organisations are an essential means of ensuring the proper functioning of such organisations, free from unilateral interference by individual governments.[525] It observed a trend towards extending and strengthening international cooperation in all domains in modern society, which would make the grant of immunities even more important.[526] The key point of the cases was again the question of proportionality. Unlike the Commission in *Spaans*, the Court was more critical of the effects immunity from suit might have upon the individual:

> (...) where States (...) attribute to these organisations certain competences and accord them immunities, there may be implications as to the protection of fundamental rights. It would be incompatible with the purpose and object of the Convention, however, if the Contracting States were thereby absolved from their responsibility under the Convention in relation to the field of activity covered by such attribution. It should be recalled that the Convention is intended

---

[525] *Waite and Kennedy v. Germany*, [GC] (no. 26083/95), Judgment of 18 February 1999; RJD 1999-I; *Beer and Regan v. Germany* [GC] (no. 28934/95), Judgment of 18 February 1999.

[526] *Waite and Kennedy v. Germany*, para. 63.

> to guarantee not theoretical or illusory rights, but rights that are practical and effective. This is particularly true for the right of access to the courts (...).[527]

Therefore, the Court considered the granting of an immunity a potential violation of Article 6 (1) which could be avoided if the applicants had available to them reasonable alternative means to protect effectively their rights under the Convention.[528] The Court pointed out that the applicants could have brought their case to the ESA Appeals Board based in Paris, which is independent of the ESA. Moreover, the Court referred to the possibility for the applicants to seek redress from the firms that hired them out to ESA. In suing those firms for damages, the Court pointed out that a judicial clarification of the nature of the labour relationship could be obtained.[529] It held that the restriction on Article 6 (1) had been proportionate, in particular in view of the following:

> The test of proportionality cannot be applied in such a way as to compel an international organisation to submit itself to national litigation in relation to employment conditions prescribed under national labour law. To read Art. 6 (1) of the Convention and its guarantee of access to court as necessarily requiring the application of national legislation in such matters would, in the Court's view, thwart the proper functioning of international organisations (...).[530]

Thus, the Court held unanimously that there had been no violation of Article 6 (1).

(2) *Discussion of the judgments*

The latter point in the judgment has been criticised as confusing the question of material law (*i.e.* the applicability of the German law in the present case) with the rather formal immunity-problem. It almost appears that the Court considered that the effect of the German Labour Provision Act (which creates *ex lege* an employment relationship between temporary workers and their hirer) to be disproportionate and that ESA had to be protected from it.[531] But this would not have been a question of jurisdiction. As Mr. Ress in his dissenting opinion (joint by fourteen other Commission members) rightly pointed out:

---

[527] *Waite and Kennedy v. Germany*, para. 67.

[528] Ibid., para. 68.

[529] *Beer and Regan v. Germany*, para. 60.

[530] Ibid., para. 62; *Waite and Kennedy v. Germany*, para. 72.

[531] See Bröhmer, *Die völkerrechtliche Immunität von der staatlichen Gerichtsbarkeit und die Verfahrensgarantien der EMRK – Einige Anmerkungen zu den Urteilen des Europäischen Gerichtshofs für Menschenrechte in den Fällen Waite & Kennedy und Beer & Regan gegen die Bundesrepublik Deutschland*, p. 90.

> (…) I find that the question as to whether and to what extent domestic legislation (…) can be held against an international organisation, which regularly enacts its own staff regulations, cannot be resolved in removing such matters from judicial review.[532]

The real weakness of the Court's judgments in the two cases was however that it failed to properly consider whether or not the applicants had alternative means at their disposal, as this was obviously the crucial point of the case. As far as the Court pointed to the applicants' option to sue their firms for damages, the implied judicial clarification of the nature of the labour relationship would not have any binding effect under German civil procedural law in subsequent proceedings. This means would have hardly been helpful for the applicants in attempting to obtain recognition of permanent employment by ESA. As one of the Commission members stated: the right of access to court cannot be interpreted in a way that it would amount to "a right to access to court (…) on another legal claim".[533]

As to the applicant's opportunity to avail themselves of the ESA Appeals Board, the Court should have asked whether the Appeals Board had jurisdiction both *ratione personae* and *ratione materiae.* According to the ESA Staff Regulations, the Board has jurisdiction "to hear disputes relating to any explicit or implicit decision taken by the Agency and arising between it and a staff member". But were the applicants "staff members" of the organisation? Practice of administrative tribunals of other international organisations suggests that "staff members" are only those employees which became staff personnell in accordance with the recruitment regulations of the international organisation. A temporary worker hired out to the European Southern Observatory for instance was not considered a "staff member" by the administrative tribunal of the International Labour Organisation.[534]

Moreover, the Court failed to properly assure itself that the ESA Appeals Board was competent to settle the question whether or not German law applied in the present dispute. The mere mentioning of the Appeals Board's existence cannot suffice unless it has been ensured that the main question in the dispute could be solved by making use of the alternative means. It has

---

532 In the dissenting opinion, concern was expressed that States could evade their responsibility under the Convention by treaties that create international organisations with specific competence and jurisdiction. In any circumstances, immunities could not be considered as a kind of general unwritten exception to the scope of the application of the Convention (*Waite and Kennedy v. Germany*, dissenting opinion by Judge Ress).

533 *Waite and Kennedy v. Germany*, Commission decision, EHHR 1999, p. 282.

534 Decision No. 1302 of 31 January 1993 by the ILO-Tribunal; cited by E. Habscheid, *Immunität internationaler Organisationen und Art. 6 I EMRK (insbesondere zum Rechtsschutz der Bediensteten)*, p. 269.

been alleged that the applicants ended up without having this decisive question determined by neither a German court, nor by the Appeals Board.[535] This criticism is however a bit misleading. The applicants later had recourse to the ESA Appeals Board which however rejected their complaint in June 2000. Regarding the applicability of the German Labour Provision Act, the Appeals Board found that:

> Pour résoudre la question de savoir si MM. Beer et Regan sont membres du personnel de l'Agence, la Commission estime nécessaire de déterminer les règles de droit applicables au présent litige. Les requérants estiment que c'est la loi allemande du 7 août 1982 [i.e. the German Labour Provision Act]. La Commission ne partage pas ce point de vue.[536]

Recalling that ESA is the successor organisation of the European Space Research Organisation (ESRO), the Appeals Board reasoned that the former had made an agreement with the Federal Republic of Germany in 1967 that ESRO's activities in Germany should be subject to German law, unless ESRO's protocol on immunities and privileges applied.[537] Labour disputes with staff members employed under ESRO's "Statut du personnel" were not subject to German law, whereas contracts of other categories of staff members were. It therefore appears that, had the applicants been hired out to ESA's predecessor, German law would have applied to the dispute. The Appeals Board however found that, when ESA was established as ESRO's successor organisation, a new regime of immunities and privileges had been introduced which eventually made the 1967 agreement redundant.[538] As a consequence, labour disputes between the organisations and all "staff members" were no longer subject to German law.

It is not decisive in the present context whether that reasoning was preferable, but it can be said that it was not unreasonable or arbitrary. Therefore, the applicant finally had their question determined by an independent tribunal (albeit not by a court). Arguably, the interference with their right of access was therefore proportionate. However, the Court should have been more precise and critical when considering the alternative remedies in the present case. It could have insisted that the labour courts had ensured themselves that the applicant's claim was decided upon elsewhere before granting

---

535 See E. Habscheid, *Immunität internationaler Organisationen und Art. 6 I EMRK (insbesondere zum Rechtsschutz der Bediensteten)*, pp. 271–272.

536 The decision is unpublished, but summarised in French in the Court's decision *Beer and Regan v. Germany* (II) (no. 70009/01), Decision of 15 May 2003. The expression in brackets was added.

537 Ibid.

538 Ibid.

immunity to the defendant organisation. Other courts have been more critical in this respect. In the *Eurocontrol* case, the Federal Constitutional Court of Germany was only prepared to grant immunity to that international organisation after it had assured itself that the respective tribunal that would provide for alternative remedies was adequate:

> [T]he status and principles of procedure of the tribunal also reflect an international minimum standard for a fair trial as it has emerged from developed systems for the rule of law and from the rules of procedure of international courts; altogether they do not contradict [...] the minimum requirements for the rule of law [...].[539]

The judgments of *Waite and Kennedy v. Germany* and *Beer and Regan v. Germany* however lack a critical assessment of the alternative remedies which were available to the applicants.

c) *The case of* Beer and Regan v. Germany (II)

After the ESA Appeals Board dismissed the applicant's claim, two of the applicants returned to the Court with a fresh application. This time they complained that they did not have access to court in order to challenge that decision. Their application was again dismissed by the Court as being manifestly ill-founded. Because the applicants had meanwhile made friendly settlements with the companies that had hired them out, they had received compensation for the loss of their employment. The dismissal of their claim by the Appeals Board could therefore not be considered as a disproportionate interference.[540] In deciding in this way, the Court avoided answering a thorny question which is closely related to the immunity of international organisations: in what way can applicants challenge before the Court acts of an international organisation which is (at least partly) composed of Contracting Parties to the Convention? This will be briefly addressed in the following section.

5. *Liability for acts of international organisations*

International organisations are not Contracting Parties to the Convention and therefore not bound by it.[541] However, one could argue that Member States of international organisations are responsible for the latter's acts because the former have created these organisations and transferred their

[539] BVerfG 59, p. 63; cited and discussed by Reinisch/Weber, *In the Shadow of Waite and Kennedy*, IOLR 2004, pp. 78 and 105.

[540] *Beer and Regan v. Germany* (II) (no. 70009/01), Decision of 15 May 2003.

[541] Grabenwarter, *Europäische Menschenrechtskonvention*, § 4, 5 et seq.

competencies in this respect. Issues have in particular arisen regarding acts of the European Commission and the European Court of Justice, but also regarding acts of Member States in order to comply with EU law.[542]

In *M. & Co. v. Germany*, the Commission found that Member States of the European Union are in principle responsible for acts of the European Union (in that case the German authorities' execution of a fine by the European Commission for a breach of the EC's competition rules which was upheld by the European Court of Justice). However, as long as equivalent protection of fundamental rights existed at EU level, Member States could not be held responsible for the manner in which EU institutions decided issues of human rights in those cases.[543] The Commission took the view that it would be contrary to the very idea of transferring powers to an international organisation to hold the Member States responsible for examining, in each individual case before issuing a writ of execution for a judgment of the European Court of Justice, whether Article 6 was respected in the underlying proceedings.[544] Hence it held that the application was inadmissible *ratione materiae* with the provisions of the Convention. This so-called "equivalent protection doctrine" resembled the *Solange II*-jurisprudence of the Federal Constitutional Court of Germany.[545]

In the case of *Matthews v. the United Kingdom*, the Court found the United Kingdom responsible under Article 3 of Protocol No. 1 (right to free elections) for the lack of elections in Gibraltar (where the applicant, a British citizen, resided) to the European parliament.[546] It found that, notwithstanding the transfer of competencies to the European Community, Contracting States remained responsible for ensuring that Convention rights were guaranteed once they ratified international treaties subsequent to the applicability of the Convention guarantees.[547] The Court also stressed that, where no other judicial body is competent to review acts of the international organisation, it will consider complaints of violations of the Convention rights.

---

542 See Schäfer, *Verletzungen der Europäischen Menschenrechtskonvention durch Europäisches Gemeinschaftsrecht und dessen Vollzug.*

543 *M. & Co. v. Germany* (no. 13258/87), Decision of 9 February 1990, D/R 64, pp. 138 et seq.

544 Ibid., pp. 138 et seq.

545 BVerfGE 73 (1986), p. 339; see also Peters, *Einführung in die Europäische Menschenrechtskonvention*, p. 32.

546 *Matthews v. the United Kingdom*, [GC] (no. 24833/94), Judgment of 18 February 1999, RJD 1999-I.

547 For a discussion of the judgment, see Peters, *Einführung in die Europäische Menschenrechtskonvention*, p. 32; Jacobs and White, *European Convention*, p. 333; Schäfer, *Verletzungen der Europäischen Menschenrechtskonvention durch Europäisches Gemeinschaftsrecht und dessen Vollzug*, pp. 40, 91 and 111.

After the *Matthews* case, the question arose whether that judgment was unique (because in that case there did not exist any "equivalent protection" at EU level) or whether the Court would from now on assume competence to fully review the compatibility of EU acts (or their execution through its Member States) with the Convention. Much hope to clarify that issue was put in the case of *Senator Lines GmbH v. all 15 EU States*.[548] In that case, the applicant company complained that Article 6 (1) had been violated, because they could not obtain from the European Court of Justice interim relief to suspend the enforcement of a fine by the European Commission. The lack of suspension of the fine allegedly would have forced the company into liquidation. Whereas the EU Member States (as well as the EU Commission which had joined the proceedings as a third party) argued that the Community's legal order sufficiently ensured respect for human rights and thus the principle of subsidiarity should exclude a review by the Court for the acts at issue, the applicant company argued that the Court had overruled the "equivalent protection doctrine" in *Matthews* in stating that it is the task of the Court to supervise the proper application of the Convention by the EU. The case finally resolved itself after the Court of First Instance quashed the fine and thus the applicant company was no longer a victim within the meaning of Article 34 of the Convention.

Consequently, the question whether or not the Court will apply the "equivalent protection doctrine" with regard to EU acts is still unresolved.[549] Where authorities of a Member State apply EU law, the Grand Chamber of the Court has however recently ruled that the "equivalent protection doctrine" still applies. In *"Bosphorus Airways" v. Ireland*, the Irish authorities seized an aircraft leased from the applicant company under an EC Council regulation which had implemented the UN sanctions regime against the Federal Republic of Yugoslavia during the Balkan wars.[550] The Court found that the protection of fundamental rights by EU law could have been considered to be "equivalent" to that of the Convention system. Hence a presumption arose that Ireland did not depart from the requirements of the Conven-

[548] *Senator Lines GmbH v. all 15 EU States* [GC] (no. 56672/00), Judgment of 10 March 2004, RJD 2004-IV. For an earlier decision on the matter which was declared inadmissible as being manifestly ill-founded for other reasons, see *Société Guerin Automobiles v. all 15 EU States* (no. 57717/99), Decision of 4 July 2000, RUDH 2000, p. 119.

[549] For a favorable view that the Court should be fully competent to review EU acts, see Schäfer, *Verletzungen der Europäischen Menschenrechtskonvention durch Europäisches Gemeinschaftsrecht und dessen Vollzug*, p. 200, and Grabenwarter, *Europäische Menschenrechtskonvention*, § 4, 5.

[550] *Bosphorus Hava Yollari Turizm Ve Ticaret Anonim Sirketi v. Ireland* [GC] (45036/98), Judgment of 30 June 2005.

tion when it implemented legal obligations flowing from its membership of the EU. That presumption could be rebutted if the Court considered that the protection of Convention rights was manifestly deficient. Dogmatically, the Court departed from the Commission's approach in *M. & Co. v. Germany* by considering that problem to be a question of justification of interference with a Convention article, and no longer as a *ratione materiae* issue at the admissibility-stage.

Case-law as to acts of other international organisations than the EU is still sparse. In *Behrami and Behrami v. France* and *Saramati v. France, Germany and Norway*, the Court recently found that French and Norwegian brigades making up the international security force presence in Kosovo (KFOR, which was mandated by the United Nations Security Council) were not responsible under the Convention: their actions were directly attributable to the United Nations. The applications were therefore incompatible *ratione personae* with the provisions of the Convention.[551] The Court distinguished the cases from *"Bosphorus Airways" v. Ireland* in that the latter case concerned an act that had been carried out by the respondent State authorities on its own territory.[552] It also found that there existed a fundamental distinction between the natures of the international organisations at issue. Because the United Nations was "an organisation of universal jurisdiction fulfilling its imperative collective security objective", the Court did not consider itself competent to review acts taken under Chapter VII of the Charter of the United Nations.[553]

That the nature of the international organisation might have some impact on the outcome of the case is not an entirely new approach. In *Lenzing AG v. the United Kingdom*, the Commission had found an application against the revoking of a patent by the European Patent Organisation (EPO) to be manifestly ill-founded. It relied on the fact that the applicant company had, by deciding not to register patents separately in a number of European countries, but rather avail itself of the EPO registration scheme, accepted the limitation on access to court in the various domestic systems which that choice brought with it.[554]

551 *Behrami and Behrami v. France* and *Saramati v. France, Germany and Norway* [GC] (nos. 71412/01 and 78166/01), Decisions of 31 May 2007. See also Sari, *Jurisdiction and International Responsibility in Peace Support Operations: The Behrami and Saramati Cases*, HRLR 2008, p. 151.

552 *Behrami and Behrami v. France*, para. 151.

553 Ibid.

554 *Lenzing AG v. the United Kingdom* (no. 38817/97). Commission decision of 9 September 1999; see also *Lenzing AG v. Germany* (no. 39025/97), Commission decision of 9 September 1999.

Given the rather unclear and complicated case-law, one might suspect that the Court avoided the answer to the question whether it could review the decision of the ESA Appeals Board in *Beer and Regan v. Germany (II)*. Instead of relying on the friendly settlement which the applicants had made with their former company, a better reasoning for dismissing the application would have consisted in pointing out that the applicants in fact had tried to put the same issue twice before the Court. In both their applications, Mr Beer and Mr Regan's main complaint was that they could not have determined their work relationship with ESA before the German courts. After the Court had rejected their first application concerning the immunity of ESA because the latter's Appeals Board constituted an alternative remedy, they addressed themselves to the Appeals Board. Not successful there either, they returned to the Court. Given that the outcome of the Appeals Board's decision was not an essential new fact in the case, the Court could have arguably rejected the application as being substantially the same (Article 35 (2) (b) of the Convention).

The case of *Beer and Regan v. Germany* (as well as *Waite and Kennedy v. Germany*) has however shown that the Court's approach – that the existence of alternative means may justify an interference with Article 6 (1) – may only be consistent if these alternative means are really efficient. The following section will investigate what is required for such alternative means to be adequate.

6. *Requirements for alternative means in order to satisfy the "proportionality" criterion*

The most exhaustive overview regarding alternative remedies, in particular the jurisprudence of the administrative tribunals of the United Nations and the International Labour Organisation, has been provided by Reinisch and Weber.[555] One can summarise from their article that certain requirements must be met before one may hold that alternative means are effective.

First, as has already been said, an applicant must be able to have the decisive questions of the dispute with the organisation determined by the respective alternative tribunal. Otherwise there is no remedy at all. Second, the alternative remedy must be of a judicial nature. Where a Committee provides mere judicial advice to the head of organisation and is not entitled to make a judgment, the proportionality criterion will not have been met.[556] Third, the level of qualification of the members of an Appeals Board (or

---

[555] Reinisch/Weber, *In the Shadow of Waite and Kennedy*, IOLR 2004, pp. 93–109.

[556] Ibid., p. 101. Reinisch and Weber give as examples the Board of Appeal of the World Health Organisation or the Internal Appeals Committee of the European Patent Organisation.

whatever remedy is available) is an important factor. The members should be required to be legally qualified, preferably with some practical experience in the field of labour law (the qualification of the judges of the newly-created European Union Civil Service Tribunal serving as a fine example). Fourth, an Appeals Board may only be truly independent if the personal interests of its members are not overly dependent on the organisation. Where the Director-General of an international organisation is both a party to disputes before the Appeals Board and at the same time has a monopoly on the presentation of candidates for appointments to serve on the Appeals Board, that independence might not be fully guaranteed.[557] Fifth, Reinisch and Weber suggest that decision of the Appeals Board should be published, that a legal aid scheme exists, that oral hearings are mandatory, and that there are no practical impediments (such as the failure to obtain a residence permit for the successor in title to a deceased Chinese staff member of the International Labour Organisation necessary in order to take part in a hearing in Geneva).[558] The list of possible criteria is not exhaustive, but it can serve as guidance for a domestic court when having to deal with an immunity case to assure itself that the alternative remedies are efficient.

7. *The "proportionality" criterion in cases against international organisations which are not employment-related: the case of the* Association of Citizens "Mothers of Srebrenica" and Others v. the Netherlands and the United Nations

The Court stated in *Beer and Regan v. Germany* and *Waite and Kennedy v. Germany* that the availability of alternative remedies was a "material factor" in determining whether granting immunity to an international organisation was permissible under the Convention. The question arises whether alternative remedies must therefore be seen as a prerequisite to the observance of Article 6 (whereas in the context of State immunity they serve as only one factor amongst others). The answer to the question will be decisive in cases against international organisations which are not employment-related and for which usually alternative remedies do not exist. Given the absolute immunity of international organisations and the fact that – unlike in the case of State immunity – the plaintiff does not have the possibility to turn to the courts of the defendant State to pursue his claim, there is a strong case for arguing that the availability of alternative remedies is *de facto* a prerequisite

[557] Ibid., p. 104.
[558] Ibid., pp. 105–109.

to justify interference with Article 6 (1) as far as international organisations are concerned.[559]

The Court did not yet have the occasion to rule on that issue, but it appears that it will have to soon. As this book went to press, a case is pending before the Dutch courts which will almost certainly be brought to Strasbourg in the near future: *Association of Citizens "Mothers of Srebrenica" and Others v. the Netherlands and the United Nations*. That association represents 6000 relatives of victims of the genocide in the Srebrenica "safe area" during the Balkan wars in 1995, when 7000 Muslim men and boys were executed by the Bosnian Serb army and 23.000 elderly men, women and children were transported in the presence of (Dutch) soldiers of the United Nations which tragically failed to take action which could have prevented the massacre.[560] The plaintiffs instituted proceedings before the District Court in The Hague, arguing that the United Nations and the Netherlands had violated their obligations to prevent genocide as laid down in the Convention on the Prevention and Punishment of the Crime of Genocide of 1948 (hereafter: the Genocide Convention).

On 10 July 2008, the District Court declared that it had no jurisdiction to hear the action against the United Nations because the latter was protected by immunity.[561] It found that the United Nations as an international organisation enjoyed absolute immunity and that that organisation could not be brought before a domestic court just on the grounds of the right of access to court guaranteed in Article 6 (1).

Citing *Al-Adsani v. the United Kingdom*, the District Court rejected the plaintiffs' argument that there were two conflicting obligations under international law: the prevention of genocide (Article 1 of the Genocide Convention) and the immunity of the United Nations.[562] That reasoning was correct: as has already been argued in the context of State immunity and torture, there is no such conflict.[563] Immunity from suit is a mere procedural rule which would only conflict with the material norms in the Genocide Convention if the latter contained an obligation on its Contracting Parties (among them the Netherlands) to provide for civil remedies for victims. This is not

[559] See also Angelet/Weerts, *Les immunités des organisations internationales face à l'article 6 de la Convention européenne des droits de l'homme*, JDDI 2007, p. 3.

[560] See Robertson, *Crimes against Humanity*, pp. 79–84. See also the case of *Bosnia and Herzegovina v. Serbia and Montenegro* by the International Court of Justice (Judgment of 26 February 2007).

[561] District Court in The Hague, Judgment of 10 July 2008 (Case number: 295247/HA ZA 07-2973); the judgment is available in English.

[562] Ibid., para. 5.19.–5.20.

[563] See pp. 72 et seq.

the case: Article 1 of the Genocide Convention obliges Contracting States to refrain from committing genocide as well as to institute criminal proceedings against the perpetrators.[564] It does not pose an obligation on national courts to enforce its standards by means of a civil action.[565]

Much more controversial, however, was the District Court's remainder of the judgment. It cited the cases of *Beer and Regan v. Germany* and *Waite and Kennedy v. Germany*, but decided to deviate from them for the following reasons:

> In these judgments the [European] Court [of Human Rights] expressed concern that the foundation of international organizations and their corresponding immunities are only compatible with article 6 ECHR if the institutions involved offer a reasonable alternative remedy for the protection of the rights under the ECHR. If this is not the case the ECHR prescribes that the international institution's immunities invoked are not respected. (...) Nevertheless, the [District Court] does not consider it necessary (...) to investigate whether an alternative remedy is available at the UN (...). The UN was founded before the ECHR came into force. There can be no question therefore of a restriction of the protection of human rights under the ECHR by transfer of powers to the UN. Moreover, the UN is an organisation with (...) an almost universal membership. The international organisation that the judgments of Beer and Regan v. Germany and Waite and Kennedy v. Germany related to, namely, the European Space Agency, was founded in 1980 and therefore some considerable time after the entering into force of the ECHR. This organisation has a restricted – European – membership. The UN's position is therefore very dissimilar to it. (...) All this justifies the conclusion that the European Court of Human Rights' motivations in the cases of Beer and Regan v. Germany and Waite and Kennedy v. Germany do not apply to the UN.[566]

The above reasoning is questionable for several reasons. First, the District Court differs according to the date of establishment of an international organisation. Since the United Nations were founded (albeit only shortly) prior to the entering into force of the European Convention on Human Rights, that organisation had to be treated differently from organisations which were established after the Convention went into force (e.g. the European Space Agency). This is not very convincing. The founding date of an international organisation remains mere coincidence and should not serve as a decisive criterion in the present conflict. It should also be noted that State immunity and parliamentary immunity have existed for centuries prior

---

[564] Article 1 of the Genocide Convention states: "The Contracting Parties confirm that genocide, whether committed in time of peace or in time of war, is a crime under international law which they undertake to prevent and to punish."

[565] District Court in The Hague, Judgment of 10 July 2008, para. 5.19.

[566] Ibid., paras. 5.23.–5.24.

to the entering into force of the Convention. The Court has never ruled that – because of that fact – there was no restriction of Article 6 (1).

Second, the District Court differed with regard to whether an organisation has universal or mere regional membership. That argument suggests to distinguish between European organisations (e.g. the European Space Agency, the European Union or the Council of Europe) and organisations with almost global membership (e.g. the United Nations, the International Monetary Fund or the World Bank). Such a distinction might be very difficult to apply in practice: organisations like the Organisation for Economic Co-operation and Development (OECD), the Organisation for Security and Co-operation in Europe (OSCE) or the North Atlantic Treaty Organization (NATO) are composed to a large extent of European Member States, but also have Member States from other continents. Moreover, from the point of view of an applicant who is denied access to court, it makes no difference whether the defendant organisation is of mere European or universal membership (nor is it relevant whether the defendant organisation already existed when the Convention went into force).

In order to underline its argument, the District Court also cited the cases of *Behrami v. France* and *Saramati v. France, Germany and Norway* in which the Court had held that the European Convention on Human Rights should not be an impediment to the effective implementation of duties by international missions under responsibility of the United Nations.[567] It should be recalled that the Court found in those cases that, because the United Nations was an organisation of universal jurisdiction fulfilling its imperative collective security objective, it did not consider itself competent to review acts taken under Chapter VII of the Charter of the United Nations. The District Court considered that the same ratio regarding the special position of the United Nations implied that Article 6 (1) could not be a ground for exception to its immunity.[568] It is very conceivable that the Court (if it ever has to decide on that case) would adopt a similar ruling, since the danger of a great number of civil suits might make the United Nations more reluctant to intervene in a humanitarian crisis.[569] In that case, the Court would presumably deviate from the "alternative remedy"-requirement in *Beer and Regan v. Germany* and *Waite and Kennedy v. Germany*.

---

[567] *Behrami and Behrami v. France* and *Saramati v. France, Germany and Norway* [GC] (nos. 71412/01 and 78166/01), Decisions of 31 May 2007; see above, p. 147.

[568] District Court in The Hague, Judgment of 10 July 2008, para. 5.22.

[569] One can imagine the problems arising for the United Nations if relatives of victims of the genocide in Rwanda were able to sue that organisation before domestic courts for the failure to prevent that genocide.

However, there appears to be a difference between the cases of *Behrami v. France* and *Saramati v. France, Germany and Norway* and the present case. In the former cases, the Court found that the actions of French and Norwegian KFOR soldiers were directly attributable to the United Nations. If France and Norway could be held attributable for those actions in Strasbourg, the effectiveness of the United Nations would be seriously undermined. While there indeed appears to be a similarity to the present case, the District Court failed to take into account Article VIII, Section 29 (a) of the Convention on the Privileges and Immunities of the United Nations which states:

> The United Nations shall make provisions for appropriate modes of settlement of: (a) (...) disputes of a private law character to which the United Nations is a party; (...).

In the present author's view, the suit against the United Nations before the Dutch courts falls into the category of "disputes of a private law character to which the United Nations is a party". Therefore, unlike in the cases of *Behrami v. France* and *Saramati v. France, Germany and Norway*, it is in the sphere of the United Nations itself to avoid outside interference by establishing such "appropriate modes of settlement" as an alternative remedy within the meaning of Article 6 (1). The fact that an alternative remedy is not only demanded by the Court's case-law on Article 6 (1) and immunities, but also by the internal rules of the defendant organisation itself, should have been taken into account when assessing the proportionality of the immunity in question.[570]

It should be added that the case of *Association of Citizens "Mothers of Srebrenica" and Others v. the Netherlands and the United Nations* is currently on appeal. The plaintiffs' legal counsel has already announced that an application with the Strasbourg Court will be filed should domestic remedies be to no avail.[571]

8. *Conclusion*

Unlike States, international organisations still enjoy absolute immunity from suit under public international law. And unlike in the case of State immunity, the plaintiff does not have the possibility to turn to the courts of the

---

[570] In this context, it should also be noted that it appears that the Dutch Advisory Commission on Issues arising under Public International Law (CAVV) had advised the Dutch government not to grant immunity to international organisations if there are no legal remedies available (see Axel Hagedorn, *UN immunity and the Genocide of Srebrenica*; 14 October 2008; only available on the website of "Radio Nederland Weredomroep").

[571] See the article of 11 July 2008 "Wounds remain unhealed on anniversary of Srebrenica" (available on the website of "Deutsche Welle").

defendant State to pursue his claim. Therefore, the immunity of international organisations may serve as a proportionate restriction on the right of access to court under Article 6 if applicants have alternative remedies within the organisation to pursue their claim. This applies to all kind of claims (not merely employment-related ones) and to all international organisations (independent of the date of their establishment or whether their membership is of universal or regional character). In order to find a restriction proportionate, it must be ensured that the alternative remedy is adequate. This requires that the main legal questions to the dispute can be addressed by the alternative tribunal, that the alternative tribunal is composed of members with legal qualification who are truly independent, and that a sufficient level of procedural rights is guaranteed.

V. *Other restrictions on the right of access to court for reasons based in public international law*

The jurisdiction of national courts can also be excluded for other reasons than the operation of an international immunity which are nevertheless based in public international law. As such restrictions interfere with the right of access to court and therefore have similar effects as State immunity or the immunity of international organisations, two cases that were recently decided by the Court's Grand Chamber will be referred to in the following.

1. *The case of* Prince Hans-Adam II of Liechtenstein v. Germany

The case concerned the exclusion of the German courts' jurisdiction under international law with regard to World War II reparation issues. The monarch of Liechtenstein, Prince Hans-Adam II of Liechtenstein, instituted court proceedings in Germany against the municipality of Cologne in order to gain possession of a painting ("A Roman Lime Quarry" by Pieter van Laer).[572] The painting had originally been owned by his father but was confiscated in 1946 by the former Czechoslovakia under the so-called "Benes Decrees".[573]

---

[572] *Prince Hans-Adam II of Liechtenstein v. Germany* [GC] (no. 42527/98), Judgment of 12 July 2001, RJD 2001-VIII. See also Gattini, *A Trojan Horse for Sudeten Claims? On Some Implications of the Prince of Liechtenstein v. Germany*, EJIL 2002, p. 513.

[573] Decree no. 12 on the "confiscation and accelerated allocation of agricultural property of German and Hungarian persons and of those having committed treason and acted as enemies of the Czech and Slovak people", issued by the President of the former Czechoslovakia on 21 June 1945. Note that the Benes Decrees were also applied to other persons allegedly of German or Hungarian origin or ethnicity; thus citizens of Liechtenstein were treated as German nationals. The application of the Benes Decrees to Liechtenstein

The municipality of Cologne received the painting on loan from the Czech Republic for an art exhibition in 1991. The applicant's claim was dismissed by the German courts because they did not have jurisdiction: they referred to Article 3 of Chapter 6 of the 1952 Convention on the Settlement of Matters arising out of the War and Occupation (the "Settlement Convention"), according to which broadly speaking any measures taken against German property (be it abroad or on German territory) in connection with reparations for the Second World War should be excluded from the adjudication of the German courts.[574] The German courts considered that the confiscation of the painting constituted a measure within the meaning of that provision which had not, unlike other provisions in the Settlement Convention, been suspended by the 1990 Treaty on the Final Settlement with respect to Germany (the so-called "Two-Plus-Four treaty").

In its judgment, the Grand Chamber of the Court found unanimously that Article 6 (1) had not been violated. The exclusion of German jurisdiction by the Settlement Convention was regarded by the Court as a consequence of the particular status of Germany under public international law after the Second World War. It accepted that after 1945 Germany had not been in a position to argue against the intention of the three Western powers to exclude a review by German courts of confiscation measures against German external assets for reparation purposes.[575] It found that the "Two-Plus-Four treaty" had not abolished this exclusion of Germany's jurisdiction, because Germany's position had not changed in 1990 when a final settlement with respect to the unification of the two German States was within reach: in the negotiations with the three Western powers, Germany had to accept that this specific limitation on its jurisdiction had not been abolished.[576] The Court stressed that the maintaining of that limitation on access to the German courts served a legitimate aim, given the unique circumstances, namely that Germany had secured the end of the occupation regime and obtained its full sovereignty over its internal and external affairs.[577] Because of Germany's particular status under public international law after the Second World War, the case was not comparable with the transfer of competences to international organisations and their immunities as considered in *Waite and Kennedy v.*

property continues to be an unresolved issue between Liechtenstein and the Czech Republic (see Gattini, *A Trojan Horse for Sudeten Claims? On Some Implications of the Prince of Liechtenstein v. Germany*, EJIL 2002, p. 513).

574 *Prince Hans-Adam II of Liechtenstein v. Germany*, para. 29.

575 Ibid., para. 56.

576 Ibid., para. 58.

577 Ibid., para. 59.

Germany.[578] In any event, the applicant had alternative measures as he could have challenged the expropriation before the Czech courts. Finally, the Court reasoned that the applicant's interest in bringing litigation in Germany was not sufficient to outweigh the vital public interest in regaining sovereignty and unifying Germany; hence the restriction on the applicant's right of access to court was considered proportionate.[579]

It should be added that Liechtenstein brought a case against Germany before the International Court of Justice in 2001, complaining that the latter violated public international law by treating as German assets which belonged to nationals of Liechtenstein.[580] On 10 February 2005, the International Court of Justice decided on the preliminary objections raised by Germany that it had no jurisdiction *ratione temporis*.[581]

2. *The case of* Markovic and Others v. Italy

The second case concerns reparation claims for alleged violations of humanitarian law by the NATO bombings during the Kosovo war in 1999.[582] As in the case of *Bankovic and Others v. Belgium and 16 other NATO States*,[583] the applicants were the relatives of persons who died as a result of a NATO air strike on a Serbian television building in Belgrade in 1999. They had brought an action in damages against Italy, which had provided major logistical support for NATO during the conflict. In a judgment that brought the applicants' action to an end, the Italian Court of Cassation held that the Italian courts had not had jurisdiction, because Italy's decision to take part in the air strikes had been a political one and could therefore not be reviewed by the courts. The Italian Court of Cassation stressed that the impugned act was an act of war and a manifestation of political decisions and no court possessed the power to review that manner in which the latter were carried out. In doing so, the court applied the doctrine of "act of government" which basically holds that domestic courts have no jurisdiction over the authorities for acts of a political nature and which therefore bears some similarities with the

578 Ibid., para. 68.

579 Regarding the relationship between the criteria of proportionality and the essence of the right in the present case, see the concurring opinions of Judge Ress (joined by Judge Zupancic) and Judge Costa as well as the discussion above, p. 19.

580 *Case concerning Certain Property*, Liechtenstein v. Germany; the decision is available at: www.icj-cji.org.

581 Ibid.

582 *Markovic and Others v. Italy* [GC] (no. 1398/03), Judgment of 14 December 2006.

583 *Bankovic and Others v. Belgium and 16 Other NATO States* [GC] (no. 52207/99), Decision of 12 December 2001, RJD 2001-XII.

doctrine of State immunity.[584] In fact, when the Grand Chamber of the Court found (by ten votes to seven) that the applicants' right of access to court had not been violated, it rejected the applicants' assertions that the decision of the Italian Court of Cassation constituted an immunity, either *de facto* or in practice, because of its allegedly absolute or general nature.[585] Instead, it found that the ruling was merely indicative of the extent of the courts' powers of review of acts of foreign policy such as acts of war. Therefore, the inability of the applicants to sue was a result of the principles governing the substantive right of action in domestic law.[586]

The seven dissenting judges noted with great concern that neither the Court of Cassation nor the Court had provided any definition of an "act of government" and thus applied a concept that was too vague and general in order to serve as a limitation on the right of access to court.[587] The judges stressed that the applicants' aim was simply to obtain compensation for the remote consequences of the political act concerned under a recognised right set out in the Italian Civil Code, and that the Italian Court of Cassation had refused to hear their claims solely because the decision to participate in the Kosovo conflict was political in nature. In finding that this interference with the right of access to court was justified, the dissenting judges considered that the Court had accepted a solution that struck "a blow at the very foundation of the Convention".[588]

The judgment reveals a problem that occasionally arises also in the conflict between Article 6 and immunities: to distinguish whether a certain rule sets a limitation on the right (as the Court found in the present case) or a limitation on the remedy (for example State immunity, which needs to be justified as a proportionate restriction on Article 6 (1) to its legitimate aims pursued). Even though the Court rightly distinguished the present case from the cases in which access to court was prevented through the operation of immunity, it nevertheless should have asked whether the restriction served

584 Strictly speaking, the restriction on the right of access to court was rather based in constitutional law than in public international law. On the other hand, the Italian Court of Cassation found itself to lack jurisdiction "since the action is brought against the Italian State as a specific (unitary) subject of international law for acts performed in the exercise of State authority (*iure imperii*) (…)". (*Markovic and Others v. Italy*, para. 17). This reasoning rather suggests the "act of government"-doctrine to be rooted in public international law.

585 Ibid., para. 113; for a discussion of the judgment, see Shah, *Seeking Remedies for Violations of International Humanitarian Law: Markovic v Italy*, HRLR 2007, p. 412.

586 Ibid., para. 114.

587 *Markovic and Others v. Italy*, dissenting opinion of Judge Zagrebelsky (joined by Judges Zupancic, Jungwiert, Tsatsa-Nikolovska, Ugrekhelidze, Kovler and Thor Björgvinsson).

588 Ibid.

a legitimate aim and was proportionate.[589] It appears somewhat inconsistent that the Court applied the *Ashingdane* test in the case of *Prince Hans-Adam II of Liechtenstein v. Germany*, but not in *Markovic and Others v. Italy*. In both cases the jurisdiction of the domestic courts was excluded for reasons based in international law. Still the Court treated the cases differently. In *Markovic and Others v. Italy*, the Court was therefore rightly criticised for having failed to regard the "act of government"-doctrine as a procedural limitation which must be justified.[590]

The difficulties in distinguishing between procedural and substantive limitations on a right, as seen in *Markovic and Others v. Italy*, is in fact a problem the Court had to deal with several times when considering the conflict between Article 6 and domestic immunities. The third part of this work, which deals with domestic immunities, will explore these problems in more detail.

[589] See the dissenting opinion of Judge Costa in *Markovic and Others v. Italy*.

[590] Shah, *Seeking Remedies for Violations of International Humanitarian Law: Markovic v Italy*, HRLR 2007, p. 417: "[T]he doctrine provides that a court is not competent to look at an issue, not that individuals do not have a claim." See also the criticism of Judge Loucaides, *ECHR – Collected Essays*, pp. 242–243.

Part III

Domestic Immunities

Whereas the previous chapters have dealt with immunities that were granted by States in order to comply with their obligations under public international law, other immunities exist in order to protect certain bodies at the domestic level. Such are for example the immunity of local authorities, the social services, the police, judges, lawyers or Members of Parliament. The following part of this work will investigate the conflict between those immunities and the right of access to court. It is divided into two parts. The first part deals with the liability of public authorities under English law. In those cases, the question which was highly debated was whether a certain exclusionary rule in fact constituted an "immunity", *i.e.* whether it could be characterised as a procedural (as opposed to a substantive) limitation on a right. As will be shown, the dividing line between these two types of limitations has proved to be a very difficult question. As the cases concerned were all applications brought against the United Kingdom and the specific problems that have arisen are not easily transferable to the legal system of other Contracting Parties, those immunities have been separated from the chapter on parliamentary immunity, another type of domestic immunity which is recognised by all Contracting Parties.

I. *The Liability of Public Authorities under English Law*

The cases concerning the liability of British public authorities are closely connected with the question whether or not a "civil right" existed within the meaning of Article 6 (1). It has already been mentioned that, although the concept of "civil rights" is an autonomous one, it is settled case-law of the Court that Article 6 (1) does not itself guarantee any particular content for "civil rights and obligations" in domestic law. Thus, the Court may not create any rights which have no legal basis therein.[1] A frequent argument, in particular in cases involving domestic immunities, was therefore that Article 6 (1) was inapplicable because, even though the right which was claimed by the plaintiff might generally exist under domestic law, the immunity in question led to the extinction of the cause of action in the particular case.

1. *The former approach by the Commission*

In earlier decisions, the Commission indeed followed this approach.[2] The Commission's decision in *Agee v. the United Kingdom*[3] might serve as a good example. The applicant had published a book in which he described his work for the CIA. While researching another book on further CIA activities, the applicant was refused re-entry to the country and received a deportation order on grounds that he had maintained regular contacts harmful to the security of the United Kingdom with foreign intelligence officers.[4] He was further accused of being involved in disseminating, and in helping others to obtain, information which was also considered harmful to the security of the United Kingdom. Those allegations were repeated in Parliament by the Home Secretary. The applicant complained to the Commission that he had no redress in respect of these allegedly defamatory statements due to their protection by parliamentary immunity. The Commission found that Article 6 (1) was inapplicable in the present case for the following reasons:

> Although a person's rights under domestic law to protection of his reputation generally constitute 'civil rights' within the meaning of Article 6 (1), the applicant does not have any right in United Kingdom law to protection of his reputation insofar as it may be affected by the statements complained of. Article 6 (1) does not therefore guarantee the right to take proceedings in respect of these statements, since the applicant has no civil right to protection of his reputation against them. It follows that the Commission has no competence to examine this complaint and must reject it as incompatible with the Convention ratione materiae (...).[5]

[1] *James and Others v. the United Kingdom* (no. 8793/79), Judgment of 21 February 1986, Series A 98, para. 81; *Lithgow and Others v. the United Kingdom* (no. 9006/80), Judgment of 8 July 1986, Series A 102, para. 192; *Holy Monasteries v. Greece* (no. 13092/87), Judgment of 9 December 1994, Series A 301–A, para. 80.

[2] *Agee v. the United Kingdom* (no. 7729/76), Commission decision of 17 December 1976, D/R 7, p. 175; *Dyer v. the United Kingdom* (no. 10475/83), Commission decision of 9 October 1984, D/R 39, p. 251.

[3] *Agee v. the United Kingdom*, p. 164.

[4] Ibid., p. 167.

[5] Ibid., p. 175.

However, the Commission's view is basically flawed. Had Parliament decided to waive the immunity of the Home Secretary, there would have been clearly a cause of action which the applicant in *Agee v. the United Kingdom* could have invoked. In this respect, the immunity in question could be likened to State immunity in which the foreign State may waive its immunity and in which the Court rightly rejected the argument that the immunity in question the a civil right which would otherwise have existed. Whereas the example of parliamentary immunity is therefore rather undisputed (the Court itself found later that Article 6 (1) applied in cases of parliamentary immunity), other cases have been more problematic.

The Commission subsequently maintained its approach in the case of *Dyer v. the United Kingdom.*[6] In this case, the applicant (a soldier) was prevented from suing the Crown in negligence because of a statutory immunity for liability in tort concerning personal injury resulting from a military exercise. Therefore, the only possible remedy remaining was to apply for a disability pension which, in the applicant's opinion, would have amounted to only a sixth of the amount of damages which would be awarded by a court in a successful tort claim. The Commission observed that it was not disputed between the Parties that there existed a general "civil right" to compensation for negligence and, thus, that the right to bring a civil action in negligence was guaranteed by Article 6 (1).[7] However, it found that where a right to compensation for negligence had been expressly removed by a statutory immunity (such as in the Crown Proceedings Act 1947), there was no "civil right" within the meaning of Article 6 (1). When a case with almost identical facts was later decided by the Court in 2005, the Grand Chamber – as will be shown – had more difficulties with the question whether or not a "civil right" was involved in the case of Crown immunity.

2. *The initial approach taken by the Court*

In earlier cases, the Court opted for the easiest solution to overcome the difficulties with the applicability of Article 6 (1) by simply avoiding to decide on the issue. In *Ashingdane v. the United Kingdom* and *Fayed v. the United Kingdom*, the Court proceeded on the basis that Article 6 (1) applied because the same questions of legitimate aim and proportionality would have in any event arisen under Article 8 which had also been invoked by the applicants.

---

[6] *Dyer v. the United Kingdom*, p. 246; for a similar application, see *Ketterick v. the United Kingdom* (no. 9803/82), Commission decision, EHRR 1983, p. 465.

[7] *Dyer v. the United Kingdom*, p. 251.

As a consequence, these cases do not give very much guidance as to the applicability of Article 6 (1).[8]

a) *The Case of* Ashingdane v. the United Kingdom

In the *Ashingdane* case, the applicant instituted civil proceedings challenging the Secretary of State's decision under the Mental Health Act 1959 to continue his detention in a mental institution. Section 141 (1) of the Mental Health Act 1959 provided immunity from liability for acts under the Act in the absence of bad faith or reasonable care.[9] Moreover, a claim in respect of such an act could not be brought unless the High Court gave leave on a finding of "substantial grounds" for believing that this condition was met on the part of the administrative authority.[10] The Court found it unnecessary to decide whether the exclusionary rule under the Mental Health Act which precluded the civil proceedings against carers defined the content of the right or imposed a restriction. Even assuming that Article 6 (1) was applicable, it found that the provision had not been violated by the existence of the immunity under the Act.[11] The Court found by six votes to one that these limitations served the "legitimate aim" of protecting carers from being unduly targeted by the claims of psychiatric patients. The availability of a claim in a case of bad faith or lack of reasonable care was seen as sufficient to meet the requirement of proportionality.[12]

b) *The case of* Fayed v. the United Kingdom

The case of *Fayed v. the United Kingdom* arose out of a takeover of a group of department stores by the applicants. The Secretary of State for Trade and Industry appointed two inspectors under the Companies Act 1985 to investigate the affairs of the applicants' company and the takeover in particular. The inspectors concluded in their report that the applicants had behaved dishonestly at the material time and had subsequently attempted to mislead the inspectors. The applicants argued that the making and publication of the

[8] See also comment on *Fayed v. the United Kingdom* in the Concurring Opinion of Lady Justic Arden as to Article 6 in *Z and Others v. the United Kingdom* ([GC] (no. 29392/95), Judgment of 10 May 2001, ECHR 2001–V, para. O-I4): "The result in that case does not therefore set any precedent for the applicability of Article 6 (1) or detract from the principle (...), namely that Article 6 does not guarantee any particular content for civil rights and obligations."

[9] *Ashingdane v. the United Kingdom* (no. 8225/78), Judgment of May 28, 1985, Series A 93; para. 57.

[10] Section 141 (2) of the Mental Health Act 1959.

[11] *Ashingdane v. the United Kingdom*, para. 54.

[12] Ibid., para. 59.

report seriously affected their civil right to reputation, but a libel suit was rejected by the British courts due to a defence of privilege available to the inspectors in action for defamation.

The Court decided unanimously that there had been no violation of the right to access to court. The immunity available to the inspectors had a legitimate aim, namely to facilitate and ensure the proper investigation of public companies in the public interest.[13] As regards the issue of proportionality, the Court held that the risk of some uncompensated damage to reputation was inevitable if investigators were to have the freedom required to carrying out their functions. The Court took also into account that the findings in the report related to matters which the applicants themselves had made great efforts to bring into the public domain. Two Commission members had earlier contested the finding of proportionality by saying that the interest of society were not safeguarded by reports which were not objectively determined by the findings of a court of law.[14] A significant feature of the case, however, was that a remedy of judicial review was available for the applicants against numerous actions, such as any exceeding of the inspectors' bounds of function or the improper drawing of conclusions without providing supporting facts.

Even though the Court (as in the *Ashingdane* judgment) avoided the issue whether or not Article 6 (1) was applicable, the *Fayed* judgment contains some very important statements on that issue which the Court has frequently repeated ever since:

> Whether a person has an actionable domestic claim may depend not only on the substantive content, properly speaking, of the relevant civil right as defined under national law but also on the existence of procedural bars preventing or limiting the possibilities of bringing potential claims to court. In the latter kind of case Article 6 (1) may have a degree of applicability. Certainly the Convention enforcement bodies may not create by way of interpretation a substantive civil right which has no legal basis in the State concerned. However, it would not be consistent with the rule of law in a democratic society or with the basic principle underlying Article 6 (1) – namely that civil claims must be capable of being submitted to a judge for adjudication- if, for example, a State could, without restraint or control by the Convention enforcement bodies, remove from the jurisdiction of the courts a whole range of civil claims or confer immunities from civil liability on large groups or categories of persons.[15]

---

[13] *Fayed v. the United Kingdom* (no. 17101/90), Judgment of 21 September 1994, para. 69.

[14] *Fayed v. the United Kingdom*, Commission decision of 15 May 1992, partly dissenting opinion of Mr Rozakis and Mr Trechsel, Series A 249, p. 68.

[15] *Fayed v. the United Kingdom*, para. 65; with reference to *Dyer v. the United Kingdom*, pp. 251–252. The statement has been repeated for example in the cases of *Fogarty v. the United Kingdom, McElhinney v. Ireland* and *Al-Adsani v. the United Kingdom.*

The last part of the statement can be seen as an acknowledgment of the Court that it was not at ease with the former approach of the Commission which widely limited the applicability of Article 6 (1). The Court has never clarified what exactly that passage meant in practice, but its importance will be discussed further below.[16] As to the difficulties in distinguishing between the procedural and substantive limitations of a right, the Court also remarked:

> It is not always an easy matter to trace the dividing line between procedural and substantive limitations of a given entitlement under domestic law. It may sometimes be no more than a question of legislative technique whether the limitation is expressed in terms of the right or the remedy.[17]

If anything, that statement was true regarding the cases which would follow *Ashingdane* and *Fayed*, both judgments in which the Court could avoid the problem because it did not find any violation of the Convention. The following case however marked the first occasion on which the Court found that a domestic immunity violated Article 6 (1), which might explain why the case has received very controversial reactions.

3. *Immunity of the police: the case of* Osman v. the United Kingdom

The application deals with the failure by the police to protect a boy and his father from attack from a teacher who had become obsessed with the boy. The teacher had behaved increasingly bizarre over the period of a year: he had followed the boy and his friend, he had spread rumours of a sexual nature about the friend and he had sprayed various graffiti with indecent remarks about the boy around the school. Moreover the boy's file had been stolen from the school office, a brick had been thrown through the window of the boy's house and his father's car had been damaged on several occasions. The teacher had also changed his name into the boy's name. The police had been made aware of these incidents and had interviewed the teacher; it appears that one officer recalled that the teacher had announced his intention of doing something that would be a "sort of Hungerford" (a reference to a massacre committed there in 1987). Despite all this, the boy's family was told by the police "not to worry". The teacher finally shot the boy's father and seriously wounded the boy in their home. Immediately afterwards, he also killed the deputy headmaster and his son. It is reported that the teacher, upon arrest by the police, asked "Why didn't you stop me from doing this?".

The applicants, the boy and the mother, tried to bring a negligence action against the police, alleging that the police had been warned that the man was

---

[16] See below, p. 180.

[17] *Fayed v. the United Kingdom*, para. 67.

a danger to the family but had not taken adequate steps to protect them. The claim was struck out by the Court of Appeal by applying an earlier House of Lords ruling, *Hill v. Chief Constable of West Yorkshire*,[18] which excluded the liability of the police from claims relating to the prevention of disorder and crime. The reason behind the rule was to maintain the effectiveness of the police service, and, broadly speaking, to prevent the risk that the availability of compensation for negligent acts might lead to defensive policing.[19]

a) *The judgment of the Court*

The judgment of *Osman v. the United Kingdom* is a frequently cited decision concerning positive obligations of Contracting Parties under Article 2 (the right to life).[20] This provision enjoins the State not only to refrain from the intentional and unlawful taking of life, but also to take appropriate steps to safeguard the lives of those within its jurisdiction.[21] This may not only require the adoption of effective criminal-law provisions, but also the taking of preventive measures to protect an individual from the criminal acts of a third party where the authorities knew or ought to have known of a real and immediate risk to the individual's life.[22] However, the Court found by seventeen votes to three that there was no decisive stage in the series of events leading up to the shooting when the police knew or ought to have known that the applicants' lives were at real and immediate risk from the teacher.[23]

More important in the present context, however, is what the Court had to say regarding the alleged violation of Article 6 (1). The Court observed that the exclusionary rule laid down by the House of Lords in *Hill v. Chief Constable of West Yorkshire* served a legitimate aim, namely to ensure the effectiveness of the police service by protecting it from the constant risk of tortious liability.[24] Turning to the criterion of proportionality, the Court found that the Court of Appeal in *Osman* had considered the rule a "watertight defence" to the police. Although there existed "several public-interest considerations which pull in the opposite direction to the application of the

[18] *Hill v. Chief Constable of West Yorkshire* [1989] A.C., p. 53.

[19] *Osman v. the United Kingdom* [GC] (no. 23452/94), Judgment of 28 October 1998, RJD 1998–VIII, para. 150.

[20] See generally Wright, *Tort Law and Human Rights*, Chapter 5 ("Positive obligations, omissions and the Convention", p. 115).

[21] *Osman v. the United Kingdom*, para. 115; *L.C.B. v. the United Kingdom*, Judgment of 9 June 1998, RJD 1998–III, para. 36.

[22] *Osman v. the United Kingdom*, paras. 115–116.

[23] Ibid., para. 121.

[24] Ibid., paras. 149–150.

rule",[25] the Court of Appeal had conferred a blanket immunity on the police regarding the investigation and suppression of crime. However, the domestic court should also have taken into account the degree of negligence, the harm suffered and the justice of a particular case.[26] In the present case, grave negligence on behalf of the police had been alleged and the harm had been of a very serious nature. The Court found that these issues should have been examined on the merits and that the applicants' were entitled to have the police account for their actions in adversarial proceedings.[27] The application of the rule by the Court of Appeal therefore amounted to a disproportionate restriction of the applicants' right of access to court. The decision that there had been a violation of Article 6 (1) was taken unanimously by a Grand Chamber composed of twenty judges.

b) *Responses to the judgment*

The *Osman* judgment caused an outcry amongst the British judiciary and academics alike,[28] but also received some approval.[29] Two points of criticism were frequently put forward against the judgment. First, that the Strasbourg Court had not adequately understood the English tort law. Secondly, as the decision finally paved the way for the applicants to sue the police in damages, the Court had ruled that the United Kingdom had failed to provide compensation out of public funds in cases in which "Strasbourg" thought it should do so. It is appropriate to deal with these issues separately.

---

[25] Ibid., para. 151.

[26] Ibid.

[27] Ibid., para. 153.

[28] Lord Hoffmann, *Human Rights and the House of Lords*, MLR 1999, p. 162; Lord Browne-Wilkinson in *Barret v. Enfield LBC* [1999] 3 WLR, p. 84; Craig/Fairgrieve, *Barrett, Negligence and Discretionary Powers*, Public Law 1999, p. 630; Weir, *Down Hill- all the way?* CLJ 1999, p. 4; Lunney, *A Tort Lawyer's View of Osman v. United Kingdom*, KCLJ 1999, p. 238; Gearty, *Unravelling Osman*, MLR 2001, p. 159; Lidbetter/George, *Negligent Public Authorities and Convention Rights- The Legacy of Osman*, EHRLR 2001, p. 599; Hickman, *The "uncertain shadow": Throwing Light on the Right to a Court under Article 6 (1) ECHR*, Public Law 2004, p. 122.

[29] Wright, *Tort & Human Rights*, p. xxxiv; ibid., *The Retreat from Osman*; Simpson, *Human Rights and the End of Empire*, p. 7; Markesinis/Auby/Coester-Waltjen/Deakin, *Tortious Liability of Statutory Bodies: A Comparative and Economic Analysis of Five English Cases*, pp. 96–104. Hickman also reported the following comments of Lord Woolf at a lecture to the British Academy in 2002 entitled "Human Rights: Have the Public Benefited?": "I have also to acknowledge that, while my original reaction was sceptical, after reflection I came to appreciate that [*Osman*] has substantial merits" (Public Law 2004, pp. 133–134, at Fn. 65).

c) *How the Court was alleged to have misinterpreted English tort law*
To understand why the British judiciary was so upset with the decision in *Osman*, one has to take a closer look at the relevant domestic law. Under English tort law, there is no single tort which imposes liability to pay compensation for civil wrongs. Instead there are a series of torts such as trespass, conversion, conspiracy, defamation or negligence.[30] The English tort of negligence is largely developed through the case-law of the domestic courts.[31] The leading authority of *Caparo Industries plc v. Dickman* established that a claim in the tort of negligence requires three elements: a duty of care, a breach of the duty of care and causation of damage.[32] The first element, the duty of care, defines the categories of relationships in which the law may impose liability on a defendant.[33] To show the existence of a duty of care, the claimant must either show that his case falls within a category of cases in which it has already been established that a duty of care exists. In novel situations, that is a situation in which a duty of care had not previously been decided to exist, the claimant is required to show that three conditions are fulfilled in order to establish a duty of care. First, that the damage to the claimant was foreseeable. Second, that there was a relationship of proximity between the claimant and the defendant. Lastly, it has to be shown that it was *fair, just and reasonable to impose liability on the defendant.* The last condition opens the door for policy considerations as to whether or not liability in negligence should be extended into a new category of cases.

The Court's view of the relevant law in *Osman* was that the applicants had a general right to sue in negligence. It found that the exclusionary rule established by the House of Lords had the effect that, no matter what the facts of the case were, the police had never owed a duty of care to the claimants and therefore claims in this respect could be struck out without any consideration of the merits of the case. This was regarded as a disproportionate blanket immunity for the police.

However, the critics of the judgment alleged that the Strasbourg judges had used the right of access to court to attack the content of substantive English law.[34] They referred to the Court's principle that Article 6 (1) does not guarantee any particular content for civil rights and obligations in the

[30] See *Z and Others v. the United Kingdom* [GC] (no. 29392/95), Judgment of 10 May 2001, RJD 2001-V; *Reid v. the United Kingdom*, (no. 33221/96), Decision of 26 June 2001, part B.
[31] *Reid v. the United Kingdom*, para. 3.
[32] *Caparo Industries plc v. Dickman* [1990] 2 AC, p. 605.
[33] *Z and Others v. the United Kingdom*, para. 58.
[34] Gordon/Ward, *Judicial Review*, 5.66.

substantive law of the Contracting States. Having regard to the above principle, a frequent objection was that English law does not recognise the right to sue the police in negligence (no matter how desirable) in respect of the investigation and suppression of crime. As there was no duty of care in the *Osman* case, an element of the tort was not present. Consequently, there was no right at all for the applicants to sue in negligence. And in the absence of a right, there could be no immunity to protect the defendant from being sued in respect of that right. As there was no legal basis in domestic law for the civil right invoked by the applicants, the Court was accused of creating one in order to bring into play Article 6.

4. *Immunity of the social services: the case of* Z and Others v. the United Kingdom

Almost two years after the *Osman* judgment, at a hearing in June 2000, this criticism was put to the Court in *Z and Others v. the United Kingdom.*[35] The case dealt with the grossly negligent failure of the social services to protect four children from horrific ill-treatment by their mother which lasted for a period of several years. The children had unsuccessfully tried to sue the social services in negligence before the British courts. *X v. Bedfordshire County Council*, as the case was called in the domestic proceedings, went all the way up to the House of Lords, where it was struck out in 1995.[36] The House of Lords held that it was not fair, just and reasonable to hold local authorities liable in negligence in situations in which they were charged with the task of protecting society from the wrongdoings of others.[37] The rule was absolute and not subject to any exception, not even in cases with catastrophic consequences such as those suffered by the four children in *X*. Like in *Osman*, the case was struck out without any consideration of its merits.

The Grand Chamber of the Court unanimously found in May 2001 that the failure by the local authority to protect the children from their mother violated Article 3 (prohibition of torture and inhuman and degrading treatment or punishment). The Court particularly stressed the contracting States' positive obligations to protect children from ill-treatment of which the authorities had or ought to have had knowledge.[38] But the applicants further invoked Article 6. They put forward that they did not have access to court in order to claim compensation from the social services for the violation found

---

[35] See *Z and Others v. the United Kingdom*, para. 98.

[36] *X (Minors) v. Bedfordshire C.C.* [1995] 2 AC, p. 633, HL.

[37] See *Z and Others v. the United Kingdom*, para. 46.

[38] *Z and Others v. the United Kingdom*, para. 73; see also *Osman v. the United Kingdom*, para. 116.

under Article 3: a situation which was very similar to the one in *Osman*. This time, however, only two judges of the original Grand Chamber which had decided *Osman* were sitting in the Grand Chamber which had heard the applicants in *Z and Others*. Twelve out of the remaining fifteen judges decided to reverse the *Osman* ruling.[39] The reason why they did so becomes obvious from the following passage of the *Z and Others* judgment:

> (...) [T]he Osman judgment was based on an understanding of the law of negligence which has to be reviewed in the light of clarifications subsequently made by the domestic courts and notably the House of Lords.... In the present case, the Court is led to the conclusion that the inability of the applicants to sue the local authority flowed not from an immunity but from the applicable principles governing the substantive right of action on domestic law.[40]

The main clarification to which the Court had referred was the House of Lords ruling in *Barrett*[41] in which Lord Browne-Wilkinson commented on *Osman* as follows:

> Although the word 'immunity' is sometimes incorrectly used, a holding that it is not fair, just and reasonable to hold liable a particular class of defendants whether generally or in relation to a particular type of activity is not to give immunity from liability to which the rest of the world is subject. It is a prerequisite to there being any liability in negligence at all that as a matter of policy it is fair, just and reasonable in those circumstances to impose liability in negligence.[42]

This is where things get complicated. If the Court in *Osman* had erred in holding that the exclusionary rule established an immunity, it had not been the only court to do so. The House of Lords in *Hill* mentioned that 'the police was immune from an action', referring to another decision which had also used the word 'immunity' in this respect.[43] The legal situation provides great potential for confusion. This led Sir Sydney Kentridge QC, on the occasion of a seminar named 'Human Rights and Tort Remedies in English Public Law',[44] to comment as follows in a speech entitled 'When is an immunity not an immunity?':

---

[39] The Commission, however, had previously found unanimously a violation of Article 6 (see Lunney, *Osman in action- Article 6 and the Commission reports in Z and Others v. the United Kingdom and TP & KM v. United Kingdom*, KCLJ 2000, p. 119).

[40] *Z and Others v. the United Kingdom*, para. 100.

[41] Lord Browne-Wilkinson in *Barrett v. Enfield LBC* [1999] 3 WLR, p. 79.

[42] Ibid., p. 85.

[43] *Rondel* v. *Worsley* [1969] 1 AC, p. 191.

[44] Hosted by the British Institute of International & Comparative Law on 19 July 2001 in London.

> The effect of the judgment of the House of Lords and now of the European Court of Human Rights is that no matter how great the damage to the child, no matter how easy it would have been to prevent it, no matter how clear the warning -even if it were rubbed under their noses- public policy must always come down in favour of the local authority. The specific facts are irrelevant: the court will not listen to them. (…) I would say that this is a good definition of an immunity. And I would say that a child faced with that exclusionary rule has been denied a fair hearing by a court.[45]

The Court in *Z and Others*, however, went even further by stating that even if the exclusionary rule had had the effect of an immunity it would not have mattered, as there was no right to sue and the Court could not create such a right. Like the critics in *Osman*, it referred to the principle that Article 6 does not in itself guarantee any particular content for civil rights and obligations in national law.[46] However, this view fails to take into account the particular circumstances of the case. The applicants did not invite the Court to create any dubious rights that national law would have never provided for. They simply wanted to sue an authority in negligence for an action for which the Court had found a violation of Article 3, a provision which reflects one of the fundamental values in a democratic society. The Court was aware of the fact that there was a gap in domestic law, but instead decided that this raised an issue under and amounted to a violation of Article 13 (which gives the right to an effective remedy).[47] But Article 13 does not provide for a *judicial* remedy, *i.e.* to claim compensation before a court. Judge Rozakis and Judge Palm, the only two judges who ruled in *Osman* and later also in *Z and Others*, pointed out in their partly dissenting opinion that if the complaint involved a violation of core Convention rights the Court should be bound to find that States are obliged not simply to offer an effective remedy, but a judicial remedy.[48] It is here that the United Kingdom might have overstepped its freedom to limit the right of access to court and the Court could have intervened without wrongfully interfering in the United Kingdom's substantive law.

The decision in *Z and Others* coincided with a further judgment by the Grand Chamber in *T.P. and K.M. v. the United Kingdom*.[49] Unlike in *Z and Others*, the social services had not been slow to take children into care in

---

45 Quoted with kind permission of Sir Sydney Kentridge QC. The speech is unpublished.

46 *Z and Others v. the United Kingdom*, paras. 87, 98, 100–101.

47 Ibid., para. 102.

48 Ibid., partly dissenting opinion of judges Rozakis and Palm, para. 2; see also the partly dissenting opinion of Judge Thomassen joined by Judges Casadevall and Kovler.

49 *T.P. and K.M. v. the United Kingdom* [GC], Judgment of 10 May 2001, EHRR 2002, p. 42.

this case. Due to a mistake, a four year old sex abuse victim was removed from her mother. The applicants' complaints that an immunity from liability prevented them from suing the social services in negligence remained unsuccessful. This was mainly because they had failed in proceedings before the House of Lords to argue that any direct duty of care was owed to them by the local authority. The Grand Chamber held that the applicants' claims were not rejected due to the application of an exclusionary rule, as the case was based on the vicarious liability of the social services.[50] Unanimously, the Court found that there had not been a violation of Article 6.

5. *The question of compensation*

When the Court found a violation of Article 6 in *Osman*, it was also criticised for having granted the applicants the possibility to claim compensation in a case for which British law did not provide for compensation. Lord Hoffmann stated that in doing so, the Court was challenging the autonomy of the domestic courts and the Parliament of the United Kingdom to deal with what are essentially social welfare questions involving budgetary limits and efficient public administration.[51]

It appears that a common fear is that compensation claims limit the resources of a public authority: the money which is spent to compensate an individual will be missing elsewhere. As a side-effect of successful compensation claims, public authorities might therefore carry out their activities more cautiously and inefficiently. In *X v. Bedfordshire County Council*,[52] it was feared that social workers would constantly be threatened by lawsuits

[50] Ibid., paras. 36 and 101.

[51] Lord Hoffmann, *Human Rights and the House of Lords*, MLR 1999, p. 162 et seq. See also the comments by Weir, *Down Hill- all the way?*, CLJ 1999, p. 7. Until the entering into force of the Human Rights Act 1998, the English tort of negligence was the only possibility for an individual to obtain compensation from a public authority which caused damage by having acted negligently. The legal situation in English law can therefore be distinguished from other legal systems in which claims against public authorities are based in public law such as the French administrative law (see Monti, *Osman v. UK- Transforming English Negligence Law into French Administrative Law*, ICLQ 1999, p. 766). From the perspective of English law, public authorities carry our services at the public expense to protect or to confer benefits on individuals. If an individual fails to receive these benefits or protection, it is not plain why he or she should be entitled to claim damages from the public authority. Monti has, broadly speaking, called the English liability rules "utilitarian- a sacrifice is allowed for the greater good and the loss lies where it falls" whereas the "collectivist" French rules pursue a greater good which requires the compensation of those who are injured as a result of a failure by the authorities to protect them (Ibid., p. 766).

[52] *X (Minors) v Bedfordshire C.C.* [1995] 2 AC, p. 633, HL.

when making difficult decisions to protect children.[53] However, a comparative study on similar cases in France and Germany revealed that the potential of civil liability in those countries did not make the public authorities less efficient and that in Germany their financial burden in relation to civil claims amounted only to 0.015 per cent of the total budget.[54] *The Guardian* rightly observed in this respect that in other contexts, judges insist on evidence whereas in cases like *X v. Bedfordshire County Council* they have been content to rely on unsubstantiated fears.[55]

Neither did the Court seem to be impressed by this criticism in *Z and Others*. The applicants in *Z and Others* were entitled to compensation, albeit through a finding of a violation of Article 13, not of Article 6. One might be inclined to ask whether the four children would have actually minded under which of the two provisions they were entitled to compensation, as long as they received compensation. The reality is that it probably was of significance for them as they could not sue the authority with direct responsibility under Article 13. Sir Sydney Kentridge QC identified this as the real weakness of *Z and Others*:

> The United Kingdom as a state is liable under Article 13 because its courts do not provide a remedy for the inhuman treatment; yet the courts are held to be entitled to refuse the obvious remedy on no ground other than that the defendant is a local authority. Where does this leave the public policy arguments which supposedly underpin the decision of the House of Lords? I would say that this contradiction demonstrates that the majority in *Z and others* fudged the issue, whereas the Court in *Osman* made a realistic assessment of where the fault truly lay.[56]

It should be added that the decisions in *Osman* and *Z and Others* go far beyond a mere dispute about Article 6 and English Tort Law. They are also a vivid example of occasional tensions between the United Kingdom and European institutions. An example are the comments by Lord Hoffmann on *Osman*.[57] Although declaring that his views should not be regarded as 'vulgar Euroscepticism', he raises serious issues such as the consideration of a possible withdrawal from the Strasbourg court, the suitability of having questions of human rights determined by an international tribunal, the cultural diversity between Council of Europe member states (especially between

[53] Clare Dyer, *The Children's Crusade* (The Guardian of 9 November 1999).

[54] Markesinis/Auby/Coester-Waltjen/Deakin, *Tortious Liability of Statutory Bodies: A Comparative and Economic Analysis of Five English Cases*, pp. 96–104; Markesinis/Fedtke, *Damages for the Negligence of Statutory Bodies*, Public Law 2007, p. 313.

[55] Clare Dyer, *The Children's Crusade* (The Guardian of 9 November 1999).

[56] Quoted with kind permission of Sir Sydney Kentridge QC. The speech is unpublished.

[57] Lord Hoffmann, *Human Rights and the House of Lords*, MLR 1999, p. 162.

'some old democracies, some former police states') and whether the Strasbourg Court 'is seeking to impose a Voltairean uniformity of values upon all the member states'.[58]

6. *Crown immunity: the case of* Roche v. the United Kingdom

The cases of *Osman* and *Z and Others* also serve as examples of how difficult the distinction between procedural and substantive limitations of a right occasionally proves to be in order to establish whether a "civil right" within the meaning of Article 6 (1) exists. As one writer observed: "(...) [T]he jurisprudence of the [Court] has become more concerned with whether a claimant has a 'civil right' than with whether democracy and the rule of law have been undermined."[59] If anything, those problems have worsened in a recent Grand Chamber-judgment by the Court on Crown immunity to which we will turn in the following.

Crown immunity is basically the application of the premise "the king can do no wrong". Prior to 1947, it was a well-established principle that the Crown was not liable in tort.[60] The Crown Proceedings Act 1947 made wide changes, both substantive and procedural, to the Crown's liability to be sued.[61] Section 2 of the Act created for the first time a right to claim damages in tort from the Crown, but subject to section 10 which was entitled "Provisions relating to the armed forces" and stated that the Crown could not be sued in tort in the case of death or injury of members if killed or injured in the course of their duties and if the Secretary of State issued a certificate that the death or injury was attributable to service for the purposes of entitlement to war pension. Both provisions are in the first part of the Act entitled "Substantive law", in contrast with the second part of the Act ("Jurisdiction and procedure"). Section 10 was later basically repealed by the 1987 Crown Proceedings (Armed Forces) Act.[62]

The applicant had been a soldier in the British army until 1968. In the 1980s he was diagnosed with hypertension, bronchial asthma and high blood pressure and was subsequently registered as an invalid. The applicant alleged that he was suffering from the effects of his exposure to toxic chemicals (mustard and nerve gas) during tests on armed forces personnel carried out in the army barracks during the period 1962–1963. He complained, *inter alia*, that he did not have adequate access to court as a result of the certificate

---

[58] Ibid., p. 164.

[59] Nicol, *Judicial Immunity and Human Rights*, EHRLR 2006, p. 562.

[60] Clayton/Tomlinson, *The Law of Human Rights*, 11.28.

[61] *Roche v. the United Kingdom* [GC] (no. 32555/96), Judgment of 19 October 2005, para. 76.

[62] Case note EHRLR 2006, p. 80.

issued by the Secretary of State under section 10 of the Crown Proceedings Act 1947.

The Grand Chamber of the Court was highly divided over the issue whether or not a "civil right" existed in order to engage Article 6 (1). Whereas the majority (nine judges) considered that the impugned restriction flowed from the applicable principles governing the substantive right of action in domestic law (with the result that Article 6 was inapplicable and there had consequently not been a violation of that provision), a minority of eight judges considered the limitation to be of a procedural nature with the consequence that Article 6 (1) had applied and possibly had been violated.

a) *The decision of the majority*

In its judgment, the Court referred to the Court of Appeal and House of Lord ruling in a parallel case, *Matthews v. Ministry of Defence*[63] in which both courts reasoned that Article 6 (1) did not apply because section 10 of the Crown Proceedings Act 1947 was a provision of substantive law delimiting the rights of servicemen from making damages claims against the Crown.[64] In particular, the House of Lords had unanimously found that section 10 of the Crown Proceedings Act 1947 maintained the existing absence of liability in tort of the Crown to servicemen. The provision did therefore not confer immunity from liability which had been previously recognised but that such a claim had never existed and was not created by the 1947 Act.[65] The decisions of the Court of Appeal and the House of Lords have to be seen in contrast to the decision of the High Court which, at first instance, had found in *Matthews* that there had been a procedural and disproportionate restriction and consequently a violation of Article 6 (1). As one of their Lordships noted: "[The] uncertain shadow of *Osman* still lies over this area of law."[66]

The Court reasoned that in the instance that superior national courts had analysed in a comprehensive and convincing manner the precise nature of the impugned restriction, it would need strong reasons to differ from the conclusion by finding, contrary to the national courts' view, that there was arguably a right recognised by domestic law.[67] Finding that it was necessary to look beyond the appearances and the language used, the Court stated:

---

[63] *Matthews v. Ministry of Defence* (Court of Appeal, 2002 EWCA Civ, p. 773; House of Lords, 2003 UKHL, p. 4).

[64] For a similar decision by the Commission on earlier applications, see *Dyer v. the United Kingdom*, D/R 1984, p. 246; *Ketterick v. the United Kingdom*, (no. 9803/82), Commission decision, EHRR 1983, p. 465.

[65] House of Lords, 2003 UKHL, p. 4.

[66] Lord Walker, 2003 UKHL, para. 140.

[67] *Roche v. the United Kingdom*, para. 120.

> The Court must not be unduly influenced by, for example, the legislative techniques used (…) or by the labels put on the relevant restriction in domestic law: as the Government noted, the oft-used word 'immunity' can mean an 'immunity from liability" (in principle, a substantive limitation) or an 'immunity from suit' (suggestive of a procedural limitation).[68]

The Court noted several reasons for its decision that section 10 of the Act was a provision of substantive law. It disagreed with the applicant that the section 10 certificate issued by the Secretary of State operated as a procedural restriction to prevent him from pursuing a right of action which he enjoyed under the 1947 Act from the moment he suffered injury; having regard to the its historical context and the legislative intent, the Court found that the object of the certification process was to facilitate the grant of a pension to injured service personnel by obviating the need to prove that the injury was attributable to service, but not to introduce the Crown's liability in tort for such injuries.[69] Such a right had never existed and was not created by the 1947 Act. This was supported by the fact that section 10 was in the first part of the Act entitled "Substantive law". Regarding the fact that the House of Lords in *Matthews* had stated that such certificates had been routinely issued in the past forty years (and any practitioner would have advised the applicant that the certificate was bound to issue), the Court considered the narrow discretion of the Secretary of State under section 10 of the 1947 Act to be fundamentally different from the discretion enjoyed by a foreign government not to waive State immunity in proceedings before the courts of the forum State to prevent a claim otherwise well-founded in domestic law.[70] The Court also distinguished the case from *Tinelly & Sons Ltd and Others v. the United Kingdom*[71] where under the relevant legislation the Secretary of State could issue a certificate to stop proceedings concerning a right which was recognised in national law (a claim of damages for religious discrimination).[72] Consequently, the Court concluded that:

> In such circumstances, the applicant had no (civil) "right" recognised under domestic law which would attract the application of Article 6 § 1 of the Convention. (…) The Court concludes that Article 6 is not applicable and that there has not therefore been a violation of that provision.[73]

---

[68] Ibid., para. 121.

[69] Ibid., paras. 122–123.

[70] Ibid., para. 123.

[71] *Tinelly & Sons Ltd and Others v. the United Kingdom* (nos. 20390/92 and 21322/93), Judgment of 10 July 1998, RJD 1998-IV.

[72] *Roche v. the United Kingdom*, para. 123.

[73] Ibid., paras. 124–125.

b) *The opinion of the eight dissenting judges*

In a dissenting opinion by Judge Loucaides (joined by the other seven dissenting judges), the minority disagreed with the Court and found that section 10 of the 1947 Act in fact served as an "immunity from suit" for the Crown. The dissenting judges basically took the approach of the High Court in *Matthews* which, unlike the Court of Appeal and the House of Lords in that case, had found section 10 of the 1947 Act to be incompatible with Article 6 because it constituted a procedural bar which was, in the light of political and social developments, disproportionate.

The argument of the dissenting judges was as follows. The applicant had a civil right in respect of the tort of negligence, subject to a procedural limitation. Consequently, there had been a right of action but the remedy was unavailable.[74] The fact that the certificate as a condition for preventing an action in tort against the Crown was routinely issued as a matter of policy did not mean that the responsible Secretary of State could not depart from this policy if he wished to.[75] Given the political status of the Secretary of State, his intervention involved the exercise of a substantial discretion and thus indicated a procedural rather than a substantive limitation. This was particularly supported because it appeared that such a certificate had not been issued in respect of another test participant in the same position as the applicant.[76] Thus, the dissenting judges stated:

> The Secretary of State may not have a wide discretion comparable to that of a foreign government in deciding whether or not to waive State immunity, but he certainly does have the possibility or the power to decide each case in one way or another. If he issues the certificate there can be no judicial action. If he does not, people in the applicant's position can bring an action on a legal basis that already exists. Indeed, it is important to stress that in such cases the existing legal basis is the general right to sue the State in tort under section 2 of the Act. (…) The legal basis of the right is there. The remedy is conditional.[77]

It appears from the dissenting opinion that the eight judges did not only consider Article 6 (1) to apply in the present case because, in their view, the applicant had a "civil right" to sue the Crown in tort, but that they also found that the Crown immunity established under section 10 of the 1947 Act could not be considered a proportionate interference with the right of access to court.

---

[74] Dissenting opinion of Judge Loucaides (joined by Judges Rozakis, Zupancic, Straznicka, Casadevall, Thomassen, Maruste and Traja) in *Roche v. the United Kingdom*.

[75] Ibid.

[76] Ibid.

[77] Ibid.

7. *Various approaches to a resolution of the conflict between "immunity from suit" and "immunity from liability"*

Given the enormous difficulties (in particular in the case of *Roche v. the United Kingdom*) in determining whether a limitation on a right is substantial or procedural, the question arises how to deal with this problem under Article 6 (1). It has become clear that the case-law of the Court is rather inconsistent and consequently that no approach can be fully consistent with or reconcile all judgments that have been discussed above.[78]

a) *The "Gearty thesis"*

Based on an alternative interpretation of the *Ashingdane* judgment, Professor Gearty has provided an important interpretation of the case-law by proposing a test to establish infringements of the right to a court that operates at two levels that are mutually exclusive.[79] The first level (the so-called "threshold" level) concerns those applications in which the applicant can show that he or she had an arguable civil claim in domestic law. If that level is met, the guarantees under Article 6 (1) are engaged, *i.e.* the Court will not so much consider the limitation on the right as such but whether the applicants had a fair and public hearing within a reasonable time by an independent and impartial tribunal. It appears that the Court took this approach in *Z and Others* when finding that the applicants were able to argue their case in several courts before which the proceedings had been fair, independent and impartial. If the applicant however cannot prove that he or she had an arguable civil right (and therefore the "threshold" level is not satisfied), the Court should ask at a second level whether the deprivation of the applicant's civil right is contrary to the *Ashingdane* criteria (legitimate aim and proportionality). This would be the so-called "European fallback test" to ensure that the Court retains a proper supervisory function.

The test has been criticised by several authors as "at odds"[80] or as "not fitting happily"[81] with the Strasbourg jurisprudence. As Wright put it:

> Thus, according to Gearty, a claimant cannot on the one hand have both an arguable case that engages Article 6 and then also seek to engage another level of supervision, the jurisprudence relating to the right of access (proportionality

[78] Hickman, *The "uncertain shadow": Throwing Light on the Right to a Court under Article 6 (1) ECHR*, Public Law 2004, p. 133.

[79] Gearty, *Unravelling Osman*, MLR 2001, pp. 159 et seq.

[80] Wright, *Tort & Human Rights*, p. xxxii; ibid., *The Retreat from Osman*, p. 70.

[81] Hickman, *The "uncertain shadow": Throwing Light on the Right to a Court under Article 6 (1) ECHR*, Public Law 2004, p. 133.

> and legitimacy) that is properly the fallback test. This approch is unduly restrictive and out of tune generally with the Strasbourg jurisprudence which echews narrow formalism.[82]

Moreover, the Court has made clear in its case-law that it is exactly in the instance that the applicant does *not* have a civil right on at least arguable grounds that it is less inclined to require the exclusion of that right to be justified.[83] Therefore, the "European fallback test" would in fact require greater justification than the test applied once the "threshold level" had been met. It is here that the approach does not appear to be very consistent.

b) *A "common sense application" of Article 6 (1)*

Nicol has proposed limiting the application of Article 6 (1) to its underlying rationale, which is "to maintain the rule of law and the separation of powers".[84] Pointing to the fact that inadequate attention has been given to the substantive rights guaranteed by Article 6, he suggests that the Court should have asked in *Osman* and *Z and Others* whether the applicants had a "fair and public hearing within a reasonable time by an independent and impartial tribunal" instead of focusing on the nature of the immunity at issue:

> In both *Z* and *Osman*, the applicants had two public hearings, in which all disputed facts had been assumed to have been found in their favour. The results in these cases should not have been determined by technical threshold tests but by a common sense application of Art.6 (1) itself.[85]

This approach is however at odds with the principle that the right of access to court must not become theoretical and illusory, but has to be practical and effective. It should be recalled that, despite the fact that the applicants in *Z and Others* had two public hearings, their claim was dismissed by the English courts because of an exclusionary rule that applied irrespective of the merits of their case. That the facts were found "in the applicants' favour" was obviously not of much help to them in the view of an absolute exclusionary rule. As Judge Thomassen rightly observed in *Z and Others*:

> It is true that (…) the applicants were not prevented in any practical manner from bringing their claims before the domestic courts. The case was litigated up to the House of Lords, the applicants being provided with legal aid for that purpose. Nor is it the case that any procedural rules of limitation had been relied on. However, the notion of 'access to a court' under Article 6 guarantees

---

[82] Wright, *Tort Law & Human Rights*, p. xxxii.

[83] Ibid., p. xxxii.

[84] Nicol, *Judicial Immunity and Human Rights*, EHRLR 2006, p. 560 (with reference to Lord Hoffmann in *Matthews v. Minstry of Defence*).

[85] Ibid., p. 560.

> not only that the applicants have their claims brought before the courts, but implies also the right to have those claims examined on the basis of the facts before the courts and to have them decided on.[86]

It is therefore not sufficient merely to point out that the applicants were not prevented from bringing their claim before the domestic courts. To hold otherwise would reduce the right of access to court to a mere "physical" access.[87]

c) *The "dual limb"-approach*
An important analysis of the case-law has also been made by Hickman.[88] Rejecting the notion that Article 6 (1) can prescribe the substantive content of domestic rights and accepting that the *Ashingdane* criteria are only applicable to procedural bars (which, in his opinion, constitutes the "first limb" right of access), he argues that the uncertainty in the Court's case-law results from the failure to recognise that Article 6 (1) has always had both procedural and substantive components.[89] His reading of the judgments of *Golder* and *Fayed* reveals that there exists a "second limb" which can be described as a constitutional safeguard which prevents States simply from removing whole tracts of civil rights. This "second limb" complements the right of access to court and the explicit protection of the independence and impartiality of tribunals and would apply without distinction between procedural and substantive abrogations. In order to satisfy this second component, the Court would (once it had found that a limitation was of a substantive nature, so the *Ashingdane* criteria would not apply) merely have to establish that the limitation was not arbitrary or unreasonable.

In the present author's opinion, the above approach is questionable from a dogmatic point of view. Assuming that a substantive limitation would not come within the "first limb" of the right of access to court, the obvious result would be that the applicant had no "civil right" and that consequently Article 6 (1) was inapplicable. That should be the end of the story. It is difficult to see how the Court should then proceed to investigate whether a constitutional safeguard as a "second limb" was satisfied. What if the Court found that the constitutional safeguard was not satisfied? The Court could not find a violation of Article 6 (1) if the previous result was that the provision was

[86] *Z and Others v. the United Kingdom*, partly dissenting opinion of Judge Thomassen joined by Judges Casadevall and Kovler.

[87] See also the concurring opinion of Judge Costa in the case of *Markovic v. Italy* (see above, p. 158).

[88] Hickman, *The "uncertain shadow": Throwing Light on the Right to a Court under Article 6 (1) ECHR*, Public Law 2004, p. 122.

[89] Ibid., p. 124.

inapplicable because there was no "civil right" in the first place. Although the Court would have already deprived itself of its jurisdiction by finding that there was no "civil right" at issue, it would then have to consider whether the restriction was in breach of Article 6 (1).[90] This does not appear very convincing.

Nevertheless, Hickman's approach is important as he recognises that the right of access to court has a constitutional component which applies to both procedural and substantive limitations on a civil right. It should be recalled that the Court noted this component in the *Fayed* judgment when stating that "it would not be consistent with the rule of law (…) if (…) a State could, without restraint or control by the Convention enforcement bodies, remove from the jurisdiction of the courts a whole range of civil claims or confer immunities from civil liability on large groups or categories of persons".[91]

In *Matthews v. Ministry of Defence*, Lord Walker stated that "the Court's wide and rather speculative observations in *Fayed* (…) marked a diversion which proved, in *Z*, to be a blind alley".[92] However, the meaning of the "constitutional safeguard" noted by the Court in *Fayed* can be explained with the following example:[93] if a legislative provision denied all women the right to bring actions in defamation, the Court would have to find under its current approach that, because the limitation on the right to sue for defamation was clearly of substantive nature, a woman had no "civil right" in this respect. Consequently, any complaint about this legislation would fall outside the scope of Article 6 (with the result that the non-discrimination provision of Article 14 would not be applicable either). Since the removal of the right to bring an action in defamation for women would however clearly be arbitrary and unreasonable, the "constitutional safeguard" established by the Court in *Fayed* would prevent such a law to escape from the Court's scrutiny.

d) *Proposal for a solution: the establishment of a "but for" test as first proposed by Francoise Hampson*

In view of the somewhat inconsistent case-law of the Court on domestic immunities and the difficulties to find an approach to reconcile this case-law, the question should be asked: where did it all go wrong? In the present author's opinion, and to paraphrase the above statement by Lord Walker in

[90] The same argument can in fact be made against the test proposed by Professor Gearty which was considered above.

[91] *Fayed v. the United Kingdom*, para. 65.

[92] *Matthews v. Ministry of Defence*, 2003 UKHL, para. 140.

[93] The example was given by Hampson, *Restrictions on Rights of Action and the European Convention on Human Rights*, BYIL 1991, p. 288, and also quoted with approval by Bröhmer, *State Immunity*, p. 180.

Matthews v. Minstry of Defence, the Court started to focus too much on the procedural/substantive-distinction which eventually proved, in *Roche v. the United Kingdom*, to be a blind alley.

(1) *The dissenting opinion of Judge Zupancic in* Roche v. the United Kingdom

As Judge Zupancic observed in his dissenting opinion in *Roche v. the United Kingdom*, the artificial separation of procedural and substantive limitations is based on a false premise which "generates hard cases, as the split in the vote demonstrates, which make bad law".[94] The reason for this might not only lie in, as the Court itself observed in *Fayed*, the fact that it might only be a matter of legislative techniques whether a limitation is phrased in a procedural or in a substantive way. The crucial point is that the Court is trying to distinguish between "immunity from liability" (a limitation on a right) and "immunity from suit" (a limitation on its remedy). Both are however so interdependent that a distinction eventually becomes impossible.[95] This was probably what led Judge Zupancic in *Roche v. the United Kingdom* to comment as follows:

> If the remedy does not exist a right is not a right; if the remedy is not procedurally pursued the right will not be vindicated. The right and its remedy are not only interdependent. They are consubstantial. To speak of rights as if they existed apart from the procedural context is artificially (...) to separate what in practical terms is inseparable. A substantive right *is* its remedy.[96]

Commenting on the very close decision (nine to eight) in *Roche v. the United Kingdom*, Judge Zupancic also observed:

> We may have muddled through another case but the underlying false premise remains. The dilemma is certain to come back. The way to address this dilemma is, obviously, to cease subscribing to the false premise.[97]

(2) *The "but for" test*

In the present author's view, a possible departure from the substantive/procedural-distinction could be achieved by adopting an approach which has originally been proposed by Francoise Hampson[98] almost twenty years

---

[94] Dissenting opinion of Judge Zupancic in *Roche v. the United Kingdom*.

[95] See also Gearty, *Unravelling Osman*, MLR 2001, who called the procedural/substantive-distinction "arid nonsense" (p. 178).

[96] Ibid.

[97] Ibid.

[98] Hampson, *Restrictions on Rights of Action and the European Convention on Human Rights*, BYIL 1991, p. 279.

ago but which has not received much attention as to date. Hampson suggests a "but for" test: when establishing whether there existed a civil right in the domestic law on arguable grounds in cases where an immunity poses a restriction on a cause of action, the Court should ask the question whether the applicant would have had a cause of action "but for" the restriction.[99] If the question is answered in the affirmative, Article 6 (1) is applicable. For example, in the case of *Roche v. the United Kingdom*, the Court – instead of determining whether section 10 of the 1947 Act was a substantive or procedural limitation – should have asked whether the applicant had a cause of action "but for" the limitation provided for by that provision: a right to sue in negligence for compensation in personal injury existed under section 2 of the 1947 Act which recognises the right to sue the Crown in tort. Hence Article 6 (1) would have applied. In *Fayed v. the United Kingdom*, the Court would simply have to ask whether in English law a person has a right to reputation in order to bring an action for defamation.[100] Using the "but for" test, Article 6 (1) would also have applied in *Osman,* given that a tort in negligence is generally recognised in English law, disregarding the fact that the applicants in *Osman* could not sue the police because the latter did not owe a duty of care to the applicants as the police were generally considered immune in this respect. It should be recalled that the applicants in *Osman* had fulfilled all prerequisites for a tort in negligence but for the duty of care.

(3) *Conclusion*

The suggested approach has several advantages. First, it shifts the main conflict between a domestic immunity (whether "immunity from suit" or "immunity from liability") and the right of access to court from the applicability stage of Article 6 (1) to the question whether the immunity at issue is justified, *i.e.* whether it is proportionate to the legitmate aim pursued. This would mark a shift of the conflict to a stage where it can be solved best. The obvious advantage would be simplicity, as the Court could avoid the investigation of complicated legislative techniques in the domestic legal system and the substantive/procedural distinction which has created such enormous

99 Ibid., p. 286.

100 It appears that Judge Martens took a similar approach in his dissenting opinion in *Fayed v. the United Kingdom* when stating that: "(...) there could be no doubt as to the applicants' right to reputation having been damaged. (...) [S]uch a right does exist, at least in principle, under all our national laws and it has not been contended that in this respect English law makes an exception by clearly and fully excluding such a right. (...) Consequently, the question whether under English law the defence of privilege constitutes a substantive limitation on the content of the right to reputation or a procedural barrrier to access to court is immaterial." (para. 7).

difficulties in the past. Second, the Court would not create any rights which have no basis in the domestic legal system, because Article 6 would only apply to rights that are generally recognised therein (e.g. the right to bring an action for defamatory remarks or the right to bring an action in negligence). Given that the Court has established that the concept of a "civil right" is autonomous, the "but for" test ("Could the applicant sue but for the restriction?") would not be inconsistent with general Convention principles. It should be noted that, by invoking the autonomy of Convention concepts, the Court has in other areas gone behind matters of form to investigate the substance of an issue.[101]

Thirdly, the approach suggested would not necessarily lead to a different outcome in the case-law, as the *Ashingdane* criteria could be applied in a manner that is consistent with the Court's jurisprudence in the past.[102] It would merely lead to a different reasoning as applications would no longer be turned down by the Court with a possible narrow majority finding that there was no "civil right" at issue. In fact, this approach is not very different from the way the Court decided in *Ashingdane* and *Fayed* when assuming that Article 6 (1) applied, but without creating insecurity by addressing this question hypothetically. For example, there would have been good reasons to find no violation of Article 6 (1) in *Roche v. the United Kingdom* because the Crown immunity at issue could have been considered proportionate. The Commission decided that way in *Dyer v. the United Kingdom* because the cause of action was substituted by a pension entitlement, which was however much lower than the damage asserted. However, the strong minority of eight dissenting judges in *Roche* and the fact that the immunity at issue was abolished in 1987 might have suggested a different outcome. On the other hand, the immunities in the cases of *Osman* and *Z and Others* could have been considered a disproportionate restriction on Article 6 (1) given that those immunities were, compared with other European countries, significantly broader and the cases involved the exclusion of remedies for issues that concerned such core Convention rights as the right to life (Article 2) and the prohibition of inhuman and degrading treatment (Article 3). Moreover, the present approach would also include the "constitutional safeguard"-clause established in *Fayed* in a manner that would be dogmatically coherent. Only if there exists a "civil right" on at least arguable grounds will Article 6 (1)

[101] Hampson, *Restrictions on Rights of Action and the European Convention on Human Rights*, BYIL 1991, p. 289; see for instance the case of *Oztürk v. Germany* (no. 8544/79, Judgment of 21 February 1984, Series A 73) regarding the autonomous meaning of a "criminal charge" under Article 6 (1).

[102] Hampson, *Restrictions on Rights of Action and the European Convention on Human Rights*, BYIL 1991, p. 288.

apply; only if Article 6 (1) is applicable can the Court safeguard that Contracting Parties do not arbitrarily remove whole tracts of civil rights.

8. *Judicial immunity in English tort law and in other legal systems*

National judges enjoy certain immunity from liability in numerous Member States of the Council of Europe. There are several reasons for that immunity. First, there is a concern that without such immunity there would be less finality in litigation and therefore less legal certainty.[103] Second, it is feared that judges would be influenced in their decision-making by the threat of personal liability.[104] In the case of *Ernst and Others v. Belgium*, the Court found that judicial immunity was a long-standing practice intended to ensure the proper administration of justice and was to be found in other domestic and international legal systems.[105] In that case, several Belgian journalists had lodged a complaint about searches of their newspapers' offices and their homes. The search warrants had been issued by an investigating judge in connection with the prosecution of members of the State legal service for breach of confidence following leaks in highly sensitive criminal cases. The journalists' application to be joined as civil parties in the proceedings which they had brought against the investigating judge and several other people was declared inadmissible by the Court of Cassation in respect of that judge because the latter enjoyed judicial immunity.[106]

The Strasbourg Court did not find a violation of Article 6 (1). Having established that judicial immunity served the legitimate aim of pursuing the proper administration of justice, the Court considered the limitation on the applicants' right of access to court proportionate, because the applicants had other remedies available to protect their Convention rights. Apart from pursuing their civil action against the other persons who were not members of the judiciary, the applicants could have also brought a civil action in damages against the Belgian State in respect of the unlawfulness of the search warrants.[107] The Court noted that the applicants had therefore not been deprived of an action to seek reparation.[108]

---

[103] For a general overview see: Olowofoyeku, *Suing Judges: A Study of Judicial Immunity*; ibid, *State Liability for the Exercise of Judicial Power*, Public Law 1998, p. 452.

[104] Nicol, *Judicial Immunity and Human Rights*, EHRLR 2006, p. 563.

[105] *Ernst and Others v. Belgium* (no. 33400/96), Judgment of 15 July 2003, para. 50. Regarding the immunity of international judges, see above, p. 134, and Koster, *Immunität internationaler Richter*.

[106] *Ernst and Others v. Belgium*, paras. 11–25.

[107] Ibid., para. 54.

[108] Ibid., para. 55.

Not everybody shares the view that a broad judicial immunity is necessary to guarantee a proper administration of justice. It has been argued that the above reasons for judicial immunity are not very convincing: neither would the relaxing of judicial immunity open the "floodgates" for disappointed litigants to sue the judges who had decided against them, nor does the fear of personal liability justify the extent to which judges are immune in the legal systems of some Member States, for example under the current English legal system where the immunity is relatively broad.[109] Whereas the House of Lords recently decided that the immunity of advocates from liability for negligence was no longer justified,[110] judges enjoy in English tort law immunity in respect of actions taken in the exercise of judicial functions unless the judge acts knowingly in excess of jurisdiction.[111] This also includes immunity from liability for corrupt or malicious acts. Nicol has therefore suggested that a qualified immunity (subjecting judges to liability only where they intended to cause harm) might be more suitable.[112] The argument deserves approval as the independence of judges would not necessarily be endangered if they were not immune from liability for corrupt or malicious acts. It appears however that the Court in *Ernst and Others v. Belgium* found that absolute immunity of judges from liability (including corrupt or malicious acts) was a proportionate restriction on Article 6 (1). The Court thus granted the Contracting States a relatively wide margin of appreciation. However, it is here that a rather broad judicial immunity might conflict with the right of access to court under Article 6 (1).

---

109 Nicol, *Judicial Immunity and Human Rights*, EHRLR 2006, p. 562.

110 *Arthur J.S. Hall & Co v. Simons* [2002] 1 AC, p. 615; see also Seneviratne, *The rise and fall of advocates' immunity*, Legal Studies 2001, p. 644.

111 Clayton/Tomlinson, *The Law of Human Rights*, 11.36; Nicol, *Judicial Immunity and Human Rights*, EHRLR 2006, p. 562.

112 Nicol (*Judicial Immunity and Human Rights*, EHRLR 2006, p. 562) assumes that the Court would probably accept the immunity under English law as a proportionate restriction of Article 6 (1) or – in the alternative – that the Court would not find Article 6 to be engaged because there was no "civil right" within the meaning of that provision. Under its current approach, the Court would possibly consider judicial immunity as being a substantive rather than a procedural limitation since the English courts have found that judges do not owe a duty of care (which is a prerequisite for a tort in negligence) in this respect. The result would be that there is no "civil right" at issue and that Article 6 (1) is consequently inapplicable. Applying the "but for"-test suggested above, one would find that there was a civil right at issue (the right to sue in negligence, disregarding the restriction imposed by judicial immunity), but that the immunity, at least as far as harm caused inadvertently or negligently is concerned, was proportionate to the above-mentioned legitimate aims pursued.

II. *Parliamentary Immunity*

The concept of parliamentary immunity was established some four hundred years ago. Today, all Contracting States protect the free speech of their parliamentarians. So does the Council of Europe and the European Parliament as regards its representatives and members.[113] The European Court of Human Rights itself has, in two cases concerning freedom of expression under Article 10 of the Convention, stressed the particular importance of free speech for Members of Parliament (MPs). In *Castells v. Spain*[114] (in which the applicant was a Spanish parliamentarian who had been convicted of insulting the government) and *Jerusalem v. Austria*[115] (which concerned an injunction against a parliamentarian for having expressed negative views about private associations that were active in a public debate on a controversial issue), the Court found that while freedom of expression is important for everybody, it is especially so for an elected representative of the people.[116] The Court stated that interference with the freedom of expression of an opposition Member of Parliament therefore calls for the closest scrutiny on the part of the Court.[117]

However, the degree to which parliamentary free speech is protected varies across the European continent. Before deciding on the case of *A v. the United Kingdom* (the first case brought before the Court on the conflict between Article 6 and parliamentary immunity), the Court conducted an extensive comparative law analysis on the scope of parliamentary immunity in the Contracting States.[118] The survey unfortunately remains confidential because the Court did not consider it appropriate to make the information available.[119] But the third-party interventions of eight Contracting States in *A v. the United Kingdom* reveal the different approaches that States chose in order to protect the work of their parliaments from outside interference.[120]

---

113 For the Council of Europe: Article 40 of the Statute of the Council of Europe and Articles 14 and 15 of the General Agreement on Privileges and Immunities of the Council of Europe; for the European Union: Article 9 of the Protocol to the General Agreement on Privileges and Immunities of the European Communities.

114 *Castells v. Spain* (no. 11798/85), Judgment of 23 April 1992, Series A 236.

115 *Jerusalem v. Austria* (no. 26958/95), Judgment of 27 February 2001, RJD 2001–II, paras. 36 and 40.

116 Ibid., para. 36.

117 *Castells v. Spain*, para. 42; *Jerusalem v. Austria*, para. 36.

118 Wildhaber, *The Role of Comparative Law in the Case-Law of the European Court of Human Rights*, in: Festschrift Georg Ress, p. 1104.

119 Ibid.

120 According to the third party-interventions in the case of *A v. the United Kingdom* (paras. 37–58), it appeared that parliamentary immunity usually may be waived, but not by the

Whereas the Commission occasionally had to decide on the conflict, the Court has issued several judgments and decisions in recent years, finding violations of the right of access to court on several occasions in cases against Italy (and on one occasion against Greece). Cases concerning parliamentary immunity can be categorised into three basic groups: first, cases concerning the content of a statement made by a Member of Parliament, and – secondly – cases concerning the occasion on which that statement was made. A third category of cases concerns the refusal of Parliament to lift the immunity of one of its members, even though that Member of Parliament explicitly requests Parliament to do so.

Cases concerning parliamentary immunity generally involved defamation proceedings brought against Members of Parliament. In this context, it should be noted that, even though Article 6 does not grant the right to institute criminal proceedings against third persons (any such complaint would be incompatible *ratione materiae* with the provisions of the Convention), the right of access to court applies when the victim joins the criminal proceedings as a civil party. From that moment the proceedings cover a "civil right" within the meaning of Article 6.[121]

1. *The case-law of the Commission*

On three occasions, the Commission declared applications inadmissible in which applicants complained of a violation of their right of access to court because their claims had been rejected by the domestic courts due to parliamentary immunity. These decisions reflect the varying approaches the Convention organs took over the years with regard to immunities.

In *X v. Austria*, a case decided in 1969, the Commission noted that parliamentary immunity was traditionally recognised in all Contracting States. It declared the application inadmissible as being manifestly ill-founded mainly because it found that it was inconceivable that the State parties would have wished to derogate from such a fundamental principle in favour of

---

individual MP as the immunity is not concerned with his or her private interests, but rather with the interests of Parliament as a whole. Some countries (Austria, France and Norway) interpret parliamentary immunity strictly as not extending to acts outside of Parliament (see also the "Italian cases" below). In several countries (e.g. Finland, Norway and the Netherlands), a warning may be issued to an MP in view of insulting or improper behaviour and, as *ultima ratio*, an MP may be excluded by Parliament from the right to speak for the rest of the debate. See also the "Comparative law"-part in the case of *Kart v. Turkey* (no. 8917/05), Judgment of 8 July 2008, paras. 41–51.

[121] *Cordova v. Italy (No. 1)* (no. 40877/98), Judgment of 30 January 2003, RJD 2003–I, paras. 13 and 49; *Tomasi v. France*, para. 121.

Article 6.[122] Seven years later, the Commission declared inadmissible the application of *Agee v. the United Kingdom*[123] because the applicant, a former CIA agent, did not have a "civil right" to sue a British Member of Parliament for defamation in view of harmful allegations because the latter was protected by parliamentary privilege. The view that, in cases where immunities apply, the claimant lacks a "civil right", has rightly been given up by the Convention organs in recent years. In the event that a Parliament decides to waive the privilege, the applicant could have pursued his claim. Thus, it cannot be said that he lacked a "civil right" to sue the Member of Parliament for defamation.[124] Around the same time as *Agee*, the Commission issued its report in *Golder*, in which it stressed that the immunity from suit of MPs concerned rather the inaccessibility of a defendant than a court; a view that is likewise questionable. Lastly, in 1996, the Commission adopted the Court's approach in the then recently decided *Fayed* case: it left open whether or not Article 6 was applicable because the "Ashingdane criteria" were also applied under Article 8. Applying these principles, the Commission briefly noted that parliamentary immunity pursued a legitimate aim, and that even blanket immunities for Members of Parliament served as a proportionate restriction.[125] The latter argument strongly resembled the reasoning of the Court in its first judgment on the matter, the case of *A v. the United Kingdom*, to which we shall turn in the following.

2. *The case-law of the Court*

As has already been said, applications before the Court concerning parliamentary immunity and Article 6 can be roughly divided up into three groups of cases. First, the content of a certain allegedly defamatory statement by a Member of Parliament is relevant. Second, the occasion on which statement has been made (*i.e.* whether it was made in or outside of Parliament) has to be determined. A third category of cases concerns the refusal of Parliament to lift the immunity of one of its members, even though that Member of Parliament explicitly requests Parliament to do so. It is appropriate to deal with these matters separately.

---

122 *X v. Austria* (no. 3374/67), Commission decision of 6 February 1969.

123 *Agee v. the United Kingdom* (no. 7729/76), Commission decision of 17 December 1976, D/R 7, p. 164.

124 See above, p. 161.

125 *Young v. Ireland* (no. 25646/94), Commission decision of 17 Janaury 1996, D/R 84–A, p. 122; *O'Faolain v. Ireland* (no. 29099/05); see also Nicol/Millar/Sharland, *Media Law and Human Rights*, p. 149.

a) *The content of the remarks by a Member of Parliament*

(1) *The case of* A v. the United Kingdom

The applicant, a young black woman with two children living in Bristol, was named by her Member of Parliament during a parliamentary debate on municipal housing policy. The Member of Parliament stated that her brother was in prison, gave her precise address and made derogatory remarks about the behaviour of both her and her children. He mentioned verbal abuse, truancy, vandalism and drug activity and called the family "neighbours from hell", a phrase which was subsequently quoted in local and national newspapers.[126] Following the speech and the reporting of it by the press, the applicant received racist hate-mail. She and her children were eventually rehoused; the children had to change schools. The applicant stated that the allegations made by the Member of Parliament had not been supported by the local authorities but that they had rather been spread by neighbours motivated by racism and spite, but her efforts to have the comments rectified were to no avail.[127]

The Court found that a rule of parliamentary immunity was consistent with and reflected generally-recognised rules within the Member States of the Council of Europe and the European Union. It served the legitimate aims of protecting free speech in Parliament and maintaining the separation of powers between the legislature and the judiciary.[128] Therefore, it could not in principle be regarded as imposing a disproportionate restriction on the right of access to court.[129] The Court also observed that parliamentary immunity as provided for in the United Kingdom was somewhat narrower than in other Contracting States as it only applied to statements made during the course of parliamentary debates.[130] Thus, it could not be said that the United Kingdom had exceeded its margin of appreciation and that the interference had been disproportionate in the present case. Although the Court recognised that the statements at issue had been "extremely serious and clearly unnecessary" and had severe consequences for the applicant, these factors could not alter its finding (by six votes to one) that there had been no violation of Article 6 in the present case.[131] It reasoned that the creation of exceptions to parliamentary

[126] Ibid., paras. 13–15.
[127] Ibid., paras. 18–20.
[128] Ibid., para. 77.
[129] Ibid., para. 78.
[130] Ibid., para 84.
[131] Ibid., para. 89.

immunity for particular circumstances would severely undermine the legitimate aims pursued.[132]

(2) *Discussion of the judgment*

It is here that the judgment is a bit overcautious as the Court should have taken into account that other Contracting States do not provide for parliamentary immunity in cases of defamatory statements. For example, Article 46 (1) of the German constitution (the Basic Law) provides for immunity of Members of the German Parliament (*Bundestag*) as follows:

> At no time may a Member be subjected to court proceedings or disciplinary action or otherwise called to account outside the Bundestag for a vote cast or any speech or debate in the Bundestag or any of its committees. *This provision shall not apply to defamatory insults.*[133]

Arguably, the comments by the Member of Parliament in *A v. the United Kingdom* therefore would not have been protected by parliamentary immunity had they been made in a debate in the German parliament. It appears that Germany is not the only country that does not extend parliamentary immunity to defamatory statements.[134] Moreover, it is not reported that the "defamatory insults" exception in the German constitution has opened the door for unreasonable or vexatious litigations against Members of Parliament, thereby "seriously undermining" the legitimate aims of parliamentary immunity as feared by the Court in *A v. the United Kingdom*. On the contrary, it is currently debated in Germany to abolish the provisions on parliamentary immunity altogether.[135] The somewhat inflexible absolute rule of parliamentary immunity and its relationship with the right to reputation (as recognised by Article 8 of the Convention) of third persons was also addressed in the concurring opinion of Judge Costa, who, although voting against a violation of Article 6, stated:

> But should this sacrosanct principle not be tempered? Since the 1689 Bill of Rights and the 1791 French Constitution (...), relations between parliaments and the outside world have changed. Parliaments are no longer solely or chiefly concerned with protecting their members from the sovereign or the executive. Their concern should now be to affirm the complete freedom of expression of

132 Ibid., para. 88.

133 Emphasis added. The provision is also repeated in section 36 of the German Criminal Code.

134 See the dissenting opinion of Judge Loucaides in *A v. the United Kingdom*. See also Loucaides, *ECHR – Collected Essays*, pp. 213–214.

135 See *Der Tagesspiegel*, "Debatte über Immunität der Abgeordneten" (29 July 2006).

> their members, but also, perhaps, to reconcile that freedom with other rights and freedoms that are worthy of respect.[136]

A more flexible approach that would deny parliamentary immunity in cases of defamatory insults might also improve the quality of parliamentary debate instead of making Members of Parliament more cautious. As Judge Loucaides (the only judge who voted for a violation in the present case) pointed out:

> The argument regarding encouragement of an uninhibited debate on public issues is understandable. But the opposite argument appears to me more convincing: the suppression of untrue defamatory statements, apart from protecting the dignity of individuals, discourages false speech and improves the overall quality of public debate through a chilling effect on irresponsible parliamentarians.[137]

(3) *Conclusion*

Given the fact that the applicant had no other realistic possibility to seek redress against the defamatory statements[138] (unlike applicants who sue an international organisation or a foreign State which are protected by immunity), and taking into account that parliamentary immunity is not an obligation imposed "from outside" by international law, the Court should have been more critical when finding that the interference with the applicant's right of access to court in the present case was proportionate.[139] The above

---

[136] Concurring opinion of Judge Costa in *A v. the United Kingdom.*

[137] Dissenting opinion of Judge Loucaides in *A v. the United Kingdom.*

[138] The Court considered that the applicant was not entirely without means of redress: she could have filed a petition through any other MP with a view to securing a retraction. Moreover, in extreme cases misleading statements may be punishable as contempt and general control during public debate is exercised by the Speaker of Parliament (*A v. the United Kingdom*, para. 86). Therefore, the Court considered these factors as relevant to the question of proportionality. In his concurring opinion, Judge Costa rightly observed that this justification was rather unnecessary once the Court had found that absolute parliamentary immunity is in principle a proportionate interference with Article 6. Instead, he suggested to point out that the applicant was a voter in the constituency of the MP who had made the statements about her and that it would ultimately be for the voters to decide at the next election whether his attacks had been excessive (Concurring opinion of Judge Costa in *A v. the United Kingdom*). However, this suggestion cannot serve as an effective "alternative remedy" either.

[139] See also Krenc, *La règle de l'immunité parlementaire à l'epreuve de la Convention Européene des Droits de L'Homme*, RTDH 2003, p. 820, and Dembour, *Who Believes in Human Rights? Reflections on the European Convention*, p. 95: "[A v. the United Kingdom] nonetheless shows the excesses to which absolutism can lead and the way absolutism refuses to consider how the 'solutions' it proposes may be very problematic."

arguments would have justified the application of a narrower margin of appreciation than the one granted to the British government.

(4) *The case of* Zollmann v. the United Kingdom

In November 2003, the judgment of *A v. the United Kingdom* was confirmed by the Court in *Zollmann v. the United Kingdom*.[140] In that case, a Member of Parliament (the Minister of State at the Foreign and Commonwealth Office responsible for Africa) had named the applicants in respect of their involvement in exporting "blood diamonds" from Africa in breach of UN sanctions and stated that "those individuals are making money out of misery".[141] The statements were reported in the press but the allegations were never verified as criminal investigations against the applicant by the Belgian prosecution were later stayed. The applicant complained under Article 6 (1) that they had been unable to bring proceedings for defamation against the Member of Parliament. The Court basically followed its reasoning in *A v. the United Kingdom*.

b) *The occasion on which the statements have been made: the "Italian cases"*

The above cases have dealt with the statements of a Member of Parliament made in Parliament, *i.e.* during a parliamentary debate. However, there have been other cases in which the behaviour which gave rise to a claim against a Member of Parliament lacked such a clear connection with parliamentary activity. In these cases, the Court rightly adopted a narrow interpretation of the proportionality criterion, also in view of the fact that the applicants had no other remedies to pursue their claims. In several applications brought against Italy (and in one case against Greece), the Court found violations of Article 6 (1) because parliamentary immunity had been granted for statements made outside of parliament. These cases are remarkable because, together with the *Osman* ruling (which the Court however has meanwhile "reversed"), they remain as to date the only occasions on which the right of access has trumped the immunity in question.

The background to the "Italian cases" can be summarised as follows. Article 68 (1) of the Italian constitution provides that "Members of Parliament shall not be required to account for the opinions they express or the votes

---

[140] *Zollmann v. the United Kingdom* (no. 62902/00), Decision of 27 November 2003, RJD 2003–XII.

[141] Ibid.

they cast in the exercise of their functions". That provision is wider than regulations in other European countries as the wording also covers statements made outside of Parliament. Under Italian law, a legislative chamber (the "Parliamentary Immunities Commission") proposes to the Senate whether or not it should declare that certain acts are covered by parliamentary immunity. The Senate's resolution on the matter may usually not be quashed by the courts. However, if a court considers that the resolution represents an unlawful exercise of the legislative chambers' discretion, a court may raise a conflict of State powers before the Constitutional Court.[142] However, a person who joined the criminal proceedings against a Member of Parliament as a civil party does not have the right to raise a conflict of State powers. Any decision that the statements at issue are covered by parliamentary immunity therefore makes it impossible for that person to pursue proceedings aimed at establishing the liability of the Member of Parliament or at securing reparation for the damage suffered.[143]

In a number of applications brought against Italy, the applicants complained about a violation of their right of access to court because the legislative chambers had adopted a broad interpretation of Article 68 of the Italian Constitution, holding it to apply to opinions expressed outside of Parliament. In *Cordova v. Italy (No. 1)*, the applicant, an Italian prosecutor, had received cynical letters and a parcel with a little wooden horse, a tricycle and detective game from a senator for life (a former Italian president) in connection with the applicant's criminal investigation against a third person who had had dealings with that senator for life. In *Cordova v. Italy (No. 2)*,[144] an Italian Member of Parliament had made two speeches at election meetings, insulting the same applicant because of his criminal investigations. The cases of *De Jorio v. Italy*,[145] *Ielo v. Italy*[146] and *Patrono, Cascini and Stefanelli v. Italy*[147] all dealt with alleged defamatory statements made by Members of Parliament during various interviews with Italian newspapers. In all these cases, the applicants unsuccessfully sought to institute proceedings for defamation against the Members of Parliament, who were found to be entitled to parliamentary immunity.

The above cases have in common that the Members of Parliament were granted parliamentary immunity for statements made outside of parliament.

142 *Cordova v. Italy (No. 1)* (no. 40877/98), Judgment of 30 January 2003, RJD 2003–I, para. 24.
143 Ibid., para. 50.
144 *Cordova v. Italy (No. 2)* (no. 45649/99), Judgment of 30 January 2003, RJD 2003–I.
145 *De Jorio v. Italy* (no. 73936/01), Judgment of 3 June 2004.
146 *Ielo v. Italy* (no. 23053/02), Judgment of 15 March 2005.
147 *Patrono, Cascini and Stefanelli v. Italy* (no. 10180/04), Judgment of 20 April 2006.

The Court was not prepared to find that there had been a proportionate restriction of the right of access to court in those cases as the behaviour in question was not connected with the exercise of parliamentary functions in their strict sense. In *Cordova v. Italy (No. 1)*, the Court observed that "(…) ironic or derisive letters accompanied by toys personally addressed to a prosecutor cannot, by their very nature, be construed as falling within the scope of parliamentary functions. Such behaviour is more consistent with a personal quarrel."[148] In such circumstances, the denial of access to court could not be justified purely on the basis that the quarrel might be political in nature or connected with a political activity.[149] The Court took the view that the lack of any clear connection with a parliamentary activity required a narrow interpretation of the concept of proportionality, especially where the restrictions on the right of access to court stem from the resolution of a political body (in that case, the "Parliamentary Immunities Commission").[150] The Court also noted that the applicants were left with no reasonable alternative means of effectively pursuing their right to privacy against the defamatory statements.[151] The narrow interpretation of parliamentary immunity which the Court took in these cases is to be welcomed. The judgments were all taken unanimously and do not give rise to much controversy.[152]

It should be added that the Court has found that a narrow interpretation of parliamentary immunity is also required *ratione temporis*. In the case of *Tsalkitzis v. Greece*, the Court found that the granting of parliamentary immunity for alleged acts of blackmail and abuse of office committed by a person prior to his election to Parliament lacked a clear link between those acts and parliamentary activity. The Court also considered unsubstantiated the Greek government's argument that the temporary nature of parliamentary immunity meant that the applicant could renew his attempt to bring proceedings against that Member of Parliament once his term had ended: in the absence of any time-limits regarding the renewal of parliamentary office in the Greek constitution, the applicant might have been definitely deprived of his right of access to court.[153] In any event, the suspending of criminal pro-

---

148 *Cordova v. Italy (No. 1)*, para. 63.
149 *Cordova v. Italy (No. 2)*, para. 63.
150 Ibid., para. 63.
151 Ibid., para. 65.
152 See also Krenc, *La règle de l'immunité parlementaire à l'epreuve de la Convention Européene des Droits de L'Homme*, RTDH 2003, p. 820.
153 *Tsalkitzis v. Greece* (no. 11801/04), Judgment of 16 November 2006, para. 50.

ceedings of any kind against a Member of Parliament resulted in a substantial amount of time elapsing between the commission of the offence and the institution of criminal proceedings which rendered a prosecution uncertain, in particular regarding evidence.[154]

c) *The refusal of the request by a Member of Parliament to have his parliamentary immunity lifted: the case of* Kart v. Turkey

A third category of cases concern the refusal of Parliament to lift the immunity of one of its members, even though that Member of Parliament explicitly requests Parliament to do so. That category differs from the above cases as it is the Member of Parliament himself – e.g. as defendant in civil or criminal proceedings – who alleges a violation of his right of access to court. Such cases might arise if the Member of Parliament wishes the immunity to be lifted in order to defend himself in court, possibly to avoid having a criminal accusation hanging over him until the end of a Parliament's term.[155]

In *Kart v. Turkey*,[156] the applicant – a member of the People's Republican Party (CHP) – was a Member of Parliament in the Turkish National

[154] Ibid.

[155] Note that the situation needs to be distinguished from cases in which Parliament *decides* to lift the immunity of one of its members. In *Ziegler v. Switzerland* (no. 27742/95, Commission decision of 3 December 1997, D/R 74, p. 234), the applicant (a member of the National Council) was accused of defamatory statements made in his publications. Both Houses of Parliament ruled that the applicant's alleged conduct was not covered by parliamentary immunity, which subsequently resulted in a criminal charge of defamation against the applicant. The Commission found that the decision of whether or not the applicant's conduct was covered by parliamentary privilege did not determine his civil rights and obligations or the criminal charge against him. Therefore, Article 6 (1) did not apply in the present case. The same conclusion was made in the case of *Sakik and Others v. Turkey* (no. 23878/94, Commission decision of 25 May 1995, D/R. 81-B, p. 86) which involved the arrest of former members of the Turkish National Assembly who were accused of having committed terrorist offences. After the Turkish Constitutional Court's rejection to set aside the lifting of their immunity, the Commission declared the complaint inadmissible under Article 6 (1) because the decision did not determine the applicants' civil rights. These cases however do not concern the conflict between immunities and the right of access to court under Article 6 (1) as discussed in this work. The applicants were not prevented from having access to court because of the operation of parliamentary immunity; they rather wanted the opposite (preventing their appearance before a court). However, Article 6 (1) does not have such a negative aspect (e.g. the right *not* to appear before a court).

[156] *Kart v. Turkey* (no. 8917/05), Judgment of 8 July 2008.

Assembly. Prior to his election, two sets of criminal proceedings for insult were brought against him. The applicant was however protected by parliamentary immunity: under Article 83 of the Turkish Constitution, no Member of Parliament suspected of having committed an offence before or after his election could be prosecuted unless the National Assembly decided to lift his immunity.

In the present case, it was the applicant himself who requested the lifting of his immunity in order to be able to defend his reputation in the criminal proceedings. His request was to no avail as the competent committee in the National Assembly decided to stay the proceedings until the end of the applicant's term of office. However, the committee had not given any reasons for its decision and had taken more than two years to take its decision. The applicant then complained that having a criminal accusation hanging over him for such a long time without being given a fair trial amounted to a violation of Article 6 (1).

The Court found by four votes to three that there had been a violation of Article 6 (1). It noted that the present case was the first time the party complaining of the effects of immunity on the right of access to court was the beneficiary of the parliamentary immunity.[157] Considering the criminal law aspect of Article 6 ("In the determination of...any criminal charge against him, everyone is entitled to a fair...hearing...by [a]...tribunal..."), the Court found that the applicant had no chance to overcome the temporary, but significant procedural obstacle that his immunity posed and to have access to court concerning the criminal charges brought against him. Therefore, that interference with the applicant's right of access to court had to be justified. The Court found in this respect that the parliamentary immunity provided by the Turkish constitution was considerably broad and had been identified as one of the main problem areas in the context of corruption.[158]

Since parliamentary immunity is a matter of public policy and not a personal privilege of a Member of Parliament, the Court found that it was not the applicant's right to waive his immunity, but only request that it be lifted. The three dissenting judges in the case opined that the decision on the applicant's request was an internal decision by the Turkish parliament which could not be assessed by the Court. Since the procedure to take that decision was regulated in the Turkish Constitution and the Rules of Procedure of the National Assembly and the applicant had had the possibility to appeal that

[157] Ibid., para. 56.

[158] Ibid., paras. 40 and 92; see also Wigley, *Parliamentary Immunity in Democratizing Countries: The Case of Turkey*, Human Rights Quarterly, August 2009, p. 567.

decision, the dissenting judges considered the interference with Article 6 (1) proportionate.[159] They also took into account that the criminal proceedings were merely deferred until the end of the applicant's term of office.[160]

The majority of the judges in *Kart v. Turkey* however rightly found that certain aspects of a fair procedure also applied to the committee's decision which would ultimately determine whether or not the applicant would be able to have access to court in the foreseeable future. Since no objective criteria had been established as regards the conditions for lifting parliamentary immunity, no reasons had been given by the committee and, in the absence of a time-limit for such a decision, the applicant's request had not been processed for more than two years without a proper explanation, the applicant had been deprived of the means of defending his rights. Given the narrow outcome of the case, it comes to no surprise that it was subsequently referred to the Grand Chamber; a hearing was held on 4 March 2009.[161]

Postscript: After work on this book was finished, the Grand Chamber of the European Court of Human Rights found on 3 December 2009 (with a majority of thirteen votes to four) that there had been no violation of Article 6 (1) in *Kart v. Turkey*. The Court based its finding on the fact that the criminal proceedings against the applicant had commenced prior to his election to the Turkish Parliament, and the applicant had been aware that he was aspiring to a status that could delay the proceedings. The Court also found that the interference was proportionate because the failure to lift the applicant's immunity had merely constituted a temporary procedural obstacle, but had not deprived him of the possibility of having his case tried on the merits once his term of office as a Member of Parliament had ended. In his dissenting opinion (joined by two other judges), Judge Bonello rightly observed that the complaint was rather about a denial of a fair hearing within a reasonable time (another guarantee under Article 6) than about a denial of access to court (the latter allowing the Court to balance the applicant's right against the general interest). Moreover, the Court had failed to take into account

159 *Kart v. Turkey*, Joint dissenting opinion of Judges Baka, Ugrekhelidze and Popovic.

160 In this context, see the Court's preliminary observations on the distinction between "non-liability" (which protects Members of Parliament from legal proceedings for things they do in the performance of their duties) and "inviolability" (which affords immunity from prosecution for acts unrelated to their parliamentary duties and which does not "expunge" the offence but merely delays the proceedings); see *Kart v. Turkey*, paras. 70–72.

161 A webcast of that hearing can be seen under: http://www.echr.coe.int/ECHR/EN/Header/Press/ Multimedia/Webcasts+of+public+hearings/

that it was not just the applicant, but also the victims of the alleged criminal offences who were deprived of their right to have a speedy trial. The majority's reasoning meant that, in exercising his fundamental right to stand for Parliament under Article 3 of Protocol No. 1 to the Convention, the applicant had basically waived his right to stand trial within a reasonable time. This obligation to choose between two fundamental rights was also criticised in the dissenting opinion of Judge Power. Conflicts such as the one in the present case could perhaps be solved best by giving Members of Parliament the possibility to waive their parliamentary immunty of their own free will – at least for minor offences – as suggested by Judge Malinverni in his concurring opinion.

3. *Conclusion*

Parliamentary immunity is recognised by all Contracting States and serves the legitimate aims of protecting free speech in Parliament and maintaining the separation of powers between the legislature and the judiciary. In its case-law, the Court has found that even an absolute rule of parliamentary immunity constitutes in principle a proportionate restriction on the right of access to court under Article 6 (1) of the Convention because the creation of exceptions for particular circumstances would severely undermine the legitimate aims mentioned above. However, it has been argued that the Court's approach is to narrow as regards defamatory statements made in Parliament. As some Contracting States provide for an exception from parliamentary immunity in those cases and thus reconcile that principle with the conflicting right to reputation as enshrined in Article 8 of the Convention without having undermined the legitimate aims of parliamentary immunity, the Court should have adopted a more flexible approach. This view is also supported by the fact that an exception for defamatory statements does not only protect the rights of private persons, but also improves the quality of parliamentary debate by discouraging deliberately false statements. As regards comments made outside of Parliament, the granting of parliamentary immunity with regard to those statements constitutes a disproportionate interference with Article 6 (1) of the Convention. Moreover, the refusal of Parliament to lift the immunity of one of its members, even though that Member of Parliament explicitly requests Parliament to do so, may lead to a violation of Article 6 (1) if there do not exist objective criteria to define the conditions under which immunity can be lifted, or if that decision is being taken by Parliament with a considerable delay.

Summary

1. Immunity from suit means that the effort of a person to bring a claim against the holder of that immunity will prove to be unsuccessful. Therefore, immunities conflict with the right of access to court under Article 6 (1) of the Convention. The present work distinguishes between international immunities (*i.e.* immunities which are granted by domestic courts in order to fulfil obligations under public international law such as State immunity) and domestic immunities (*i.e.* those immunities which are granted to legal bodies or persons at the domestic level such as Members of Parliament).

2. There is no express restriction on the right of access to court which itself has been "read" into Article 6 (1) of the Convention ever since the landmark judgment of *Golder v. the United Kingdom*. The Court has established the so-called *Ashingdane* criteria (named after the first case involving immunities in which that test was applied): the right of access to court is not absolute and may be subject to limitations if the restriction pursues a legitimate aim, is proportionate and does not have the effect of extinguishing the applicant's right of access to court altogether (the "very essence" criterion). That test is applied uniformly to all kinds of immunities. However, immunities *de facto* eliminate the right of access to court. Therefore, it is inconsistent to apply the "very essence" criterion as immunities *per definitionem* touch upon the very essence of the right of access to court. A case analysis shows that the Court often lists the third criterion without actually discussing it. Therefore, it is suggested that that criterion be abandoned as a part of the test. Consequently, there should be a mere twofold test when considering complaints of an alleged immunity-related violation of the right of access to court: immunities do not amount to a violation of Article 6 (1) of the Convention if they serve a legitimate aim and if they are posing a proportionate restriction on the right of access to court.

3. Whether the immunity in question serves a legitimate aim has to be considered in a general way. For example, the Court considers that State immunity as such serves legitimate aims, namely to promote comity and to maintain an interchange of good relations between States. The particular facts of the application (e.g. whether the proceedings in question concerned claims for serious human rights violations) are brought into play

when assessing whether the granting of State immunity was proportionate. When determining the proportionality of an interference with the right of access to court, the Court allows the State a certain "margin of appreciation" in applying the relevant law. That is primarily the domestic law, but it also includes the application of norms of public international law (other than the Convention itself).

4. With regard to State immunity, one has to distinguish between the State which benefits from immunity (the foreign State) and the State which grants immunity (the forum State). In cases in which State immunity is granted to the foreign State, the forum State does not lack jurisdiction but merely refrains from exercising it. Consequently, an applicant who complains about a violation of access to court comes "within the jurisdiction" of the forum State within the meaning of Article 1 of the Convention. His or her complaint cannot be considered as incompatible *ratione materiae* with the provisions of the Convention. This is because the word "immunity" presupposes jurisdiction of the forum State, which can be demonstrated by the situation in which the foreign State waives its immunity. In that instance, the forum State may always exercise its jurisdiction. On the other hand, the foreign State – when raising the defence of State immunity as the defendant in proceedings before the courts of the forum State – does not have any responsibility under Article 6 (1) of the Convention because the claimant does not come within its jurisdiction pursuant to Article 1 of the Convention. In that respect the foreign State could be likened to a private individual against whom proceedings are instituted.

5. The conflict between Article 6 (1) of the Convention and State immunity needs to be solved by balancing the competing interests. Approaches that the right of access to court always trumps State immunity or *vice versa* do not have a sufficient basis in international law. It is questionable to argue that the Contracting Parties have waived their right to invoke or grant State immunity when ratifying the Convention. Under public international law, a waiver needs to be declared explicitly (which was not the case) or implicitly (there is however no indication that a waiver of their immunity was intended by the Contracting Parties). On the other hand, the Convention puts obligations on the Contracting States which they have to fulfil and which cannot be delegated to other States. Thus, it cannot be argued that there is no interference with Article 6 (1) of the Convention if it is possible for the claimant to bring proceedings in the courts of the foreign State.

6. The basis for the interpretation of the Convention as an international treaty is the Vienna Convention on the Law of Treaties of 1969. Article 31 (3) (c) of the Vienna Convention provides that an international treaty shall be interpreted while taking into account "any relevant rules of international law applicable in the relations between the parties". These rules include the

principles of State immunity. While the meaning of the wording "taking into account" remains somewhat unclear, this study has rejected the notion that the Convention operates as a *lex specialis*, *i.e.* that the Court's task is in the first place to apply the Convention articles while general principles of public international law have to be disregarded unless where they are expressly referred to in the Convention. To hold otherwise would ultimately mean to regard the Convention as a separate and self-sufficient legal system instead of an integral part of public international law. This is what the Court means when finding that the Convention cannot be interpreted "in a vacuum". It is important to keep the Convention within the general framework of international law and to interpret it – in the words of the Court – "so far as possible in harmony with other principles of international law". That approach takes into account that the Contracting Parties do not only have obligations towards individuals, but also towards other States which have not ratified the Convention. At the same time, it seems appropriate to recognise that in the past fifty years the principle of State immunity has been increasingly restricted, whereas the position of the individual in international law has been strengthened.

7. To settle the issue of proportionality of an interference with Article 6 (1) of the Convention by the granting of State immunity (or any other international immunity) requires an in-depth assessment and analysis of the applicable public international law. That includes the jurisprudence and legislation of States, but also international treaties such as the European Convention on State Immunity, the United Nations Convention on Jurisdictional Immunities of States and their Property or the draft Conventions of both the International Law Association and the Institute of International Law. While such an analysis naturally requires a case-by-case approach, some general principles can be formulated. Where all international treaties and materials suggest that State immunity is accepted in a particular situation (for example in the case of *Fogarty v. the United Kingdom* regarding the recruitment processes in foreign embassies), there is a strong indication that the granting of State immunity in such a situation still reflects international law and that the interference with Article 6 (1) of the Convention was thus proportionate. If, on the other hand, all international treaties and materials (as well as national legislation and jurisprudence in numerous countries) recognise a certain exception from State immunity, one may conclude that States are no longer obliged to grant State immunity in that case. The forum State is thus not faced with a conflict between two legal obligations (both to grant access to court and to apply the principle of State immunity) as the latter obligation no longer exists. An example of this category of cases is the judgment of *McElhinney v. the United Kingdom* which involved State immunity for torts committed by the foreign State on the territory of the forum State. The

Court's finding in that case that the forum State "was certainly not alone" in applying the principle of State immunity unnecessarily widened the Contracting Parties' margin of appreciation.

8. With regard to serious human rights violations such as torture committed by the foreign State outside the territory of the forum State, international practice does not yet recognise an exemption from the rules of State immunity, however desirable such an exemption may be. As long as international practice has not changed in that respect, the granting of State immunity in cases concerning torture is a proportionate interference with Article 6 (1) of the Convention (as found by the majority of the Grand Chamber in the case of *Al-Adsani v. the United Kingdom*). The fact that the prohibition of torture is a *jus cogens* norm (*i.e.* a peremptory norm of international law) does not require a different result. The prohibition of torture as a *jus cogens* norm does not trump the rules of State immunity because the norms do not conflict with each other. State immunity is a procedural rule and would only interfere with the prohibition of torture if the latter included an obligation for States to grant access to their courts in civil proceedings to a person who has been tortured by a third State on the latter's territory. This is not (yet) the case. Even though the wording in Article 14 of the UN Torture Convention – a provision which puts obligations on States to provide for civil remedies for torture victims – is wide enough to cover torture inflicted abroad by another State, a systematic and historic interpretation of that provision shows that such obligations are limited to torture committed within a State's own territory. The case-law of the Court also demonstrates that the prohibition of torture in Article 3 of the Convention does not put positive obligations on a Contracting State to provide civil remedies for individuals tortured by a third State and outside the territory of that Contracting State.

9. Acts of torture cannot be qualified as *acta jure gestionis* (*i.e.* they are so illegal that they fall outside the scope of official activity) with the consequence that Article 6 (1) of the Convention trumps the rules of State immunity which is granted only for *acta jure imperii*. Article 1 of the UN Torture Convention defines torture as an official act. It would create an asymmetry between the UN Torture Convention and the rules of State immunity if the same act was official for the purposes of the definition of torture but not for the purposes of State immunity.

10. Nevertheless, neither the UN Torture Convention nor Article 6 (1) of the Convention prohibits States from refusing to apply the rules of State immunity in cases involving torture. Such cases would serve in their turn as evidence of a new State practice regarding a "human rights exception" from State immunity. Therefore, a real change in practice of the rules on State immunity has to come from States which shape international law through their legislation and jurisprudence, or through respective amendments of the

international treaties on State immunity. The Court should however refrain from acting as a moderniser of public international law by demanding Contracting States to grant access to court under Article 6 (1) of the Convention where international practice currently requires the opposite. Having said that, it is however deplorable that the Court occasionally appears to shy away from deciding upon questions of public international law which are decisive for the outcome of the immunity-cases under Article 6 (1). An example is the problem whether immunity forms part of or merely serves as an exemption to the term "jurisdiction" (the outcome being decisive for the admissibility of all cases involving international immunities because of the term "within [the Contracting Parties'] jurisdiction" within the meaning of Article 1 of the Convention).

11. The right of access to court does not only provide for the right to institute civil proceedings before a court, but also includes the right to enforcement of a judgment or a decision. That aspect of Article 6 (1) of the Convention conflicts with State immunity from enforcement measures such as execution, arrest or attachment. The two principles have conflicted with each other in a series of cases in which plots of land which had been expropriated by Communist regimes were later returned but had meanwhile been sold or rented to foreign embassies. The right to enforce a judgment may likewise be restricted if that restriction pursues a legitimate aim and is proportionate.

12. While Heads of State hold office, they traditionally enjoy absolute immunity (*ratione personae*), without distinction between criminal or civil proceedings. Efforts by the Institute of International Law to restrict the immunity in civil matters to official acts have been criticised for not being a strict statement of the law in force and cannot be said to have authoritative value that would contradict clear jurisprudence of national and international courts. Moreover, exemptions from Head of State immunity for international crimes in the statutes of international criminal tribunals do not necessarily support an exemption from immunity in civil proceedings before national courts for those crimes. This is because international criminal tribunals do not concern the exercise of national authority of one State over another. As a consequence, Contracting States do not violate the right of access to court under Article 6 (1) of the Convention if they apply the present rules of Head of State immunity.

13. Once Heads of State leave office, only their official acts will be covered by immunity (*ratione materiae*). The decision of a Contracting State not to extradite a former Head of State on the grounds that the latter is protected from immunity does not violate the right of access to court of claimants who brought civil proceedings against that former Head of State in the courts of another Contracting Party. There is no jurisdictional link within the meaning

of Article 1 of the Convention between those claimants and the State which refuses to extradite. Contracting States are not obliged under the Convention to grant the claimants effective access to foreign courts by extraditing the defendant in those proceedings.

14. Unlike States, international organisations still enjoy absolute immunity from suit under public international law. And unlike in the case of State immunity, the plaintiff does not have the possibility to turn to the courts of the defendant State to pursue his claim. Therefore, the immunity of international organisations may serve as a proportionate restriction on the right of access to court under Article 6 (1) if applicants have alternative remedies within the organisation to pursue their claim. This applies to all kind of claims (not merely employment-related ones) and to all international organisations (independent of the date of their establishment or whether their membership is of universal or regional character). In order to find a restriction proportionate, it must be ensured that the alternative remedy is adequate. This requires that the main legal questions to the dispute can be addressed by the alternative tribunal, that the alternative tribunal is composed of members with legal qualification who are truly independent, and that a sufficient level of procedural rights is guaranteed.

15. In order for Article 6 (1) of the Convention to apply, applicants need to demonstrate that they pursued a "civil right" on a least arguable grounds. The "civil" character of a right is usually unproblematic in cases involving immunities, unless they concern employment disputes in foreign embassies or international organisations. This is because the applicability of Article 6 (1) of the Convention to disputes relating to the recruitment, employment and retirement of civil servants traditionally raises legal problems under the Convention. In the recent case of *Vilho Eskelinen and Others v. Finland*, the Grand Chamber of the Court considerably reviewed its jurisprudence on the issue and widened the applicability of Article 6 (1) of the Convention with regard to civil servants. It is suggested that this approach is also applied to civil servants in foreign embassies or international organisations.

16. Article 6 (1) of the Convention does not guarantee any particular content for civil rights in domestic law, and the Court does not possess the power to create any legal rights which have no basis in the legal system of a Contracting State. Therefore, arguments have frequently been submitted to the Court that immunities have the effect of extinguishing the civil right on which the applicant's claim was based. To find that Article 6 (1) of the Convention was applicable in these cases would ultimately mean to create civil rights for which there is no basis in domestic law. With regard to international immunities, that argument can be easily rejected. The rules of State immunity and the immunity of international organisations are entirely procedural rules which may be waived. In the case of a waiver, the applicant

may proceed with his or her claim. Consequently, international immunities do not extinguish a civil right. The case is more difficult when it comes to domestic immunities. In a number of cases involving the liability of public authorities under English law, the Court has adopted a distinction between "immunity from liability" (a substantive limitation, *i.e.* a limitation on a right) and "immunity from suit" (a procedural limitation, *i.e.* a limitation on its remedy). Whereas the categorisation as a substantive limitation eventually means that there is no civil right (with the consequence that Article 6 (1) of the Convention is strictly speaking not applicable), procedural limitations must be justified under the *Ashingdane* criteria. Even though the Court acknowledged that the difference between the two categories might sometimes only be a question of legislative techniques, it based its jurisprudence on that distinction with the consequence of a series of controversial judgments and a case-law which becomes increasingly inconsistent. The present study has suggested a departure from the substantive/procedural distinction and to adopt instead an approach which was originally proposed by Professor Hampson in 1991. When establishing whether there existed a civil right in the domestic law on arguable grounds in cases where an immunity poses a restriction on a cause of action, the Court should ask whether the applicant would have had a cause of action "but for" the restriction (hence the test is called the "but for" test). Given that the concept of "civil rights" is autonomous, that approach would not create any rights which have no basis in the domestic legal system, because Article 6 (1) of the Convention would only apply to rights that are generally recognised therein. The test would greatly simplify the dealing with domestic immunities while not necessarily leading to different outcomes. On the other hand, cases in which applicants sought to institute claims for damages for alleged violations of core human rights (such as the right to life in the case of *Osman v. the United Kingdom* or the prohibition of inhuman and degrading treatment in *Z and Others v. the United Kingdom*) could have been considered as involving disproportionate restrictions on Article 6 (1) of the Convention. This is particularly the case because the immunities in question were considerably broader than those in the legal systems of other European countries. In this context, this study has also argued that it is insufficient to merely point out that the applicants were not prevented in any practical manner from bringing their claim before the domestic courts, referring to the fact that they often had had several court hearings before their claim was dismissed because of the operation of an exclusionary rule. To hold otherwise would reduce the right of access to court to mere physical access.

17. Parliamentary immunity is recognised by all Contracting States and serves the legitimate aims of protecting free speech in Parliament and maintaining the separation of powers between the legislature and the judiciary. In

its case-law, the Court has found that even an absolute rule of parliamentary immunity constitutes in principle a proportionate restriction on the right of access to court under Article 6 (1) of the Convention because the creation of exceptions for particular circumstances would severely undermine the legitimate aims mentioned above. However, it has been argued that the Court's approach is to narrow as regards defamatory statements made in Parliament. As some Contracting States provide for an exception from parliamentary immunity in those cases and thus reconcile that principle with the conflicting right to reputation as enshrined in Article 8 of the Convention without having undermined the legitimate aims of parliamentary immunity, the Court should have adopted a more flexible approach. This view is also supported by the fact that an exception for defamatory statements does not only protect the rights of private persons, but also improves the quality of parliamentary debate by discouraging deliberately false statements. As regards comments made outside of Parliament, the granting of parliamentary immunity with regard to those statements constitutes a disproportionate interference with Article 6 (1) of the Convention. Moreover, the refusal of Parliament to lift the immunity of one of its members, even though that Member of Parliament explicitly requests Parliament to do so, may lead to a violation of Article 6 (1) if there do not exist objective criteria to define the conditions under which immunity can be lifted, or if that decision is being taken by Parliament with a considerable delay.

Bibliography

Adams, Wendy: “In Search of a Defence of a Transnational Human Rights Paradigm: May *Jus Cogens* Norms be Invoked to Create Implied Exceptions in Domestic Immunity Statutes?”, in: Scott (ed.) *Torture as Tort- Comparative Perspectives on the Development of Transnational Human Rights Litigation*, Oxford/Portland Oregon 2001, p. 247.

Alkema, E.A.: “The EC and the European Convention on Human Rights- Immunity and Impunity for the Community?”, in: *Common Market Law Review* 1979, p. 501.

Angelet, Nicolas/Weerts, Alexandra: “Les immunités des organisations internationales face à l’article 6 de la Convention européenne des droits de l’homme”, in: *Journal du Droit International* 2007, p. 3.

Arai-Takahashi, Y: “The Margin of Appreciation Doctrine and the Principle of Proportionality in the Jurisprudence of the ECHR”, Antwerpen 2002.

Badr, Gamal Moursi: “State Immunity- An Analytical and Prognostic View”, The Hague/Boston/Lancaster 1984.

Bantekas, Ilias: “Case note: *Prefecture of Voiotia v Federal Republic of Germany*”, in: *American Journal of International Law* 1998, p. 765.

Bartsch, Kerstin/Elberling, Björn: “Jus Cogens v. State Immunity, Round Two: The Decision of the European Court of Human Rights in the *Kalogeropoulou et al. v. Greece and Germany* Decision”, in: *German Law Journal* 2003, p. 477 (only available online).

Bates, E.: “The Al-Adsani Case, State Immunity and the International Legal Prohibition of Torture”, in: *Human Rights Law Reports* 2003, p. 193.

Beddard, Ralph: “Human Rights and Europe”, 3rd edition, Cambridge 1993.

Bederman, David J.: “Dead Man’s Hand: Reshuffling Foreign Sovereign Immunities in US Human Rights Litigation”, in: *Georgia Journal of International and Comparative Law* 1995–96, p. 255.

Bernhardt, Rudolf (ed.): “Encyclopedia of Public International Law”, Amsterdam 1997.

Bianchi, Andrea: “Denying State Immunity to Violators of Human Rights”, in: *Austrian Journal of Public International Law* 1994, p. 195.

Bianchi, Andrea: “Immunity versus Human Rights: The *Pinochet* Case”, in: *European Journal of International Law* 1999, p. 194.

Bianchi, Andrea: “Overcoming the Hurdle of State Immunity in the Domestic Enforcement of International Human Rights”, in: Conforti/Francioni/Francesco (eds.): *Enforcing Internatinal Human Rights in Domestic Courts*, The Hague/Boston/London 1997.

Bianchi, Andrea: “State Immunity and Human Rights- The Italian Supreme Court Decision on the *Ferrini* case”, in: *European Journal of International Law* 2005, p. 89.

Bianchi, Andrea: “Ferrini v. Federal Republic of Germany” (Case note), in: *American Journal of International Law* 2005, p. 242.

Bianchi, Andrea: “Human Rights and the Magic of Jus Cogens”, in: *European Journal of International Law* 2008.

Blackburn, Robert/Polakiewicz, Jörg (eds.): "Fundamental Rights In Europe: The European Convention on Human Rights and its Member States, 1950–2000", Oxford 2001.

Bothe, Michael: "Die strafrechtliche Immunität fremder Staatsorgane", in: *Zeitschrift für ausländisches öffentliches Recht und Völkerrecht* 1971, Vol. 31, p. 246.

Bratza, Sir Nicholas: "The Implications of the Human Rights Act 1998 for Commercial Practice", in: *European Human Rights Law Review* 2000, p. 1.

Brazier, Margaret/Murphy, John: "Street on Torts", 10th edition, London/Edinburgh/Dublin 1999.

Brody/Ratner: "The Pinochet Papers: The Case of Augusto Pinochet in Spain and Britain", London 2000.

Bröhmer, Jürgen: "State Immunity and the Violation of Human Rights", The Hague/Boston/London 1997.

Bröhmer, Jürgen: "Diplomatic Immunity, Head of State Immunity, State Immunity: Misconceptions of a Notorious Human Rights Violator", in: *Leiden Journal of International Law* 1999, p. 361.

Bröhmer, Jürgen: "Die völkerrechtliche Immunität von der staatlichen Gerichtsbarkeit und die Verfahrensgarantien der EMRK- Einige Anmerkungen zu den Urteilen des Europäischen Gerichtshofs für Menschenrechte in den Fällen *Waite & Kennedy* und *Beer & Regan gegen die Bundesrepublik Deutschland*", in: Bröhmer (ed.) *Der Grundrechtschutz in Europa- wissenschaftliches Kolloquium aus Anlass des 65. Geburtstages von Prof. Dr. Dr. Dr. mult. h.c. Georg Ress*, 2002: p. 85.

Brown, Jonathan: "Diplomatic Immunity: State Practice under the Vienna Convention on Diplomatic Relations", in: *International and Comparative Law Quarterly* 1988, p. 53.

Brownlie, Ian: "Principles of Public International Law", 7th edition, Oxford 2008.

Buergenthal, Thomas/Maier, Harold G.: "Public International Law", St. Paul, Minn. 1990.

Burxton, Richard: "The Human Rights Act and Private Law", in: *Law Quarterly Review* 2000, p. 48.

Byers, Michael: "Decisions of British Courts During 1996 Involving Questions of Public or Private International Law: *Al-Adsani v. Government of Kuwait and others*", in: *British Yearbook of International Law* 1996, p. 537.

Byrnes, A.: "Civil Remedies for Torture Committed Abroad: An Obligation Under the Convention Against Torture?", in: Scott (ed.) *Torture as Tort: Comparative Perspectives on the Development of Transnational Human Rights Litigation*, 2000.

Caflisch, Luzius/Cancado Trindade, Antonoi A.: "Les Conventions américaine et européenne des droits de l'homme et le droit international general", in: *Revue Générale de Droit International Public* 2004, p. 5.

Caflisch, Luzius: "Immunité des États et droits de l'Homme: Evolution récente", in: *Internationale Gemeinschaft und Menschenrechte, Festschrift für Georg Ress*, Berlin/Köln/ München 2005, p. 935.

Caflisch, Lucius: "The Law – Substantive and Procedural Questions", in: *The Law and Practice of International Courts and Tribunals* 2008, Special Issue – Selected Papers from the Conference "International Courts and Tribunals – The Challenges Ahead", Lancester House, London, 6–7 October 2008, p. 289.

Cane, Peter: "Accidents, Compensation and the Law", 6th edition, London/Edinburgh/Dublin 1999.

Caplan, Lee M.: "State Immunity, Human Rights and Jus Cogens: A Critique of the Normative Hierarchy Theory", in: *American Journal of International Law* 2003, p. 741.

Carnwath, Robert: "Welfare Services- Liabilities in Tort after the Human Rights Act", in: *Public Law* 2001, p. 210.

Cassesse, Antonio: "When May Senior State Officials be Tried for International Crimes? Some Comments on the *Congo v Belgium* Case", in: *European Journal of International Law* 2002, p. 869.

Clapham, Andrew: "Revisiting *Human Rights in the Private Sphere*: Using the European Convention on Human Rights to Protect the Right of Access to the Civil Courts", in: Craig Scott (ed.) *Torture as Tort- Comparative Perspectives on the Development of Transnational Human Rights Litigation*, Oxford/Portland Oregon 2001, pp. 513 and 717 (Postscript).

Clapham, Andrew: "The Jus Cogens Prohibition of Torture and the Importance of Sovereign State Immunity", in: Kohen (ed.) *Promoting Justice, Human Rights and Conflict Resolution through International Law, Liber Amicorum Lucius Caflisch*, Leiden 2007, p. 151.

Clayton, Richard/Tomlinson, Hugh: "The Law of Human Rights", Oxford 2000.

Clayton, Richard/Tomlinson, Hugh: "The Law of Human Rights- First Annual Updating Supplement", Oxford 2001.

Clements, Luke/Mole, Nala/Simmons, Alan: "European Human Rights: Taking a Case under the Convention", London 1999.

Collums, H.D.: "The *Letelier* Case: Foreign Sovereign Liability for Acts of Political Assassination", in: *Virginia Journal of International Law* 1981, p. 251.

Council of Europe: "Privileges and Immunities of International Organisations", Strasbourg 1970.

Crawford, James: "Execution of Judgments and Foreign Sovereign Immunity", in: *American Journal of International Law* 1981, p. 820.

Dahm, Georg: "Völkerrechtliche Grenzen der inländischen Gerichtsbarkeit gegenüber ausländischen Staaten", in: *Festschrift für Arthur Nikisch*, Tübingen 1958, p. 153.

Damian, Helmut: "Staatenimmunität und Gerichtszwang", Berlin/Heidelberg/New York/Tokyo 1985.

Deen-Racsmany, Z.: "Prosecutor v. Taylor: The Status of the Special Court for Sierra Leone and Its Implications for Immunity", in: *Leiden Journal of International Law* 2005, p. 299.

Delaume, Georges R.: "The State Immunity Act of the United Kingdom", in: *American Journal of International Law* 1979, p. 18.

De Wet, Erika: "The Role of European Courts in Reviewing Conflicting Obligations under International Law", in: *International Organizations Law Review* 2008, p. 359.

Dembour, Marie-Bénédicte: "Who Believes in Human Rights? Reflections on the European Convention", Cambridge 2006.

Denza, Eileen: "The 2005 UN Convention on State Immunity in Perspective", in: *International and Comparative Law Quarterly* 2006, p. 395.

Dickinson, Andrew: "Status of Forces under the UN Convention on State Immunity", in: *International and Comparative Law Quarterly* 2006, p. 427.

Doehring, Karl: "Völkerrecht", Heidelberg 1999.

Doehring, Karl/Ress, Georg: "Diplomatische Immunität und Drittstaaten", in: *Archiv des Völkerrechts* 1999, p. 68.

Dolzer, Rudolf: "Der Areopag im Abseits", in: Neue Juristische Wochenschrift 2001, p. 3525.

Dutertre, Gille: "Key case-law extracts, European Court of Human Rights", Strasbourg 2003.

Eissen, Marc-Andre: "The Principle of Proportionality in the Case-Law of the European Court of Human Rights", in: Macdonald, R.St.J./Matscher, F./Petzold, H. (eds) *The European System for the Protection of Human Rights*, Dordrecht/Boston/London 1993, p. 125.

Emberland, Marius: "Case note: *McElhinney v. Ireland/ Al-Adsani v. the United Kingdom/ Fogarty v. the United Kingdom*", in: *American Journal of International Law* 2002, p. 699.

Erdal, Ugur/Bakirci, Hasan: "Article 3 of the European Convention on Human Rights- A Practitioner's Handbook", Geneva 2006.

Feldman, David: "Civil Liberties and Human Rights in England and Wales", 2nd edition, Oxford 2002.

Fairgrieve, Duncan: "The Human Rights Act 1998, Damages and Tort Law", in: *Public Law* 2001, p. 695.

Fox, Hazel: "State Responsibility and Tort Proceedings Against A Foreign State In Municipal Courts", in: *Netherlands Yearbook of International Law* 1989, p. 3.

Fox, Hazel: "Enforcement Jurisdiction, Foreign State Property and Diplomatic Immunity", in: *International and Comparative Law Quarterly* 1985, p. 115.

Fox, Hazel: "Employment contracts as an exception in respect of employment disputes", in: *British Yearbook of International Law* 1997, p. 97.

Fox, Hazel: "The First Pinochet Case: Immunity of a Former Head of State", in: *International and Comparative Law Quarterly* 1999, p. 207.

Fox, Hazel: "The Resolution of the Institute of International Law on the Immunities of Heads of State and Government", in: *International and Comparative Law Quarterly* 2002, p. 1.

Fox, Hazel: "Where Does the Buck Stop? State Immunity from Civil Jurisdiction and Torture", in: *Law Quarterly Review* 2005, p. 353.

Fox, Hazel: "In Defence of State Immunity: why the UN Convention on State Immunity is important", in: *International and Comparative Law Quarterly* 2006, p. 399.

Fox, Hazel: "State Immunity and the International Crime of Torture", in: *European Human Rights Law Reports* 2006, p. 142.

Fox, Hazel: "The Law of State Immunity", 2nd edition, Oxford 2008.

Frowein, Jochen/Peukert, B.: "Europäische Menschenrechtskonvention", 2nd edition, Kehl/Strasbourg 1996.

Gaeta, Paola: "Ratione Materiae Immunities of Former Heads of State and International Crimes: The Hissène Habré Case", in: *Journal of International Criminal Justice* 2003, p. 186.

Gaillard, Emmanuel/Pingel-Linuzza, Isabelle: "International Organisations and Immunity from Jurisdiction: to Restrict or to Bypass", in: *International and Comparative Law Quarterly* 2002, p. 1.

Gardiner, Richard: "UN Convention on State Immunity: Form and Function", in: *International and Comparative Law Quarterly* 2006, p. 407.

Garnett, Richard: "The Defence of State Immunity for Acts of Torture", in: *Australian Yearbook of International Law* 1997, p. 97.

Garnett, Richard: "State Immunity in Employment Matters", in: *International and Comparative Law Quarterly* 1997, p. 81.

Gattini, Andrea: "A Trojan Horse for Sudeten Claims? On Some Implications of the *Prince of Liechtenstein v. Germany*", in: *European Journal of International Law* 2002, p. 513.

Gattini, Andrea: "War Crimes and the *Ferrini* Decision", in: *Journal of International and Comparative Law* 2005, p. 224.

Gearty, Conor A.: "Unravelling *Osman*", in: *Modern Law Review* 2001, p. 159.

Geimer, Reinhold: "Immunitätsrecht als Hindernis für effektiven Rechtsschutz", in: *Zeitschrift für Rechtsvergleichung und Internationales Privatrecht und Europarecht* 1992, p. 321.

Gergen, J. A.: "Human Rights and the Foreign Sovereign Immunities Act", in: *Virginia Journal of International Law* 1996, p. 765.

Gery, Yoav: "The Torture Victim Protection Act: Raising Issues of Legitimacy", in: *George Washington Journal of International Law and Economics* 1993, p. 597.

Gomien, Donna: "Short Guide to the European Convention on Human Rights", 3rd edition, Strasbourg 2005.

Gordon, Richard QC/Ward, Tim: "Judicial Review and the Human Rights Act", London/Sydney 2000.
Grabenwarter, Christoph: "Europäische Menschenrechtskonvention", 3rd edition, Munich/Vienna 2007.
Grabenwarter, Christoph: "Probleme paralleler Rechtsverbürgungen durch Vertrag und Gewohnheit", in: Klein (ed.) *Menschenrechtsschutz durch Gewohnheitsrecht*, Berlin 2003, p. 147.
Graf Vizthum, Wolfgang (ed.): "Völkerrecht", 4th edition, Berlin/New York 2007.
Grosz, Stephen/Beatson, Jack/Duffy, Peter: "Human Rights- the 1998 Act and the European Convention", London 2000.
Habscheid, W.J.: "Immunität internationaler Organisationen, internationales Schiedsverfahren und anzuwendendes Verfahrensrecht", in: *Festschrift für Anton Heini zum 65. Geburtstag*, 1995, p. 147.
Habscheid, Edgar J.: "Die durch Art. 6 I EMRK beschränkte Immunität internationaler Organisationen im Erkenntnisverfahren", in: *Praxis des internationalen Privat- und Verfahrensrechts* 2001, p. 396.
Habscheid, Edgar J.: "Immunität internationaler Organisationen und Art. 6 I EMRK (insbesondere zum Rechtsschutz der Bediensteten)", in: Rolf A. Schütze (ed.) *Einheit und Vielfalt des Rechts - Essays in Honour of Reinhold Geimer*, Munich 2002, p. 255.
Hafner, Gerhard/Kohen, Marcelo G./Breau, Susan: "State Practice Regarding State Immunities", Leiden/Boston 2006.
Hall, Christopher Keith: "UN Convention on State Immunity: the need for a human rights protocol", in: *International and Comparative Law Quarterly* 2006, p. 3411.
Hall, Christopher Keith: "The Duty of States Parties to the Convention against Torture to Provide Procedures Permitting Victims to Recover Reparations for Torture Committed Abroad", in: *European Journal of International Law* 2008, p. 921.
Hampson, Francoise J.: "Restrictions on Rights of Action and the European Convention on Human Rights: The Case of Powell and Rayner", in: *British Yearbook of International Law* 1990, p. 279.
Harris, DJ.: "Cases and Materials on International Law", 5th edition, London 1998.
Harris, DJ./O'Boyle, M./Warbrick, C.: "Law of the European Convention of Human Rights", Edinburgh 1995.
Herdegen, Matthias: "Völkerrecht", 8th edition, Munich 2009.
Herdegen, Matthias: "Internationales Wirtschaftsrecht", München 1995.
Hess, Burkhard: "Staatenimmunität bei Distanzdelikten", Munich 1992.
Higgins, Rosalyn: "The Role of Domestic Courts in the Enforcement of International Human Rights: The United Kingdom", in: Conforti, Benedetto/Francioni/Francesco (eds.): *Enforcing Internatinal Human Rights in Domestic Courts*, The Hague/Boston/London 1997.
Higgins, Rosalyn: "The International Court of Justice and the European Court of Human Rights: Partners for the Protection of Human Rights" (speech given on the occasion of the Opening of the Judicial Year at the European Court of Human Rights, 30 January 2009), in: *Dialogue between Judges - Fifty Years of the European Court of Human Rights Viewed by its Fellow International Courts*, Strasbourg 2009, p. 97.
Hobe, Stephan: "Durchbrechung der Staatenimmunität bei schweren Menschenrechtsverletzungen- NS-Delikte vor dem Areopag", in: *Praxis des internationales Privat- und Verfahrensrecht* 2001, p. 368.
Hockl, Doris: "The State Immunity Act 1978 and its Interpretation by the English Courts", in: *Austrian Journal of Public and International Law* 1995, p. 121.

Hoffmann, Lord: "Human Rights and the House of Lords", in: *Modern Law Review* 1999, p. 162.

Human Rights Committee, International Law Association (British Branch): "Report on Civil Actions in the English Courts for Serious Human Rights Violations Abroad", in: *European Human Rights Law Review* 2001, p. 129.

Jacobs, Francis G./White, Robin C.A./Ovey, Clare: "The European Convention on Human Rights", 3rd edition, Oxford 2002.

Jacobs, Francis G.: "The Right to a Fair Trial in European Law", in: *European Human Rights Law Review* 1999, p. 141.

Janis, Mark: "An Introduction to International Law", 1988.

Janis, Mark/Kay, Richard/Bradley, Anthony: "European Human Rights Law – Text and Materials", 2nd edition, Oxford 2000.

Jenks, E.: "International Immunities", 1961.

Jones, David Lloyd: "Article 6 ECHR and Immunities arising in Public International Law", *International and Comparative Law Quarterly* 2003, p. 463.

Kempen, Bernhard: "Der Fall *Distomo*: griechische Reparationsforderungen gegen die Bundesrepublik Deutschland", in: Cremer, H.-J./Giegerich, T./Richter, D./Zimmermann, A. (eds): *Tradition und Weltoffenheit des Rechts-* Essays in Honour of Helmut Steinberger, Berlin/Heidelberg/New York/Barcelona/Hongkong/London/Milano/Paris/Tokyo 2002.

Kimminich, Otto/Hobe, Stephan: "Einführung in das Völkerrecht", 7th edition, Tübingen/Basel 2000.

Klein, Eckart: "Menschenrechte und Ius Cogens", in: *Internationale Gemeinschaft und Menschenrechte, Festschrift für Georg Ress*, Berlin/Köln/München, p. 151.

Kloth, Matthias: "Immunities and the Right of Access to Court under the European Convention on Human Rights", in: *European Law Review* (Human Rights Survey) August 2002, p. 33.

Kokott, Juliane: "Mißbrauch und Verwirkung von Souveränitätsrechten bei gravierenden Völkerrechtsverstößen", in: Beyerlein et al. (eds.) *Recht zwischen Umbruch und Bewahrung*, Essays in Honour of Rudolf Bernhardt, Heidelberg/Berlin/New York 1995, p. 135.

Koster, Martina: "Immunität internationaler Richter", Heidelberg 2002.

Krenc, F.: "La règle de l'immunité parlementaire à l'epreuve de la Convention Européene des Droits de L'Homme", *Revue trimestrielle des droits de l'homme* 2003, p. 813.

Lauterpacht, H.: "The Problem of Jurisdictional Immunities of Foreign States", in: *British Yearbook of International Law* 1951, p. 220.

Leach, P.: "Taking a Case to the European Court of Human Rights", 2nd edition, Oxford 2005.

Leigh, Monroe: "1996 Amendments to the Foreign Sovereign Immunities Act with Respect to Terrorist Activities", in: *American Journal of International Law* 1997, p. 187.

Le Sueur, Andrew: "Access to Justice Rights in the United Kingdom", in: *European Human Rights Law Review* 2001, p. 457.

Levy, Jack Allan: "As between Princz and King: reassessing the law of foreign sovereign immunity as applied to ius cogens violators", in: *The Georgetown Law Journal* 1998, p. 2703.

Lidbetter, Andrew/George, James: "Negligent Public Authorities and Convention Rights- The Legacy of *Osman*", in: *European Human Rights Law Review* 2001, p. 599.

Lininger, Tom: "Recent Developments: Overcoming Immunity Defences to Human Rights Suits in US Courts", in: *Harvard Human Rights Journal* 1994, p. 177.

Lord Hoffmann: "Human Rights and the House of Lords", in: *Modern Law Review* 1999, p. 159.

Loucaides, Loukis: "The European Convention on Human Rights – Collected Essays", Leiden/Boston 2007.

Lüke, Monika: "Die Immunität staatlicher Funktionsträger", Berlin 2000.

Lunney, M.: "A Tort Lawyer's View of *Osman v. United Kingdom*", in: *King's College Law Journal* 1999, p. 238.

Lunney, M.: "*Osman* in action- Article 6 and the Commission reports in *Z v. United Kingdom* and *TP & KM v. United Kingdom*", in: *King's College Law Journal* 2000, p. 119.

Maierhöfer, Christian: "Der EGMR als 'Modernisierer' des Völkerrechts?", in: *Europäische Grundrechtezeitschrift* 2002, p. 391.

Maierhöfer, Christian: "Weltrechtsprinzip und Immunität: das Völkerstrafrecht vor den Haager Richtern/ Urteil des IGH Demokratische Republik Kongo gegen Belgien", in: *Europäische Grundrechtezeitschrift* 2003, p. 545.

Mann, Frederik A.: "The State Immunity Act 1978", in: *British Yearbook of International Law* 1979, p. 43.

Marasinghe, Lakshman: "The Modern Law of Sovereign Immunity", in: *Modern Law Review* 1991, p. 664.

Markesinis, B.S./Auby, J.-B./Coester-Waltjen, D./Deakin, S.: "Tortious Liability of Statutory Bodies: A Comparative and Economic Analysis of Five English Cases", Oxford and Portland, Oregon 1999.

Markesinis, B.S./Fedtke, Jörg: "Damages for the Negligence of Statutory Bodies: The Empirical and Comparative Dimension to an Unending Debate", in: *Public Law* 2007, p. 299.

Marks, Susan: "Torture and the Jurisdictional Immunity of Foreign States", in: *The Cambridge Law Journal* 1997, p. 8.

Matscher, Franz: "Methods of Interpretation of the Convention", in: Macdonald, R.St.J./ Matscher, F./Petzold, H. (eds) *The European System for the Protection of Human Rights*, Dordrecht/Boston/London 1993, p. 63.

McClanahan, Grant V.: "Diplomatic Immunity", 1989.

McGregor, Lorna: "Torture and State Immunity: Deflecting Impunity, Distorting Sovereignty", in: *European Journal of international Law* 2008, p. 903.

McRae, Donald: "Approaches to the Interpretation of Treaties: the European Court of Human Rights and the WTO Appellate Body", in: Kohen (ed.) *Promoting Justice, Human Rights and Conflict Resolution through International Law, Liber Amicorum Lucius Caflisch*, Leiden 2007, p. 1407.

Meyer-Ladewig, Jens: "Europäische Menschenrechtskonvention", 2nd edition, Baden-Baden 2006.

Monti, Giorgio: "*Osman v. UK*- Transforming English Negligence Law into French Administrative Law", in: *International and Comparative Law Quarterly* 1999, p. 757.

Müller, Jörg Paul/Wildhaber, Luzius: "Praxis des Völkerrechts", 3rd edition, Bern 2001.

Muller, A.S.: "International Organisations and their Host States", The Hague/London/Boston 1995.

Murphy, John F.: "Civil Liability for the Commission of International Crimes as an Alternative to Criminal Prosecution", in: *Harvard Human Rights Journal* 1999, p. 1.

Murphy, Sean D.: "Contemporary Practice of the United States Relating to International Law-State Jurisdiction and Jurisdictional Immunities; the *Flatow* Case: Suit Against Iran for Act of Terrorism", in: *American Journal of International Law* 1999, p. 161.

Nedjati, Z. N.: "Human Rights under the European Convention", Amsterdam/New York/ Oxford 1978.

Nicol, Andrew/Millar, Gavin/Sharland, Andrew: "Media Law and Human Rights", 2002.

Nicol, Andrew: "Judicial Immunity and Human Rights", in: *European Human Rights Law Review* 2006, p. 558.

Nouwen, Sarah M.: "The Special Court for Sierra Leone and the Immunity of Taylor: the Arrest Warrant Case Continued", in: *Leiden Journal of International Law* 2005, p. 645.

Novogrodsky, Noah Benjamin: "Immunity for Torture: Lessons from *Bouzari v. Iran*", in: *European Journal of International Law* 2008, p. 939.

Nowak, Manfred: "UNO-Pakt über bürgerliche und politische Rechte und Fakultativprotokoll" (ICCPR-Commentary), Kehl/Strasbourg/Arlington 1989.

Nowak, Manfred/McArthur, Elizabeth: "The United Nations Convention Against Torture – A Commentary", Oxford 2008.

Olowofoyeku, A.: "Suing Judges: A Study of Judicial Immunity", 1993.

Olowofoyeku, A.: "State Liability for the Exercise of Judicial Power", in: *Public Law* 1998, p. 444.

Orakhelashvili, Alexander: "Restrictive Interpretation of Human Rights Treaties in the Recent Jurisprudence of the European Court of Human Rights", *European Journal of International Law* 2003, p. 549.

Orakhelashvili, Alexander: "State Immunity and Hierarchy of Norms: Why the House of Lords Got it Wrong", *European Journal of International Law* 2008, p. 955.

Paech, Norman: "Der juristische Schatten der Wehrmachtsverbrechen in Griechenland" (only available online).

Pahr, Willibald: "Die Staatenimmunität und Art. 6 Absatz 1 der Europäischen Menschenrechtskonvention", in: *Problemes des droits de l'homme et l'unification européenne. Melanges offerts a Polys Modinos*, Paris 1968, p. 222.

Parlett, Kate: "Immunity in Civil Proceedings for Torture: the Emerging Exception", in: *European Human Rights Law Reports* 2006, p. 49.

Parlett, Kate: "Universal Jurisdiction for Torture", in: *European Human Rights Law Reports* 2007, p. 385.

Parmar, Sejal: "*Vilho Eskelinen v Finland*: The Further Extension of ECHR Article 6 to Disputes concerning Civil Servants", in: *European Human Rights Law Review* 2007, p. 456.

Parry, Clive/Grant, John P./Parry, Anthony/Watts, Arthur D.: "Encyclopaedic Dictionary of International Law", New York/London/Rome 1988.

Paust, J.: "Draft Brief Concerning Claims to Foreign Sovereign Immunity and Human Rights: Non-Immunity for Violations of International Law under the FSIA", in: *Houston Journal of International Law* 1985, p. 49.

Peters, Anne: "Einführung in die Europäische Menschenrechtskonvention", Munich 2003.

Pittrof, Sabine: "Compensation Claims for Human Rights Breaches Committed by German Armed Forces Abroad During the Second World War: Federal Court of Justice Hands Down Decision in the Distomo Case", in: *German Law Journal* 2004, p. 15 (only available online).

Rabkin, J.: "Universal Justice: the Role of Federal Courts in International Civil Litigation", in: *Colombia Law Review* 1995, p. 2120.

Rau, Markus: "Schadensersatzklagen wegen extraterritorial begangener Menschenrechts-verletzungen: der US-amerikanische Alien Tort Claims Act", in: *Praxis des Internationalen Privat- und Verfahrensrechts* 2000, p. 558.

Rau, Markus: "After Pinochet: Foreign Sovereign Immunity in Respect of Serious Human Rights Violations – The Decision of the European Court of Human Rights in the *Al-Adsani* Case", in: *German Law Journal* 2002 (only available online).

Redress Trust: "Immunity v. Accountability: Considering the Relationship between State Immunity and Accountability for Torture and other serious International Crimes", 2005.

Reece Thomas, Katherine/Small, Joan: "Human Rights and State Immunity: Is there Immunity from Civil Liability for Torture?", in: *Netherlands International Law Review* 2003, p. 1.

Reed, Robert/Murdoch, Jim: "A Guide to Human Rights Law in Scotland", London 2001.

Reid, Karen: "A Practitioner's Guide to the European Convention on Human Rights", 2nd edition, London 2004.

Reimann, M.: "A Human Rights Exception to Sovereign Immunity: Some Thoughts on *Princz v Federal Republic of Germany*", in: *Michigan Journal of International Law* 1995, p. 403.

Reimann, M.: "Nazi-Verbrechen und Staatenimmunität: Kann die Bundesrepublik Deutschland von KZ-Gefangenen vor US-amerikanischen Gerichten verklagt werden?", in: *Praxis des Internationalen Privat- und Verfahrensrechts* 1995, p. 123.

Reinisch, August: "Case note: *Waite and Kennedy v. Germany/Beer and Regan v. Germany*, in: *American Journal of International Law* 1999, p. 933.

Reinisch, August: "International Organisations before National Courts", Cambridge 2000.

Reinisch, August: "European Court Practice Concerning State Immunity from Enforcement Measures", in: *European Journal of International Law* 2006, p. 803.

Reinisch, August/Weber, Ulf Andreas: "In the shadow of *Waite and Kennedy*- The jurisdictional immunity of international organizations, the individual's right of access to the courts and administrative tribunals as alternative means of dispute settlement", in: *International Organizations Law Review* 2004, p. 59.

Rensmann, Thilo: "Internationale Verbrechen und Befreiung von staatlicher Gerichtsbarkeit", in: *Praxis des Internationalen Privat- und Verfahrensrechts* 1999, p. 268.

Ress, Georg: "Entwicklungstendenzen der Immunität ausländischer Staaten", *Zeitschrift für allgemeines ausländisches Recht und Völkerrecht* 1980, p. 271.

Robertson, A.H./Merrills, J.G.: "Human Rights in Europe", 3rd edition, Manchester/New York 1993.

Robertson, Geoffrey: "Crimes against humanity", 2nd edition, London 2002.

Roht-Arriaza, Naomi: "The Foreign Sovereign Immunities Act and human rights violations: one step forward, two steps back?", in: *Berkeley Journal of International Law* 1998, p. 71.

Rozakis, Christos L.: "The Contribution of the European Court of Human Rights to the Development of the Law on State Immunity", in: Caflisch/Callewaert/Liddell/Mahoney/Villiger (eds.) *Human Rights – Strasbourg Views; Liber Amicorum Luzius Wildhaber*, Kehl 2007, p. 387.

Sari, Aurel: "Jurisdiction and International Responsibility in Peace Support Operations: The *Behrami* and *Saramati* Cases", in: *Human Rights Law Review* 2008, p. 151.

Schäfer, Patrick: "Verletzungen der Europäischen Menschenrechtskonvention durch Europäisches Gemeinschaftsrecht und dessen Vollzug", Baden-Baden 2006.

Schermers, Henry G.: "International Institutional Law", 2nd edition, Alphen aan den Rijn/Rockville 1980.

Schönfeld, Ulrich von: "Die Staatenimmunität im amerikanischen und englischen Recht", Berlin 1983.

Schreuer, Christoph H.: "State Immunity: Some Recent Developments", Cambridge 1988.

Schreuer, Christoph H.: "Die Durchsetzung zivilrechtlicher Ansprüche gegen ausländische Staaten", in: *Österreichische Juristenzeitung* 1991, p. 41.

Sears, Jill M.: "Confronting the 'Culture of Impunity': Immunity of Heads of State from Nuremberg to *ex parte Pinochet*", in: *German Yearbook of International Law* 1999, p. 125.

Seidl-Hohenveldern, Ignaz/Stein, Thorsten: "Völkerrecht", 10th edition, Cologne/Berlin/Bonn/ Munich 2000.

Seidl-Hohenveldern, Ignaz/Loibl, Gerhard: "Das Recht der internationalen Organisationen einschließlich der Supranationalen Gemeinschaften", 6th edition, Cologne/Berlin/Bonn/Munich 1996.

Seneviratne, Mary: "The rise and fall of advocates' immunity", in: *Legal Studies* 2001, p. 644.

Shah, Sangeeta: "Seeking Remedies for Violations of International Humanitarian Law: *Markovic v Italy*", in: *Human Rights Law Review* 2007, p. 412.

Shaw, Malcom N.: "International Law", 5th edition, Cambridge 2003.

Shorts, Edwin/De Than, Claire: "Civil Liberties", London 1998.

Simon, Jean-Marie: "The Alien Tort Claims Act: Justice or Show Trials?", in: *Boston University International Law Journal* 1993, p. 1.
Simor, Jessica/Emmerson, Ben Q.C.: "Human Rights Practice", London 2000.
Simpson, A. W. B.: "Human Rights and the End of Empire: Britain and the Genesis of the European Convention", Oxford 1999.
Singer, Michael: "Jurisdictional Immunity of International Organisations: Human Rights and Functional Necessity Concerns", in: *Virginia Journal of International Law* 1995, p. 53.
Starke, J. G.: "Introduction to International Law", 10th edition, London 1989.
Steiner, Henry Jr./Alston, Philip: "International Human Rights in Context", 2nd edition, Oxford 2000.
Stephens, B./Ratner, S.: "International Human Rights Litigation in US Courts", 1996.
Stewart, David P.: "The UN Convention on Jurisdictional Immunities of States and their Property", in: *American Journal of International Law* 2005, p. 194.
Sucharitkul, S.: "State Immunities and Trading Activities in International Law", 1959.
Sundikas, Andrias/Goldammer, Yvonne: "The Restrictive Theory of State Immunity in Lithuania: Reality or Illusion", in: Baltic Yearbook of International Law 2005, p. 111.
Sutter, Patrick: "Fällt nun auch die Staatenimmunität? Von einer 'unbemerkten' Revolution im Völkerrecht", in: *Jusletter* of 14 January 2002 (only available online).
Tams, C. J.: "Schwierigkeiten mit dem Ius Cogens", in: *Archiv des Völkerrechts* 2002, p. 331.
Tregilgas-Harvey, M.: "*Osman v. Metropolitan Police Commissioner*: The Cost of Police Protectionism", in: *Modern Law Review* 1993, p. 732.
Trooboff, P.: "Foreign State Immunity: Emerging Consensus on Principles", in: *Recueil Des Cours* 1986, p. 235.
Van Alebeek, Rosanne: "The Immunity of States and Their Officials in International Criminal Law and International Human Rights Law", Oxford 2008.
Van Dijk, Pieter: "The Maze of Paragraph 1 of Art. 6 of the European Convention on Human Rights; New Openings or Dead Ends", in: *Hague Yearbook of International Law* 1988, p. 141.
Van Dijk, Pieter: "Access to Court", in: Macdonald, R.St.J./Matscher, F./Petzold, H. (eds) *The European System for the Protection of Human Rights*, Dordrecht/Boston/London 1993, p. 345.
Vicuna, Francisco Orrego: "Diplomatic and Consular Immunities and Human Rights", in: *International and Comparative Law Quarterly* 1991, p. 34.
Villiger, Mark E.: "Handbuch der Europäischen Menschenrechtskonvention (EMRK)", 2nd edition, Zürich 1999.
Villiger, Mark E.: "Articles 31 and 32 of the Vienna Convention on the Law of Treaties in the Case-Law of the European Court of Human Rights", in: *Internationale Gemeinschaft und Menschenrechte, Festschrift für Georg Ress*, Berlin/Köln/München 2005, p. 317.
Voyiakis, Emmanuel: "Access to Court v State Immunity", in: *International and Comparative Law Quarterly* 2003, p. 297.
Wallace, Rebecca: "International Law", 3rd edition, London 1997.
Watts, Sir Arthur: "The Legal Position in International Law of Heads of States, Heads of Government and Foreign Ministers" in: *Recueil des cours* 1994–III, p. 57.
Weintraub, R.: "International Law: Establishing Incredible Events By Credible Evidence: Civil Suits for Atrocities that Violate International Law", in: *Brooklyn Law Review* 1996, p. 753.
Weir: "Down *Hill*- all the way?", in: *Cambridge Law Journal* 1999, p. 7.
Wenckstern, M.: "Handbuch des internationalen Zivilverfahrensrechts, Vol. II/1: *Die Immunität internationaler Organisationen*", 1994.

Westerdiek, Claudia: "Le Tribunal Administratif du Conseil de l'Europe : Présentation et apercu de la Jurisprudence", in: Kohen (ed.) *Promoting Justice, Human Rights and Conflict Resolution through International Law, Liber Amicorum Lucius Caflisch*, Leiden 2007, p. 951.

Wheatley, Steven: "State Immunity for Acts of Torture", 1996.

Wigley, Simon: "Parliamentary Immunity in Democratizing Countries: The Case of Turkey", in: *Human Rights Quarterly* 2009, p. 567.

Wildhaber, Luzius: "The Role of Comparative Law in the Case-Law of the European Court of Human Rights" in: *Internationale Gemeinschaft und Menschenrechte, Festschrift für Georg Ress*, Berlin/Köln/München 2005, p. 1101.

Wildhaber, Luzius: "The European Convention on Human Rights and International Law", in: *International and Comparative Law Quarterly* 2007, p. 217.

Wirth, S.: "Immunity for Core Crimes? The ICJ's Judgment in the *Congo v. Belgium* Case", in: *European Journal of International Law* 2002, p. 877.

Wright, Jane: "Local Authorities, the Duty of Care and the European Convention on Human Rights", in: *Oxford Journal of Legal Studies* 1998, p. 1.

Wright, Jane: "Tort Law and Human Rights", Oxford/Portland (Oregon) 2001.

Wright, Jane: "The Retreat from Osman: *Z v. United Kingdom* in the European Court of Human Rights and Beyond", in: Fairgrieve/Andenas/Bell (eds) *Tort Liability of Public Authorities in Comparative Perspective*, London 2002, p. 55.

Yang, X: "State Immunity in the European Court of Human Rights: Reaffirmations and Misconceptions", in: *British Yearbook of International Law* 2003, p. 333.

Yang, X: "Universal Tort Jurisdiction over Torture?", in: *Cambridge Law Journal* 2005, p. 1.

Yourow, Howard Charles: "The Margin of Appreciation Doctrine in the Dynamics of European Human Rights Jurisprudence", The Hague/Boston/London 1996.

Zaffuto, Warren D.: "A 'pirate's victory': President Clinton's approach to the new FSIA exception leaves the victory empty-handed", in: *Tulane Law Review* 1999, p. 685.

Zappalà, S.: "Do Heads of State in Office Enjoy Immunity from Jurisdiction for International Crimes?", in: *European Journal of International Law* 2001, p. 595.

Ziemele, Ineta: "Case-Law of the European Court of Human Rights and Integrity of International Law", in: Huesa Vinaixa/Wellens (eds.) *L'influence des sources saur l'unité et la fragmentation du droit international*, Bruxelles 2006, p. 187.

Zimmermann, A.: "Sovereign Immunity and Violations of *Jus Cogens*: Some Critical Remarks", in: *Michigan Journal of International Law* 1995, p. 433.

Index

Alternative remedies, 15, 35, 52, 54, 98, 129, 143–154, 191, 204
Amnesty International, 126, 131
Armed forces, 59f., 93, 99, 173

Charter of the United Nations, 76, 134, 147, 152
"Civil rights and obligations" (Article 6 of the European Convention on Human Rights), 3–11, 28, 88, 159–162, 167, 170, 179, 184, 195, 204f.
Council of Europe, 23, 47, 57 n. 154, 84 n. 290, 133 n. 494, 134 n. 501, 135 n. 507, 152, 172, 184, 186, 189
Crown immunity, *see* Immunity of the Crown
Customary international law, 23f., 28, 61, 69, 73, 82–86, 107, 112f., 121–125, 135f.

Employment disputes, 7–10; 41f., 48–54, 136f., 204
European Commission, 145f.
European Commission of Human Rights, 8
European Convention on State Immunity, 23–25, 43, 45f., 49, 52, 55–57, 59f., 82, 90, 93, 201
European Court of Justice, 9, 100, 145f.
European Space Agency, 8, 19, 27, 141–144, 148, 151f.
European Union, 137, 145, 149, 152, 186, 189
European Union Civil Service Tribunal, 137

German Federal Constitutional Court, 17, 99, 101, 104, 144f.
Greek Supreme Court, 59, 82f.

House of Lords, 28, 31, 69, 71, 75, 77, 80, 83f., 85, 110, 112, 115f., 123, 126f., 130–132, 165–176, 178, 185

Immunity from execution, 82, 88–93, 95, 97, 99, 101–107, 121
Immunity from liability, 2, 162, 169, 171, 174f., 177, 181f., 184f., 205
Immunity from suit, 1f., 12, 22, 73, 132, 135, 139f., 150, 153, 175f., 177, 181f., 188, 199, 204f.
Immunity of
  Consular agents, 119f.
  the Crown, 161, 173, 176, 183
  Diplomats, 119–124
  Foreign ministers, 59, 81, 108, 119, 123f., 126
  International organisations, 1, 6f., 10, 12f., 22, 36, 38, 48, 54, 132–137, 139–145, 147, 149–151, 153–155, 204
  Judges, 134, 184f.
  Members of Parliament, 1, 6, 13, 159, 186–199, 206
  Police, 1, 6, 9 n. 41, 33, 41, 159, 164–169, 173, 182
  Social services, 1, 41, 159, 168, 170f.
  State agencies, 103f.
  States, 1f., 9, 12, 14–16, 21–108, 111, 115f., 119, 121, 124, 126, 129–136, 149–151, 153f., 157, 161, 175f., 180, 199–204
International Labour Organisation, 137, 142, 148f.
International Law Association, 23, 46, 58, 60f., 64, 70, 201
International Court of Justice, 24, 29, 76, 81f., 84f., 95, 107f., 112, 114, 123f., 150, 156
International Criminal Court, 64, 109f., 112, 134
International Criminal Tribunals for the former Yugoslavia and Rwanda, 64, 70, 125
International Law Commission, 24, 40, 57, 59, 61, 70, 73, 135

Jurisdiction, 1, 4f., 14, 21–23, 25–32, 42, 46–55, 57f., 61f., 64–66, 69, 71, 74–76, 78–80, 87f., 92, 94, 96, 100, 104, 107, 109, 111–119, 121, 123–126, 129–131, 133, 136–142, 147, 150, 152, 154–158, 163, 165, 173, 180, 185, 200, 203
Jus cogens, 23, 33, 66–70, 72–77, 80–83, 86, 92f., 96f., 99, 105f., 130, 132, 202

Legitimate aim, 2, 13–15, 17–20, 28, 31, 49, 95, 97f., 106, 140, 155, 158, 161–163, 165, 177, 184, 188, 199, 203
Length of proceedings, 29, 122

Margin of appreciation, 16f., 30, 32, 45, 63, 85, 185, 189, 192, 200, 202

Parliamentarty immunity, *see* Immunity of Members of Parliament
"Personal injury exception" (tort exception) to State immunity, 53f., 56–61, 63, 66, 68, 82, 93
Positive obligations (under the European Convention on Human Rights), 5, 70, 165, 168, 202
Prohibition of torture, 69f., 72–77, 105, 130, 168, 202
Proportionality, 13–16, 18–20, 31, 38, 62f., 78, 80, 98, 102f., 140f., 148f., 153, 161f., 163, 165, 177, 191f., 194, 200f.
Public international law, 30, 32, 34, 36, 39–41, 46, 53f., 56, 62, 66, 69, 74–76, 84, 94, 107, 112–114, 119f., 124, 135f., 153–157, 159, 199–201, 203f.

Right to a fair trial, 2, 3, 5, 6, 87, 96 n. 342

State immunity, *see* Immunity of States

United Nations, 24, 33, 45–47, 51, 57, 60f., 63, 73, 76, 78–81, 90, 109, 125, 134f., 137, 139, 147–153, 201
United Nations Commission on Human Rights, 79
United Nations Convention Against Torture, 33, 73–75, 77, 79–81, 106, 115, 127–131, 202
United Nations Convention on Jurisdictional Immunities of States and Their Property, 45–47, 51, 90, 201
United Nations Convention on the Prevention and Punishment of the Crime of Genocide, 150
United States Supreme Court, 22, 66

Very essence of the right of access to court, 13, 17–19, 199
Vienna Convention on Consular Relations, 119f.
Vienna Convention on Diplomatice Relations, 43, 90, 101, 108, 111, 119f., 122, 124 n. 453
Vienna Convention on the Law of Treaties, 3, 17, 31–33, 39f., 73 n. 228f., 200

Waiver of State immunity, 12, 25f., 37, 51, 67, 71 n. 218, 90f., 106, 111, 119 n. 429, 200, 204

www.ingramcontent.com/pod-product-compliance
Lightning Source LLC
LaVergne TN
LVHW080847300926
849162LV00003B/365